CO

Preface

My search for my father's story began shortly after his death. He left us with so many unanswered questions about his life and only a sketchy outline of key moments. We knew he was a Barnardo's boy in the 1930s and that he once had a younger brother whom he had lost touch with before he went to war.

There were whispered talks of a scandal surrounding his parentage. Dad thought his mother was called Katherine or Kate Jones. He had not heard from her since he was sent into the children's home at a young age.

There was little known of our grandfather or any of his family for that matter. When he married my Mum in the early 1950s, Dad had no one on his side of the church, apart from his friends.

As the new millennium approached and I was a young father of two boys myself I had a strong yearning to find out the answers to all our family's questions. What had happened to my Dad's brother – my uncle Fred? All we knew was that he had been sent to Australia as a child, leaving my Dad alone. Had he, like my Dad, survived the Second World War, and how was it that neither he nor my Dad ever found each other again.

This book is the product of that twenty-year search. Incredibly, despite years of research there are still many unanswered questions.

What I did find as I delved deeper was a sad story of missed connections but also a tale of heroism, patriotic duty and love that is unique to that wartime generation of young men and women to whom we owe so much. Seeing the war through my Dad's eyes for the first time and trying to make sense of his childhood experiences helped explain the broken man I knew as my father.

Fred Wilson's story is one of immense resilience and service. A short life well lived. Tragically cut short at a time he had found love and happiness in his personal life with the family he had always wanted.

This book is written to hopefully ensure that the memory of the Wilson brothers and their, at times, extraordinary lives is held in the hearts and minds of future generations of our family – in England and now, thankfully, Australia.

It is dedicated to the memory of my Dad, Philip Charles Wilson (1922-88) and my late Uncle, RSM Frederick Alexander Wilson (1924-68).

Chapter One

Orphaned

77 Westminster Bridge Road, London, SE1 was a grand address for such a humble beginning. A short stroll from the dark and dirty brown River Thames and across the historic Westminster Bridge from the imposing Houses of Parliament and past Florence Nightingale's St Thomas's Hospital. Their shared home was squeezed at the end of a small section of Georgian terraced housing just around the corner from Kennington Police Station. Dwarfed by the imposing towers attached to the smelly Wellington Mills factory and the Lincoln Tower of Christ Church next door.

At night the young boys would go to sleep hungry, haunted by what they were convinced were the piercing screams from the lunatics at nearby 'Bedlam' Bethlem Asylum ringing in their ears. The three Wilson boys, the oldest, Henry (named in memory of his paternal grandfather), Philip and Frederick, were all born here in the poverty and grime of 1920s South East London, as was their younger sister Mabel Louisa, named after their mother Kate's sister and her late mother. A second daughter, Lavinia, died in infancy in 1926.

Where the poor and the powerful rubbed shoulders in this corner of London, the Wilson family at times felt like they were in hiding. Their mother Kate was well aware that she and the children's father Alfred were out of wedlock, despite Kate's attempts to persuade Alfred to do the right thing by her and divorce his wife.

For Kate Flippence, London never properly felt like home. The seemingly endless bustle of the trams at St George's Circus and the noise and the stink of the Oakey and Sons emery board factory next door to their Westminster Bridge Road house, which they shared with Frank and Lily Ward, were a million miles away from the sleepy Wiltshire village of Burbage that she had left behind. Kate had travelled a long way, physically and emotionally, from the quiet of the country farm where her father Jasper had laboured as a shepherd and where Kate had lived until leaving home desperate to find work.

She had struggled to find employment again after her first job as a 'tweeny', a between-stairs maid, to the Yorkshire widow Mary Ellison and her three children in the West London respectability of Ealing, had come to an end. Mrs Ellison hit hard times before the Great War and Kate was forced to visit the Hackney Workhouse to apply for poor relief. The Workhouse had sent her back to the care of her hometown in Wiltshire, to the Pewsey Poor Law Guardians and the shame of returning to her family home and the Pewsey Workhouse.

Kate was no stranger to shame. When she was in her twenties her firstborn son had been cruelly described, in this very same Pewsey workhouse where he was delivered, as 'base born' – the illegitimate result of her brief ill-fated coupling with the son of the Lord of the Manor and the owner of the farm where Kate's father had worked. Kate was distraught when her first born son Cuthbert, who everyone called Bertie, had been given away for good to a trusted Burbage neighbour to raise as their own.

It was so painful for her, each time she returned to Wiltshire to visit her shepherd father Jasper and his young second wife Louisa, to learn of Bertie's progress and see him playing in the dusty road outside her Father's tumble-down cottage. She had confided to Louisa, whom Kate felt was more of an older sister than a stepmother, that she wished she was strong enough to raise Bertie as her own but she was afraid of bringing shame on the family in such a small, tight-knit village.

Kate knew only too well the damage that shame could do.

She had been sent back to that Pewsey Workhouse when she had fallen on hard times as a young woman in East London. She had discovered to her cost that the paves of London were not made of gold. When two of her brothers had left the Wiltshire family cottage to seek a better life in America with the Mormon Church, Kate knew she too had to make her own way.

The New World was not an option for her so being 'in service' in London was her route out of Burbage. Sadly the work was hard to find and Kate soon fell on the parish. She was distraught when the Hackney Union Workhouse instructed her that she had to seek parish relief in her own Parish which they knew from the way she spoke was not in London.

She was also still haunted by the case of 'the Wiltshire Well murder' that had made national news when a woman she knew from school, Mary Anne or 'Annie' Nash as she was known to her friends, had been falsely accused of killing her own five year old 'base born' son Stanley in the village. When a child's body was found by two farm labourers floating in a well at the nearby Southgrove Farm, some of the locals were convinced that the body must be that of Annie's poor Stanley who had 'disappeared' two years earlier. An anonymous letter had been sent to the Police.

The wretched young woman was unfairly tried, sentenced to be hanged and unjustly imprisoned and, though subsequently pardoned, was still the talk of Burbage whenever Kate heard from any of her friends or family.

Poor Stanley's body had never been found and Doctor Farquhar, the popular local Scottish doctor who had falsified evidence in court to incriminate her had long retired in disgrace from his job as the village doctor. An appeal to Home Secretary Winston Churchill had seen Annie eventually pardoned when it was clear that the body found was that of a much older boy, but Kate knew that the mob had turned against Annie - her friend whose sister had married Kate's cousin - simply because she had not conformed. She was the talk of the Burbage ale houses and the churches because she did not fit in or play by the Parson's rules. Though Kate thought that Annie was daft to lie to the police, seven years languishing in a London gaol for a crime you did not commit was a high price to pay simply for bearing children alone and out of wedlock.

Annie had not only lost her Stanley forever, God had also taken her two other newborn children, 'base' borne alone, and for this she was cast off by the ignorant villagers as some kind of immoral and wicked woman. Even though she knew that she had travelled a long way to metropolitan Kennington from sleepy Burbage, Kate did not want to contemplate Annie's tragic fate befalling her.

To give away one child was painful enough, though at least she was assured that he was happy and healthy, even if his name had changed and he knew nothing of her as his mother. So long as she had her Alfred to help her, for all his gallivanting and golfing, Kate felt she could hold things together for her remaining children.

In her early thirties herself but fourteen years his junior, Kate was a little in awe of the Captain from the moment she met him whilst working as a cleaner in the War Office. She had suspected he was married when she first fell for his south London charms. Her cousin, also called Kate and working in service for a flamboyant wealthy family, had warned her not to get involved with a married man but it was too late by then. By the first Christmas of the 1920s she was already pregnant with Henry.

To remain 'respectable' in London and to escape the prying eyes of the authorities, at the urging of the boys' father, Alfred, Kate adopted the surname Jones, as Alfred said it was common enough to be un-noticed. Her real name Flippence marked her out as a country bumpkin, from a long line of Wiltshire peasants, at least that is what born and bred Londoner Alfred had once insisted during one of his drunken rants. It was agreed between them that their children would take a variant of their father's surname – dropping one of the L's in Willson to mark them out from his other 'legal' family – his common law wife Agnes and their five surviving children.

You see Alfred, or 'the Captain' – as the boys had known their father – wanted to keep up an air of Victorian respectability in public.

For Phil and Fred's father, soon to be retired Captain Alfred Henry Willson, had lived the Victorian dream long before the boys were born. He had travelled to the South Africa of Boers and the Old Empire. From his brief early Army career as a twenty-year-old engineer fitter with the Royal Artillery at Woolwich Arsenal, which did not work out for him and where he bought himself out after two years having contracted gonorrhoea, Alfred had taken a posting to Livingstone's Africa with the Royal Army Ordnance Corps where he spent fourteen years on a long service. His young wife Agnes had travelled to Cape Town with him. His drinking tales with the freemasons in Woodstock were those of the Boys' Own Africa of lions and other wild things. He may be a true South London boy from a strict Christian family, but the short and stocky Alfred had worked his way up through the ranks from his humble beginnings as an engineer at the Woolwich Arsenal and he had medals to prove it.

Though never exactly in the front line in the garrison town of Roberts Heights in the Eastern Cape, where his children George and Phyllis were born, he became a fine marksman and winner of many Army shooting competitions which were held to fight off the boredom and train the men at the same time.

Captain Willson serving in Sierra Leone
(Middle Row, Second from the left)

The Great War saw him posted with 11th Company to Freetown in hot and damp Sierra Leone, to the Cameroon and then to the Western Front in France. By the time he had retired in 1928, on his 55th birthday, he had held the rank of Captain for two years and proudly acquired seven medals.

His new family cherished those seven medals and for many months, even though her boys were constantly hungry, Kate resisted the urge to pawn them for money to buy food. She was, however, to lose them for good when Alfred's 'legal' wife took them away when she learnt that the Captain had died. His illegitimate sons, Philip and Frederick, remembered their older brother Henry demanding that his 'muvver' Kate was the Captain's 'deserving' wife. She was the one that had nursed him after his many drunken nights at the Golf Club. She was the one who had suffered the social events that required a retired army captain to have a trophy 'wife' on his arm, on the nights the boys were left in the charge of their 'auntie' Lily Ward.

It was Kate who had insisted they try to put money away each week for a pension when the Army had stripped Alfred of his army annuity. She feared that Alfred's age would catch up with her eventually. There was nothing Kate wanted more than to be the Captain's legal wife to protect herself and the boys.

But Alfred was refused a divorce from Agnes. Even though his love for her had long gone. His brief affair in Normandy at the end of the Great War which had resulted in his young French lover Marie Jeanne giving birth to a baby girl, she had named Louise Lucienne Angele - their 'little angel' born on Christmas Day in 1919 - had confirmed to Alfred his marriage to Agnes was all but over but he didn't want to involve the expensive lawyers. That would take money away from his golf and his gallivanting. Nor did he want his missioner late father Henry's churchy family or Kate's 'Sally Army' sisters to judge him as a moral failure more than they already did. But Agnes wanted more than his name.

For Alfred, as his lifestyle caused him to pile on the pounds, this life of deception piled on the pressure, which was only compounded by the Army's removal of his pension in November 1929, eighteen months after he had retired, when they struck him off their list and stripped him of his title as Captain. He was discharged and it was not an honourable one. He had failed to keep up payments to Agnes, convicted in court and been sent to prison for two months as a result.

He could feel his chest tightening and he was sweating more than normal as he boarded the tram on a clammy morning in July 1931 but stubbornly ignored what he dismissed as indigestion caused by him devouring his fried bacon too quickly at breakfast, as he wanted to get to the golf club. But this pain was not like any other he had felt before and it was not going away. Alfred's heart was giving up and as he collapsed on the tram it was too late to save him despite being rushed by ambulance to University College Hospital.

The 'Captain's' complicated personal life and now disgraced Army career had ended abruptly at the age of fifty-eight. The women he left behind were far from convinced as to whether Alfred would follow his missioner father Henry to heaven, or not. They had seen too much of his darker side to be sure of that.

Kate was beside herself. She was in despair at how she might cope with the young family Alfred had bequeathed her. Though also upset that her children had lost their father too, albeit already an absent one, Agnes had more immediate practical concerns at getting back from Kate what she felt was rightfully hers as she remained his wife in the eyes of the law.

As both women were grieving Alfred's sudden death following this fatal heart attack – Agnes sent two of her older sons Ernest and George - part of the Captain's other 'proper' family - to Kate's south London home — and demanded back his precious War medals – the only real trophies the smaller Wilson boys cared about. And she demanded her widow's pension too.

Kate protested that she had helped keep up the payments while Alfred had been alive and been stripped of his War Pension in disgrace on his discharge by the Army.

After the authorities got involved the compassionate side of Agnes did force her to concede, having won the insurance claim that the policy was her legal entitlement as his common-law wife, that Kate could retain the meagre ten pounds she had paid in as premiums over the past eleven years– a pound a week for ten weeks - to try and keep a roof over her children's heads and food in their hungry stomachs. Agnes knew in her heart that both she and Kate had been the innocent party here and would not want the poor mites to suffer.

But it was the War Office cleaner Kate 'Jones' who, having given up her job through ill health after contracting influenza; pneumonia, and the stress of losing her lover, was once more left to queue to claim for parish relief opposite Kennington Police Station, to receive her 25 shillings a week, of which 9 shillings a week had to go towards her rent.

The food she received on the relief was unappetizing to say the least, meat as black as your hat, potatoes with whiskers all growing out of them. Black sugar. Black, almost, bread. Lambeth at least had the tot stalls selling second, third- and fourth-hand clothes and the Congregational Church next door with its imposing Lincoln Tower honouring the reforming American President, which would have provided some succour. Like all good mothers, Kate wanted to put her children first.

It was the Church in the guise of Reverend Cartwright of the London City Mission that first alerted Doctor Barnardo's of the boys' plight. An inquiry Officer was sent to interview Kate and though an application was made for all three boys, Barnardo's decided to offer admission to their Woodford Garden City home to her younger boys Philip, then aged nine and a half, and Fred, who had then just turned eight. It was clear to them that Kate was not coping. The children were as clean as could be expected, under the circumstances, although Phil did seem a little sickly with bandy legs that hinted at rickets and all three boys were clearly a little undernourished. The chapped ruddiness in their cheeks was the result of them having the run of St George's Fields, Waterloo and the Cut in which to play.

The Wilson boys weren't exactly feral, but they loved nothing more than hanging around the entrance to the Necropolis Railway, up the road towards the river, or under the railway arches near Waterloo Station, where the coffins were sometimes stored before making their last earthly journey to Brookwood Cemetery in the Surrey countryside. This macabre pastime gave the younger boys nightmares as Henry would regale them at bedtime with ghost stories of skeletons arising from their wooden boxes, which risked the boys waking up in their shared bed with a damp and smelly sheet, again.

Henry took a perverse enjoyment from scaring his brothers with his stories. He liked to play with their young minds. It made him feel powerful. Put him in charge.

One winter evening when they had found their way to the Tower of London along the river as the light was fading and Phil was fretting about being late home and suffering his mother's wrath, Henry spooked his younger brothers with a story of the dark ravens of the White Tower picking at the bodies of the two boy princes, Edward and Richard, in the dungeon. They ran all the way home without looking back.

On the long days of the summer school holidays the boys would lie in St George's Fields in Kennington just round the corner from their house and Henry would conjure up images of the wailing lunatics in the now-closed Bedlam Asylum. As they clambered around the empty Victorian building, in his head the nervous Phil could hear the ghostly rattling of chains and the screams of the long since departed inmates.

Fred preferred Henry's re-enactments of when his beloved Grenadier Guards were despatched to the Fields to put down the 'Wilkes and Liberty' mob. Despite being the shortest of the three brothers, in his mind Fred stood tall posing as a Grenadier Guardsman and dreamt one day he too would be guarding Buckingham Palace in a scarlet tunic, a gleaming belt polished to perfection and an imposing bearskin.

At the age of eleven it was judged by Barnardo's that the talkative storyteller Henry – the oldest of the three sons – could soon fend for himself and hopefully in time his mother and their poorly younger sister Mabel. But sickly Mabel was too unwell and was sent by the doctors out of London to Darenth Valley Hospital in the Kent countryside to try to give her a hope of getting better in the cleaner air. Sadly, in June, their fragile four-year-old sister lost her fight for life and Kate was again left to mourn the loss of a beloved daughter, who was buried alongside her baby Lavinia in a pauper's grave in a Lambeth cemetery.

It was after one of her long walks with the children to the cemetery to place stones on the spot that marked Mabel's pauper's grave - on 27th July 1932 – just three days after the first anniversary of the loss of their father – after the pre-arranged visit to Kate from the sympathetic Doctor Barnardo's Inquiry Officer, that the two younger Wilson brothers were to be taken to Dr Barnardo's Boys Garden City in Woodford, Essex, to begin their new lives as 'orphans'.

As she gently urged the boys to say 'God Bless' to Mabel and Lavinia beyond the grave, Kate was torn. She knew deep down that she could not offer the boys the life they deserved. Unable to save her beloved daughters despite her frantic prayers to a God she sometimes felt had abandoned her, she wanted her boys to be given a chance of a better life, of three meals a day and a bed away from their damp-ridden room in a shared house.

But Kate's heartbreak at giving away her Bertie when she was younger still hit her hard nearly ten years on, even though she had not been allowed time to grow to love him and care for him in the way she loved her Fred and Phil. Now she faced losing her beloved young boys forever. Never seeing them grow up into fine young men she could be proud of. Becoming the brave young soldiers her Alfred would have wanted them to become.

Chapter Two

Barnardo's Boys

Kate knew she had to try to be strong for all three of her boys as the DBH bus parked up the street from Number 77 and the stern looking Matron stepped down from the vehicle to collect her two younger sons to take them away to the orphanage in the Essex countryside to start their new lives, without her and their brother Henry. She whispered in Phil's ear 'to take care of her Freddie' and turned to young Freddie as Matron firmly loosened his grip on Kate's arm with a tearful 'be good' and 'remember what the Captain taught you'.

For Phil, then aged nearly ten and Freddie just eight, the Barnardo's Boys' Garden City must have been a mixed blessing. Barely a year after the Captain's death, and only a month after their poor younger sister Mabel's death at the age of four from convulsions, whooping cough and diphtheria, and aware of their mother's obvious distress, they faced a future without their Mum and their older brother Henry to protect them. Henry would curse at the boats on the Thames carrying the leftovers from the swanky chop houses and restaurants at the end of their road while they were left starving and sucking on a handkerchief dipped in sugar. They may have annoyed him a lot, but Henry loved his little brothers. They were his army. His Grenadier Guards. His little men. And now they were marching off forever. Henry was old enough to understand that his life would never be quite the same again.

His younger brothers had no choice. Their mother had said this was all for the best. Through their teary eyes London seemed to get greener as their hour-long bus journey took them further away from the busy, noisy streets of south London and out towards the suburbs of Essex. With the bus window pulled down just enough to allow the breeze outside to drown out the petrol fumes, Phil could taste and smell the change in the atmosphere as more and more trees were visible and the air somehow felt different to him. When the bus stopped in the traffic and Fred had stopped coughing for a moment, Phil could even hear birdsong like he had never heard before. Not just the shrieks of wayward seagulls blown inland from the river but other bird calls he did not recognise.

As the Barnardo's DBH bus shuddered its way up the shady tree-lined entrance drive to the imposing ivy-clad main house, belching out fumes, Phil held his little brother's hand extra tight. The boys fought back the tears from the black-clad Matron accompanying them as they faced their uncertain future in this new home.

Though they were fearful of change and distraught to be parted from their Ma, the Garden City was for the green—fingered Phil also a strange kind of verdant paradise. Phil had never seen so many trees and flowers. In place of the slums and poverty of Lambeth, and the stench of the Oakey and Sons emery board factory on their doorstep, the brothers now had the security and stability of an organised, disciplined life in a place that felt a bit like the countryside.

300 boys lived on the 39-acre Gwynne House estate in Woodford Bridge. The regime was strict but the boys at least had the space to breathe in fresh air. The boy's cottages – with 34 boys in dormitories in each house - were called King Edward VII, Union Jack, Empire, New Zealand and Britannia and the vast dining hall which doubled as the sports hall and gymnasium was called Canada Hall. A large Union flag suspended from the ceiling at one end of the Hall was saluted on Empire Day.

The boys learnt that they were to be empire-builders or 'pioneers and picnickers.' The 'garden city' had its own swimming bath and hospital, with the children's health overseen by the committed Scottish Christian Doctor James Milne. 'Dr Jim', drawn to Barnardo's to tackle the outbreak of scarlet fever that had blighted Barnardo's Stepney home, was a popular figure.

Though the boys continued their schooling outside the home they could also learn to bake in the Garden city's own steam bakery that churned out 5000 loaves a week. Baking was to remain a passion for the older Phil throughout his life.

The two brothers lived in the same 'cottage' initially, sharing the same 'cottage mother' and were allowed to sleep in the same dormitory. Though they were to be toughened up, with their precious moth-eaten teddies being taken away on arrival, they were also protected from the vagaries of street urchin life and the pangs of hunger would be less frequent.

Soon, going to school hungry would be a distant memory. Their basic Barnardo's diet of 'pongy', a lumpy porridge, for breakfast, bread and dripping and 'skilly' a greasy fat stew served with gritty 'greens' grown in the gardens in the grounds among the cottages, for lunch, and a hot milk and shared biscuit before bedtime was a strangely comforting routine for them. They knew what day of the week it was by the meals they were given at lunchtime. They even had a fresh boiled egg to look forward to on their birthdays.

It was a tough regime for the boys. It would make men of them if it didn't break them. Woken at 06:30 by a bugle call reveille, their first job was to polish the dormitories and clean the bathrooms before breakfast, they were then marched to school. They never could escape that smell of polish. What was once a fond attachment to their mother, being the smell she brought home on her apron from her cleaning job at the War Office, now simply became a painful reminder that their Ma had given them away.

Saturdays were devoted to games – either in the purpose-built gymnasium or outdoors. Fred enjoyed the soccer and cricket more than his older brother. Phil preferred it when he could wander alone exploring the orchards and gardens around the estate. He loved to mark the changes of the seasons and Autumn was his favourite.

Sundays were special. The boys even got an extra hour in bed. The monthly parade to the church on the green at Woodford Bridge saw the boys in their cottage group, after the service, in crocodile walks, two-by-two to fill in time before dinner. They would look out for the brakes drawn by scary looking steaming, heavy horses pulling up the hill outside the White

Hart pub, with passengers aboard enjoying an outing from the East End. The boys were commandeered to hurry past the jolly singing crowd of East Enders lest they 'learn to prize the pleasures of the flesh'. Marching bands were encouraged. Phil loved these the most. He loved the sound of the band as it echoed around the imposing Chapel of the Good Shepherd.

Phil, though only two years older than Fred, was the quieter of the two. He worked hard at school, joined the cub scout troop, and had few problems with the discipline at the home. His later loves of gardening and cooking were fostered in the grounds and the bakery of the Woodford Bridge estate. The Barnardo's superintendent was very keen on growing vegetables for the boys' own needs – potatoes, greens and cabbages – and Phil enjoyed the outdoor life immensely. There was nothing he liked more than having mud-encrusted fingers tingling with the cold as he worked the soil. Indeed, for most of his working life he was to work outdoors and his modest garden was always a source of peace and inspiration to him. He was blissfully unaware of it then of course, but his mastery of the art of digging would come in handy later too, when he was at war on the Western Front.

The younger Wilson boy Freddie was a different story. He just could not settle. He clearly suffered more from the boys' recent traumas and the loss of their parents. He proved more of a challenge for the Doctor Barnardo's staff. He did not want to be there. It was decided that a fresh start would be the best course of action for both boys. They were to be sent to Australia through the Barnardo's partners, the Child Emigration Society, to live and be schooled at the Fairbridge

Farm School in Pinjarra, Western Australia, until they were old enough to work as farm hands "Down Under".

But Fairbridge had strict requirements about the health of the children they accepted so the brothers would need to be in the best of health if they were to be allowed to board the steam ship to travel around the world later that year.

However, within a few months of being sent to the Boys Garden City the sickly Freddie was despatched to the newly-opened Barnardo's convalescent home in Bognor Regis on the Sussex coast for a month, as much for the Woodford Garden City's staff's relief as his own. He had a fever that would not go away, and it was hoped that the sea air would sort him out in time for his long journey to the Fairbridge Farm School.

The Margaret Convalescent Home run by the indomitable Matron Fairbairn with her clarion call of 'close in, close in you boys. There is a time and a place for all things, but this is neither the time nor the place'. Nurse Nevell would look on as the boys got better putting colour in their cheeks playing their improvised games like 'Toe In The Ring' and 'Shoot, Buddy Shoot'.

Miss Donald, the kitchen matron, would ring two bells at six thirty in the morning and after breakfast, the boys that were well enough would don their boots and navy blue raincoats to set off for school. There was no escaping church here either. Just as at Woodford, the boys would be shepherded on a Sunday, this time to St Richard's Church of England church in Aldwick where Reverend Mosse would preach physically and spiritually, way over the boys' heads.

Freddie's physical condition must have improved enough to pinch apples from 'Daddy Whiskers' orchard or to play endless games of cricket to the sounds of the seagulls, mimicking Douglas Jardine's England team at the forthcoming Ashes tour of Australia and scraping his knees on the adapted tennis court playground in Bognor, as he ran as fast as his hero Harold Larwood. However, the authorities remained sufficiently worried for Freddie's health – knowing Fairbridge's strict health criteria, that, despite their excitement at the prospect, both boys' names were struck off a ships' list bound for Australia.

On 14th October 1932 the P&O steam ship, the SS Balranald, the ship that had previously had their names on its passenger list, departed from Tilbury Docks on the Thames and sailed round the world to Australia without either of the Wilson boys on board. Both names had been struck through with a black line as thick as the Greenwich meridian. The boys were being denied their assisted passage to a sunnier new life Down Under…for now.

The two brothers grew much closer together on Fred's return to the Boys Garden City and the following year they were boarded out together for seven weeks to a local foster family in Woodford Bridge where they celebrated Phil's eleventh birthday as a part of a 'proper' family. Phil even got to help his foster mother bake a proper birthday cake just for him. He yearned for that cosiness that came from baking in a warm Autumnal kitchen in a family home. Both boys had quietly dared to hope that this was to be their permanent home but barely a month after Phil's birthday, on the 27th November

1933, they were moved once more – this time to a newly-opened Barnardo's home. The grandly-named and imposing Dalziel of Wooler Memorial Home in Gloucester Road, Kingston was only just the other side of a sprawling London from Woodford Garden City, but for the young Wilson brothers it might as well have been the other side of the world. They had been uprooted once again.

Chapter Three

Dickies

Dalziel of Wooler House, Gloucester Road, Kingston-upon-Thames

Escorted again by a Barnardo's Welfare Officer in the DBH bus across London, this time they were travelling East to West through the north London suburbs around the noisy newly-finished North Circular Road. As they neared their destination and the London streets got greener again the driver pointed out the Royal Botanic Gardens at Kew and later Phil was sure he had glimpsed deer as they drove near Richmond Park. The small group of boys sat silently on the Barnardo's bus as it shuddered to a halt outside a grim three-storied building on Kingston Hill, built from black brick with its distinctive yellow brick tower with 'Dr Barnardo's' glittering in gold. This was to be the Wilson boys' last 'home' together.

As they arrived at the imposing main door of their new home, which Phil felt at first glance resembled a prison or a workhouse, the boys were greeted by the Barnardo's superintendent Richard 'Dickie' Gardener. He was a thin man, a voracious smoker with a slight stoop and a hairy green suit, who they were to discover had only three obsessions. The three B's - Brentford Football Club, boxing and his band – the musical troupe with handbell ringers and bagpipes played by boys in Stuart tartan. The 'Gaffer' as the boys were to come to call him, and his almost entirely male staff, provided a more robust environment designed to make men of the boys at 'Dickies'. It would be make or break for the Wilson boys.

The brothers had each been kitted out with two shirts, an ill-fitting suit, two sets of underclothes, socks, working boots and overalls and a pair of hard pyjamas, smelling of ironing and musty mothballs – this blue bundle of clothes across their shoulders were their only worldly goods apart from Phil's treasured moth-eaten copy of Pilgrims Progress, wrapped in a parcel. As they entered the House with its constant smell of floor polish, echoing with boys' voices from remote dormitories, the two new boys nervously took the short flight of red steps leading to a lobby which seemed to soar up into the central tower which itself was lined with a staircase. The iron balustrades on the landings added to the institutional feel of the place, as did the glistening thick linoleum floors.

The two young brothers at least were allowed to stay together in their vast 30-boy dorm with its three long rows of beds. Each bed had a blue and white counterpane, neatly folded and tucked. Phil fought back tears as he carefully placed his battered copy of Pilgrims Progress into his penknife-scarred wooden locker by his bed.

For the growing lads, the food at 'Dickies' seemed less generous than Woodford. Breakfast was two slices of bread and beef dripping and a cup of unsweetened cocoa. Tea was two slices of bread and margarine and a mug of tea – both meals served in the dining hall under the baronial spread of stags' horns. On your birthday, they were informed, you would get a boiled egg as a treat – presented with some ceremony. The highlight for the boys, food wise, was the midday meal served hot at St Luke's elementary school on Kingston Hill.

Fights with the 'outside' boys at school were common as the two hundred or so 'Doctor Banana boys', as they were dubbed by the cruel local lads, refused to take it lying down. The more timid Phil tried to keep out of trouble with the almost entirely male staff at the home, but Fred was having none of it. The four Barnardo's essentials – religious instruction (the Pilgrims Progress the only book the boys possessed) education, sport and moral principles, were at the core of 'Dickies'. The Gaffer added his own personal motto, 'give a boy a sense of humour and a sense of proportion and he can go anywhere.' Punishment was strict if you stepped out of line – painful caning on the hand that would sting for ages and was feared by all but the toughest of boys. Scout uniform was to be worn on parade on Sundays.

If, like Phil, you loved the outdoors and wanted a sense of freedom you could ramble in the nearby woods full of songbirds, squirrels, rabbits and, if you were lucky and very quiet, the occasional deer. You just had to be careful not to get caught bunking off.

The Home's 'Musical Boys' bagpipe troupe that was the Gaffer's pride and joy was popular with Barnardo's and was used by them to raise money for all the children's homes. Concerts took place all over the country and there were even staged appearances on Pathe newsreel profiles filmed with heart rending messages of boys yearning for a 'muvver' for Christmas.

That first Christmas at Dickies for Phil and Fred, saw them appearing on the big screen as 'Father Christmas' was piped in by the troupe adorned in kilts and quickly mobbed by the excitable cheering boys playing up to the camera. In addition to the skirl of the pipes, the boys added their own colour. The Kingston song 'there is a mouldy shack on Kingston Hill where we get goshy soup that makes us ill' which was still being sung in the 1940s, when the author Leslie Thomas recalls his days at Dickies, would have started in the Wilson boys' era.

The brothers would have baulked at the phrase used by the newspapers and Pathe Newsreel at the time, that Barnardo was 'the Father of Nobody's children'. They were their mother Kate's children. They knew that. They just could not understand why they could not go back to her.

Fred remained a worry for Barnardo's. He just did not settle. So early in 1934, barely a few months after their move to Kingston, it was proposed once again that both the Wilson boys would be shipped to Australia. The teachers again prepared them for the journey with tales of life Down Under and of the exciting journey they were to undertake. They met as a group with the small number of other children due to make the voyage. They started to feel nervous excitement at the prospect of such a long journey with such exotic stop-offs en-route. They waited nervously in line for their smallpox injections that stung like mad.

Once more, they were driven into the centre of London and through the West End to the imposing Australia House at the top of the Strand, to learn more about the country that was to become their home. As they walked into the lobby of the huge white building Phil wondered if all Australian buildings would look like this. Very similar to the other posh buildings around them in London.

As they joined a party of other children their age who they were informed were from other children's homes, a big man with a booming voice that was speaking English but sounded like he was from a different land showed them a map of the world and highlighted Australia, pointing out the port of Fremantle where, he said, their steamship from Tilbury Docks would take four weeks to sail to and marked the beginning of their new life in the sun.

Phil was more excited about the Farm School than he could imagine. He had always loved the outdoors and though he was afraid of being so far away from their mother Kate and Henry, in case they came searching for them, he knew that the change of surroundings could only be good for Fred. He was ready to leave and though he wasn't sure about looking after the animals, he did think it sounded exciting. They talked animatedly about the life that lay ahead of them and planned for their future together on the other side of the world.

He started to prepare himself for leaving England. He would look after his younger brother and they would always have each other even in this strange new land. They could work on a farm together. If they worked hard and the farming did well they could find Ma and Henry and they could come and live with them in the sunshine. They would have a home and a garden of their own and grow their own greens.

However, when the time came for the welfare officer at Barnardo's to confirm their place on the ship, cruelly, it was Phil who took ill. The Gaffer thought it might be a reaction to his injections but to be on the safe side it was Phil's turn to be transferred to the seaside at Bognor to convalesce for three weeks, with his younger brother Fred in tow. Their future in Australia was now once again in doubt. Phil was sorry as he assumed that they would once again miss out on the journey round the world. But Fred was so 'unsettled' at Kingston the momentous decision was taken by Barnardo's to leave Fred on the passenger list and strike Phil off. They were going to leave him behind and send Fred, the only person he had left in this world to care for and to love him, halfway around the world without his big brother to look after him.

On his return to Dickies, the Gaffer, Mr Gardiner, tried to explain to Phil that Fairbridge only wanted children that were fit and well to help build the new Australia. It was resolved that the nine-year-old Fred was to sail alone in a small party of 22 other 'orphans' to a fresh start Down Under. Why the Barnardo's authorities felt it appropriate to send the younger brother alone is still not known. He would be the youngest boy of the Ballarat 1934 party. Perhaps they felt unable to cope with Fred and saw the new life in Australia as his best hope of getting him on the straight and narrow.

Whatever the reasons, this momentous decision was to change the lives of the Wilson brothers forever.

Chapter Four

The Longest Voyage

Torn apart from his dear brother, the only person he felt he had left in the world and after the first of many incredible journeys, Fred was to be toughened up into a man and schooled to become a farm hand to help build the new Australia that was emerging after the Great War.

The late Kingsley Fairbridge was described to the children on the boat by the two 'old' farm hands Frank and Bob Sandilands, deputed to give them a flavour of the life they had to come, as 'a down-under Doctor Barnardo'. Fairbridge and his wife Ruby had created the Farm School bearing their name, on the 3200 acres of the former Paterson estate in Pinjarra, in the image of Woodford Garden City. Oxford-educated Fairbridge wanted to give the children the same taste of The Empire. They raised money from wealthy English benefactors and built cottages named after the same great Empire builders and saluting the same flag on Empire Day. Only this was a real working farm in the heart of the hot Western Australian countryside with the South Dandalup River running through it.

For the nine-year-old Fred this incredible journey was exciting at first. The Group photographs of the twenty-three strong Ballarat party from different children's homes dressed in their smartest Fairbridge Farm School (FFS) suits and ties at the noisy and crowded Fenchurch Street station, while the boys laughed and joked and tried to hide their nerves from the tearful girls, made them all feel very special. Fred looked up at the imposing zig-zag canopy outside the main entrance of the station and thought it reminded him of a huge snake. He hoped he would not see too many of those for real in Australia.

SS Ballarat Party April 1934

Fred, aged 9, is pictured fourth from the right in the back row

After what seemed to the excited young Fred like a very long time waiting for their train to be called, and after the children were encouraged by the Deaconess to use the toilet on the cavernous main concourse before their journey, the Fairbridge Party boarded the LNER steam train which soon after slowly puffed and edged its way out of the grey city. As their train slowed on approach to Tilbury railway station Fred was excited and a little scared by the noise and the sheer scale of the sprawling Docks. Everywhere he looked there seemed to be loud uniformed young porters shouting to make their way through the melee with trunks and other bags.

As he struggled to play hopscotch whilst carrying his brown FFS-issue suitcase on the wooden planks of the walkway linking the station to the landing stage, the noise was deafening and the ship that was to carry them across the sea looked imposing moored alongside the quay. He had never seen a ship this large up close or even in his imagination. Fred was surprised to see so many other passengers preparing to get on board. In his mind the Barnardo's children were the only people travelling so far around the world on this long adventure. Why would anyone want to travel quite so far if they were not being made to? Some of his newfound friends were the saddest to leave behind the familiar surroundings of the children's homes. All the talk of the strangeness and difference of Australia had scared them a lot. The thought of snakes and strange spiders in such a hot country kept them awake at night in the weeks running up to their planned departure. Fred could not make his mind up.

The children caught sight of the dirty water from the Thames below as they gripped the wooden handrails and gingerly clambered on board, along what felt like a very precarious wooden gangway. The screeching seagulls overhead seemed to be mocking them with their laughter-like cries. Fred so wanted to explore the ship, but the Deaconess had warned them that they all had plenty of time during the six-week voyage to get to know their temporary home. The smell of the polished wood was overpowering and for Fred another painful reminder of his mother's War Office cleaning apron and how much he missed her.

There would be no need on the farm for the smart suit and panama hat that Fred was lent for the voyage to keep up appearances at the Captain's table. No need for the smart shoes at all, that he wore when he boarded. To be sure, it was an exciting journey. No doubt a romantic voyage for some passengers, aboard a beautiful old steamship that had seen many former glories. The SS Ballarat, even this had an exotic sounding Aussie name, set off from London's Tilbury Docks to the sound of a brass band, red white and blue streamers blowing in the breeze, wishing all aboard a noisy 'bon voyage'. This 'single-class' steamer was a popular P&O service, transporting mostly hopeful migrants seeking something better, as their families stood on the quayside lined up to tearfully wave them off to their new life Down Under.

But there was no one waving just for Fred or seeking him out among the throng on the passenger deck. No one at the dockside crying at their loss or happy for his future. No one holding their end of the streamer to be released on the breeze on departure to brighten the sky with the rainbow colours of the Empire. He was making the longest journey of his life, from the grey shores of England to the sun-scorched earth of Australia, utterly alone at the age of nine.

With the top deck crowded with passengers waving their goodbyes to the people they were leaving behind on the Tilbury quayside, who seemed to be shrinking in the distance as the ship headed along the Thames for the open sea, uniformed stewards dressed in pressed whites with buttons that shone in the sunshine, took the boys down to the depths of the Ballarat through what seem like a maze of corridors to find their four berth cabins. Fred made a token effort to 'bagsy' the top bunk but secretly felt relieved when one of the older boys, George Tanner, got their first as he wasn't sure being up top would be safe during what he feared might be a rough passage when they hit the open seas.

For the Fairbridge children on board, for that was how they were to be defined from now on, it was a fearful journey in many ways. It was bad enough that it was Friday 13th April 1934 when they left England. The sixty-six-year-old slightly stern Deaconess looking after the children, Miss Bell, shared a nervous joke with another passenger that it was just as well they were not superstitious. Though the Ballarat seemed sturdy enough, the ocean could be a dangerous place. He may not be totally aware of it, but Fred was, for the first time in his life, alone in the world, seeking solace in the tears and hugs of other children facing the same fate. The innocent grandmotherly attentions of Miss Bell somehow unable to make up for a mother's hug, that gentle pat on the head or stroke of the hair that signals unconditional love. The further he was to travel away from London, the harder it would be for Ma and Henry (and now even his big brother and only true friend, Phil) to find him.

To make matters worse for Fred there were two sets of tight-knit brothers in the group on board to remind him of how much he was missing Phil. Like Phil and Fred, the Sandilands brothers and Michael and Tony Arnott were two years apart in age and Miss Bell said they were joined at the hips just like the Ashton sisters Ivy and Lucy who were the same age as he and Phil. On the positive side, two other boys, Stan Trigg and

George Tanner, were both from Kingston too and were happy to look out for Fred.

As Fred lay on his bottom bunk bed, marking out his territory in his temporary home, careful not to mess up his smart new suit he had been given for the journey, the dipping and gentle swaying of the Ballarat threatened to send him to sleep but he was too excited for that. He had time to empty his FFS suitcase of the few belongings he had been allowed to bring with him from Dickies. Thankfully the crude drawing of an aboriginal boy with a boomerang his brother Phil had given him with its pretty colouring to prepare him for the voyage was still intact, if a little crumpled. He placed it carefully under the smartest of pillows he had ever seen to press it neat again. It wasn't long before the travelling gong called the party to the posh State Room restaurant for the first dinner sitting.

Compared to their regimented life at Dickies, this really did feel like being on a swanky floating hotel or one of those London chop houses that Henry used to curse for wasting food as the barges sailed down the Thames full of the stuff the 'posh knobs' had left on their plates. They were not going to waste a morsel. The Fairbridge children were to be feted at Captain Tickell's table at dinner in the State Room. He told them the ship was built in 1921, which Fred knew made it the same age as his brother Henry and just older than Phil. They were served real food so rich and so far from the Barnardo's 'goshy' it almost made Fred sick, and there was lots of it. Fred just was not used to having fresh fruit to choose from for breakfast, in addition to sausages and eggs. He had to check himself not to steal it all away.

The Deaconess told them there was no need while they were being treated so well on board and that they should check their behaviour to repay the captain's kindness. Fred quickly worked out which of the waiters were kindly and would be able to serve him seconds of his favourite rice pudding if he asked him nicely. The smiley cabin stewards looked after the children too and offered them extra blankets when it got a bit nippy at night-time.

As the journey went on, time was spent exploring the ship and learning new skills through playing exciting new games like deck quoits and deck tennis, and some of the old favourites like hide and seek. Fred was good at this as his size helped him hide in the most compact of places on deck. This all took the children's minds off the constant swell of the waves. Enduring early morning reveille and a deck-side drill in their regulation grey swimming trunks became the boys' newest routine.

When he had the chance, and once he had decided he wasn't going to fall overboard, Fred liked to roam the deck with some of the other older boys and try to stay out of mischief. At times he was lost in his own thoughts. He would lay on the deck and look up at the cloudless sky and marvel at just how blue it was.

The Deaconess told Fred that the Saxons called the sea 'the Whale Road'. After their first few days at sea, and the disappointment of seeing no whales in the Bay of Biscay despite Fred and his friends keeping watch from the passenger desk, the Ballarat passed through what Miss Bell explained was the Straits of Gibraltar and docked for the first time at the Port of Naples. The children were not able to leave the ship and had to be content with a brief sighting of the city from behind the dockside buildings, but at dinner the children were treated to incredible Italian ice cream like Fred had never tasted before. Miss Bell tried to teach them how to say 'tri-colore', which Fred remembered means three colours. Three ice cream flavours, three colours on the flags they could see surrounding the port. One of the passengers who had gone ashore in Naples brought back on board the strangest looking puppet in a white suit with a sinister black mask covering its face which she told Fred was called something like 'pulchy nella' and was where we got Punch and Judy shows from. Fred didn't really understand and in any case he was quietly relieved when she put the scary puppet safely away in its box.

There was the very whiff of the British Empire about the Fairbridge children in their suits and hats that got Fred strange looks when the boat docked again after a long stretch through the beautifully blue Mediterranean Sea, and this time the group went ashore at Port Said. He was captivated by the smells and the vivid colours of this new world that they had only ever read about in school textbooks. For sure this was the Africa they had read about in school in Kingston and where the Captain had served in the Army.

His pulse quickened at the sight of camels' heads dripping with blood in the place they called the medina. The old and oddly smelling 'Gully-gully' men charming the scariest of snakes from their baskets with music from a strange instrument that Fred thought even Phil's beloved Barnardo's musical boys might struggle to play.

Fred's young senses were assaulted from all sides. He had not felt heat like this before and squinting at the sun made his eyes water. He was glad of his ill-fitting FFS Panama. As they walked around the noisy medina strangely dressed men, some with their heads covered, sat cradling small cups of steaming coffee while staring back at their young white faces. They seemed very interested in Miss Wigan and Miss Joynes, the two younger ladies helping Miss Bell look after the children.

It was a frightening and almost overwhelming experience that at once had him yearning to get back to the charmed existence of the steamship but at the same time to his young mind was strangely captivating. He stuck close to Miss Wigan as a young man pushed past them pursuing a tired looking donkey carrying baskets on its back, shouting something in a language Fred did not understand.

Local children, surely no older than him, sun-drenched and happy in their simple, shoe-free existence, made him sad for the life he had left behind. Running free, without hats, boys holding hands, running kites, brothers in arms leaving him aching inside to be dragging his older, quieter brother Phil reluctantly around the medina. He remembered how he and his brothers would run across Westminster Bridge and explore the posher London streets, dodging policemen, or trying to nick sweets from the market stalls at the Cut, avoiding a clip round the ear if they could.

He had the same pangs of jealousy later on the journey when he watched the Aden boys, diving for coins as their fathers and older brothers carefully steered their small boats near the old lighthouse in the Gulf of Aden – manoeuvring alongside the Ballarat to sell food and trinkets to the richer white folk on board. Fred wanted their freedom. He wanted to be diving with them. They seemed free not only of clothes but of all inhibitions. Fred loved feeling the warmth of the lapping waves against his stinging skin. He wanted to keep that olive skin on his face too that he was picking up on this long voyage. Not the 'Watneys Pale Ale' south London skin his dad used to tease him about.

The children were feted wherever the ship docked in port to refuel or allow passengers to disembark. Once they had navigated the deep and narrow Suez Canal where they had been besieged by flies, and crossed the Arabian Sea to disembark at Colombo in Ceylon, they boarded a bus that had once boasted brilliant colouring but was now faded and wilted in the tropical heat.

The Fairbridge Party were captivated by the rickshaws running through the streets. They saw what seemed to them like giant trees, mosses of twisted vines creating black canopies of much-needed shade.

The bus blew red dust clouds as it shunted across the city, passed oriental shops of vivid colours, wooden wagons and thatched carts full of strange-looking fruit and vegetables, finally arriving at the huge iron gates at the entrance to Colombo Zoo.

Once they had all dismounted from the dusty old bus and ambled open-mouthed through the imposing Zoo gates, the sweating Fairbridge party took shelter from the searing sun under coconut trees and were offered the chance to sip coconut milk for the very first time. These coconuts were nothing like the ones Fred had seen at the funfair. These were green but their flesh tasted so much sweeter than he remembered. Fred marveled at the striking colours – the mauve, red , orange and apricot flowers that Miss Wigan said were called bougainvillea, the large butterflies floating around the children as they sat slurping fruit and noisily dripping watermelon juice onto the cloth-covered tables set out for them in the shade of the most exotic palm trees.

When he looked back it felt to Fred that Colombo was the last hurrah of this amazing journey before the authorities readied the party of 23 children for the stark realities of Farm School life.

The mood among the children on deck seemed to change over the following nine days of the voyage as they came to realise that this was the last stop on this great holiday before the start of the rest of their lives.

This was the last week of what had seemed like an endless dreamy voyage across the beautifully blue Indian Ocean where the cloudless skies and the sea seemed to be joined together, broken only by the swirls of waves caused by the bow of the steamship that looked like vapour trails. The land mass of Australia slowly came into their eyeline. The children were so excited at their arrival that they had been awake since daybreak even though Miss Bell warned them that they would have a long hot day ahead of them before they finally reached the Farm school.

Fred was already sweating as he put on his new ribboned gold and brown Fairbridge tie with some help from George. He hadn't quite mastered the knot and his Phil had always been around to help him before. His white Panama hat with its FFS cloth badge was a little too big for Fred's head but Miss Bell said that was just as well as it would help keep the hot sun off his thick little neck.

As the sun slowly rose higher into the sky Australia looked to Fred so dry and desolate after the colourful tropical heat of Colombo. The stone breakwaters of Fremantle Harbour came into view and as the Ballarat approached the dock Fred caught the cries from what he later realized were out-of work dockers shouting to the children. They did not sound like friendly voices to Fred. Miss Bell had warned the children that not everyone was pleased to welcome this party of newcomers who were here to help build the 'White Australia' of the future.

Fred was a little sad to be finally leaving the SS Ballarat. The voyage had been like a dream world filled with images and smells he would remember forever. It had given him a flavour of a world way beyond foggy grey London. He had tasted ice cream like no other, in Naples. From now on whenever he clasped the tin whistle he had acquired in Port Said he would think of the gully-gully men charming the slowly coiling snakes. As his meagre coin collection grew, he would remember fondly the brown boys diving off the boats in Aden. And if he ever got to taste the delicious watermelon juice again, he would think of the amazing zoo in Colombo and the green coconut trees. Whatever lie ahead in Pinjarra, Fred knew that this long journey had changed him forever.

After their fingerprints had been taken, with George Tanner whispering to Fred that it made them feel like the convicts that Australia was famed for, and a short period the Deaconess explained was to assess whether they had to 'quarantine', Fred's party of tired and excited children noisily boarded a steam train from Fremantle towards Perth. Lulled into a slumber as the train wound its way slowly through the Perth suburbs Fred recalled a green and pleasant countryside he had once caught a glimpse of as a small boy when jumping the Necropolis train out of Waterloo. But whereas the Necropolis railway was taking people to their final resting place, this journey was the start of Fred's whole new life down under.

He stared at the tidy green spaces between the red-roofed bungalows with their well-kept lawns and brightly coloured flowerbeds that he knew Phil would have loved. He had expected Australia to be hot and arid but arriving in their Autumn time Fred was surprised at how fresh and green the countryside was as the train gradually left the Perth suburbs behind and headed into the countryside.

He could almost have been in England if it wasn't for the strange name of Pinjarra on the station stop at the small country town where the excited Fairbridge party were to leave the train for the last leg of their tiring and memorable journey.

Clambering onto the flat top Fairbridge Farm School bus, the party then faced a ride along a hot and bumpy Pinjarra dusty dirt track of white Western Australia sand that went on for miles before eventually reaching the Farm School nestled among the Darling Range. Fred had finally reached the place that was to be his home for the rest of his life.

Chapter Five

Left Behind

The young Phil was heartbroken. On his return to the Kingston Barnardo's home from the Convalescent Home in Bognor, he withdrew into himself as he thought about the journey his younger brother was making, all the way around the world to Australia without him. He cursed himself that he had got ill at just the wrong time. He promised himself he would try as hard as he could to stay well in case another chance came for him to join his brother on the other side of the world. In the evening at Dickies after he had finished his schoolwork and dorm chores, Phil would pore over the map he had been given to track the Ballarat's passage and visualize Fred and the other children at the different stop-off ports.

He wrote long letters to his little brother in the hope that Fred would get to read them at some point and at least not forget about his old Phil. Even though he knew that his news, of bagpipes lessons, cub scouts and school work was going to be a lot less exciting than Fred's journey around the world, Phil felt he had to let Fred know that he was thinking of him. When Mr Gardiner said that the post to Australia was unreliable, Phil concocted a grand plan in his head to get messages there by an unconventional route.

He had heard on the wireless that the famous Australia tennis player and reigning Wimbledon champion, Jack Crawford, was coming to London again in June to defend his title from the challenge of Phil's tennis hero Fred Perry. Phil knew it was risky, but he had a plan to get a message to his Fred. He had met a boy through the Scouts – Will Brown - who had boasted that he had been a Wimbledon ball boy and was going to be one again this summer. Will was a Shaftesbury lad the same age as Phil – living at the Fortescue House in Twickenham, and Shaftesbury, Will had told him, provided the volunteers to be ball boys on the big occasion. Will was 'quid's in' to be picked.

The Dickies' boys believed that the Gaffer should have insisted that they were also given the chance to volunteer but he was only really interested in football and being a ball boy at Brentford FC was nowhere near as exciting for the boys as the legendary Wimbledon lawn tennis finals. Phil put that animosity towards the Shaftesbury lads aside now as from playing footie with him in the Scouts he thought Will could be trusted to carry a message from him to give to Jack Crawford who could carry it back to Australia and hopefully onto his Fred. All he had to do was hope that Brown was chosen to be a ball boy for one of Crawford's big matches.

Sadly, Phil's plan had only one flaw; it relied on the sickly Brownie being well enough to be chosen to ball boy this year. Despite Phil encouraging him and receiving his assurance on a cub's honour, that he would do his best by him, Brown did not make it to Wimbledon. He was taken ill the night before the selections in the dining hall and did not make it. Phil was beside himself. He took the long letter he had written to Fred and carefully folded it inside the cover of his Pilgrim's Progress.

He would have to find another way to get a message to him. It was with mixed feelings that Phil was glued to the wireless to listen to the men's final and heard commentator announce that his favoured Fred Perry had beaten the Australian Jack Crawford, the reigning champion, in three straight sets 6-3, 6-0, 7-5. As the commentator said that Crawford was returning to Australia empty-handed, Phil knew it was true - in more ways than one.

It was July now and though Fred should have arrived in Pinjarra in May Phil had still not received any news from abroad. He had read a headline in the Evening Standard in the Kingston library, of children who were lost at sea. He knew that the ship would stop at African ports and in Ceylon where the library encyclopaedia said snakes and spiders could kill you with their bites. He prayed hard that Fred would be safe.

He would not give up trying to reach his brother. Only this time he would have to come up with a plan that did not rely on anyone else. He would have to get his message to Fred in person.

Just as the school summer holidays started, Phil learnt about the Great MacRobertson trophy Air race to Australia. It was, the poster at Kingston Railway station exclaimed, the World's Greatest Air Race, from London to Melbourne, 11,300 miles in total, to mark the Victorian and Melbourne Centenary,

1934-5.

When he found a copy of the Times in the Kingston Library, he read more about it. Commencing at dawn on the 20th October from the Mildenhall aerodrome in the flat Suffolk countryside east of London, glamourous teams of daring amateur aviators were being invited to pitch themselves in to be the fastest to reach Melbourne by air. The boys in Dickies were talking of little else, comparing notes and taking matchstick wagers on the twenty teams racing and putting their hopes on a British victory. Would Amy Johnson make history?

Phil's hopes were elsewhere. Even though Melbourne was some distance from Fremantle where Fred had sailed to, it was at least in the same country. He decided he would write another letter – this time to the de Havilland Comet team of record-holder CWA Scott and his co-pilot T Campbell Black, offering to go with them. He had nothing to lose. There was no one here to miss him if he went. The race was due to start just a week or so before his twelfth birthday, in late October 1934, six months after Fred had sailed, and his eleven-year-old self had taken it upon himself to make up for being ill when he should have been on that steamship chugging out of

Tilbury Docks – he should have been there for Fred. This was his chance to get to Australia. He agonized over the letter and it took a number of attempts to get it into a state he was happy with.

It read.

Dear Sirs

My name is Philip Wilson and I am eleven years old. My brother Fred was sent away to Australia but he is not a convick. I was suposed to travel with him but was poorly. Can I pleese fly with you to Melborne so I can be with Fred again. I dont way a lot. Thank you.

Philip Wilson. Barnardos Homes. Kingston Hill

The days following his posting of the letter passed so slowly. After a week, Phil had convinced himself he was to hit the jackpot and Scott and Campbell Black would be writing back to invite him to join them on their epic flight. He was happy to take the risk. Though the Comet aircraft were tiny he was still small enough to stow away on board and it would make a great story that would hit the headlines all over the world and on Pathe Newsreel – daredevil pilots reuniting two brothers while winning the race! Day after day as he returned from school Phil would check to see whether he had any letters. Nothing came. He convinced himself that today would be the one even as he was running out of days and the excitement about the race among the boys in Dickies was growing.

As he resigned himself to not getting a reply he wondered if he could get on board another way. He would have to head to Mildenhall, break past the police cordon and appeal to the pilots directly. When they heard Phil's plight, they could not fail to be moved and would be only too happy to take him with them. He just had to work out how to get there in time for the start in just a few days' time.

Suffolk looked a long way from Kingston on the map. If only they were still at Woodford he at least would be the right side of London. He just could not see how he would get to the airfield for the race start in time without help. He daren't discuss his plan with any of the other boys in his dorm. They just would not understand and if they let on to the Gaffer he would get the strap.

He had heard on the wireless that the King was going to start the race so there was only one thing for it. He would send a telegram to the King at Buckingham Palace asking to travel with him to start the race. It was a great plan. It would guarantee that he would be past the police cordon and close to the aircrews before they could do anything to stop him stowing away.

Time was of the essence. He raided his money box and ran to the Kingston Post Office. He had limited funds so the wording of the telegram was tight.

> Barnado's Boy (stop) requests to help His Majesty (stop) start the Air Race.

Thanks. Philip Wilson, Dalziel of Wooler Memorial Home, Kingston Hill (stop)

As he ran back to Dickies, Phil thought that surely the Palace will reply. The King was a kindly man and would want to help a Barnardo's Boy.

No response was forthcoming. Phil was so sad. He had convinced himself that his plan was bound to work and soon he would be on the way to seeing his little brother again. In time for his twelfth birthday. He didn't want to give up hope and right until the day before the Air Race was due to begin he held out for a miracle. Prayed for it. It was not to be.

When the wireless news broadcast that the King had hailed the start of the Air Race, Phil listened with the other boys and so wished he could have been part of that crowd of thousands of Londoners described by the reporter who had travelled up to Suffolk to witness this amazing spectacle. To walk among the planes as they prepared for take-off. To chat to the aircrews. Phil wasn't that bothered about meeting the King or the Lord Mayor of London as they started the race off. He just dreamt of stowing away with Scott or in Amy and Jim Mollinson's DH Comet for the 11,300-mile journey.

As the news broadcasts on the orphanage wireless in the days that followed were full of the race's progress and he mapped their five compulsory stops in the vivid world map in his mind, Phil grew more and more upset at the missed opportunity – especially when Scott and Black made it to Melbourne in less than 72 hours in their de Havilland Comet

'Grosvenor House' and were greeted by the cheering Australian crowds.

He just wanted to be with his brother again. Every time he passed the now fading poster of the be-goggled aviator in the bright blue sky heralding the race Phil was reminded of how far away his younger brother was from the London home of their birth.

As time went on Phil had to adjust to life without Fred. They were both on their own in the world now. Though his memory of him was to fade a little as time went on, he worried about his younger brother a lot and he was never far from his mind. Phil felt responsible. Had he not been ill before Fred was sent away, they would have travelled together and he would be there for him now. It was all the more frustrating for Phil that none of his letters were replied to by Fred. He had to get on with his life.

The Gaffer said he should stick to his schoolwork as he showed great promise. He worked on his bagpipe playing as he tried to convince the music teacher Mr Huskisson that he was good enough to join the musical troupe. Phil knew that the Musical Boys travelled all around the country playing for posh folk who gave money to Barnardo's. They had once even been to Australia handing round the hat at concerts as there were pictures on the wall of the Gaffer's office.

Phil liked the Music master Mr Huskisson. The down to earth Geordie had a sense of humour and was really encouraging when the boys made real efforts to try to master their instruments. He said that Phil had a good ear for music and though he struggled to learn the reading of sheet music he could pick up tunes and recognize their notes easily. Huskisson said it was a gift that Phil had, and he smiled as he thought he hadn't been given many gifts in his young life. He had best make the most of it. His piano playing was not brilliant, but he practiced as much as he could. The instrument he loved was the mandolin. In addition to the Gaffer's prized bagpipes, the musical troupe had accumulated a fascinating range of percussion instruments with long names including carillochimes, marimbaphones, tubephones and tubular bells.

Just after his fourteenth birthday Phil got the news he had been hoping for. He was to join the Musical Boys for their 1937 tour. It was to take the boys across the country, including visits to Scotland, Wales and Ulster. Phil would need to overcome his travel sickness as the boys would be travelling miles in a DBH bus around the country, but he was too thrilled to be chosen to worry about that now. Secretly he was disappointed that they would not be sailing to Australia but the Gaffer had said that times were hard for everyone, so they needed to raise the money close to home.

It was to be a punishing tour. Two concerts in each town and city they visited. One in the afternoon for local children and the evening performance for grown-ups and what Mr Huskisson called local dignitaries, Mayors and the like.

They could not have had a grander start to the tour. After an excited early start from Dickies, they drove through the cold rain to the northern city of Sheffield in the South of Yorkshire.

The steel city. They were in no doubt of this as they approached the smoky steelworks that dominated the skyline.

As they lugged their instruments up the steps of the entrance to the magnificent newly built City Hall made of Darley Dale stone and stood to admire its grand Palladian columns, Mr Huskisson told them that the last musician to perform in the grand hall there was a young American violinist called Yehudi Menuhin, so they were treading on auspicious ground. Phil could not have felt more nervous as the Boys were introduced by the Lord Mayor of Sheffield and someone called the Master Cutler.

It helped that the first concert was for the children as the boys did not feel as judged by the younger ones who always took some time to settle down into their seats but were soon enraptured by the music. They particularly liked the Highland sword dancing that accompanied the screel of the bagpipes. With Mr Huskisson on the portable organ and piano, the twelve strong group of boys worked their way through the varied programme with few wrong notes or missed beats. Their weeks of practice had paid off and the applause at the end was thrilling.

Everywhere they went, the boys got a brilliant reception. The children's concerts were always the most fun, once the audience had got over their excitement of being in what for most of them was an unusual venue.

For the evening performances Mr Huskisson was a little more serious in his introductions, especially if Major Rees from Barnardo's Head Office was accompanying them, but he still found time for amusing stories to entertain the audience. If Major Rees was unavailable, a local dignitary, usually a member of the Barnardo's Helpers League, would talk about the Boys Homes and the need for money to keep Doctor Barnardo's work alive. The boys would swell with pride as they were often cited as examples of young men taken from the streets and given new opportunities. Phil knew that his own story was a little more complicated than that and often wondered what his mother had gone through to lead to her giving up Phil and Fred when he was eleven.

After each concert the boys were paired off and billeted in local homes of Barnardo's Helpers. Phil loved this part as he got to sleep in a warm bed for the night with blankets that weren't scratchy and not in a noisy dormitory, and their breakfasts were usually well worth waiting for. Sausages were the boys' favourite and though Mr Huskisson had warned them not to be greedy their hosts were usually very generous with their helpings and seconds were common. They also got a glimpse of normal home life, though the homes they stayed in were always so different wherever they went.

After such a grand debut performance, the boys drove across the Pennines to the wet and cold Lancashire cotton towns of Colne and Nelson, where the local accents were so different to Sheffield, but the welcomes were just as warm. The boys were treated to a 'Lancashire Hotpot' after their evening performances. Hailing from Newcastle, Mr Huskisson always seemed more relaxed in these Northern towns. After a less than perfect performance in Lancaster Town Hall the boys faced a long drive across the country to Durham where they played in one of the smallest venues on the tour.

The Durham Miners Hall was packed to the rafters and the children here gave the loudest cheers. Mr Huskisson beamed as he welcomed his elderly Mam and Dad in the audience and Phil could see they too were very proud that their gifted son had become a band leader – even if it was with a band of orphans.

The boys were growing in confidence as the tour progressed and it was hard not to let it go to your head when you were introduced as the famous Barnardo's Musical Boys. Phil loved some of the grand venues they performed in. The Gloucester Corn Exchange with its Palladian columns dominating the City Centre. Bradbury Hall in Chesterfield which Mr H described as the poshest works canteen in the country. One of the most memorable for Phil was the Easter performance they gave in the old chapel of the Rye Monastery. Playing underneath the ancient wooden beams against whitewashed walls of the Chapel where the Austin Friars had sung prayers for generations gave the boys the willies but the acoustics were amazing.

After a break for the summer, when Phil was able to join the Scout summer camp in Sussex, they travelled to Scotland in September where they were to play in some places with names Phil had never heard of. Tillicoultry Town Hall, with its square tower and octagonal belfry with a clock. Cupar Corn Exchange, the Adam Smith Hall in Kirkcaldy, Arbroath (where the boys sampled smelly kippers for the first time and

Phil loved them) Markinch, and the wonderfully-named Burntisland Music Hall. In all of these small towns the boys had the best of receptions and often made the local newspapers as Mr Huskisson would tease them about their growing popularity.

They tried not to let it get to their heads, but it was hard not to feel special when you were courted like this around the country. Phil was just happy to be seeing so much of the country and he particularly loved the Scottish scenery as they drove through the Kingdom of Fife. The buildings may have been grey and brown in the rain but the people they met were always so friendly if a little reserved at first. The Scottish breakfasts were always the best though Mr Huskisson told them to wait until they had an Ulster Fry.

They had the opportunity in November, when after performing on Phil's fifteenth birthday in the Bath Pump Rooms, they travelled by ferry to Ulster and performed for Orangemen in Randalstown and at the grand wooden altar of the Kilkeel Presbyterian Church. In Carrickfergus they played in the Jubilee Hall of the old Town Hall.

On the way back to London the boys last leg of the tour was one of the most memorable as they visited coalmining towns in the South Wales Valleys. In Llanhilleth and Troedyrhiw, Rogerstone, Carmarthen and Newport, they were amazed by the hymn singing they encountered. Phil was taken with the grandeur of the Miners Institute in Llanhilleth that was bigger than many of the chapels and churches they had performed at that year.

It had been an amazing experience for the young Phil. He had loved travelling all over the country and seen how people in every part of the United Kingdom lived. From the miners in Durham and the Welsh Valleys to the cotton mill workers in Lancashire. Steelmen in Sheffield to God-fearing Orangemen in Ulster. Warm mothers who had welcomed the boys into their modest homes and fed them well even when they may not have had a lot for themselves. He had seen that there was kindness everywhere.

Their 'Notes of Happiness' concerts had brought joy to the greyest of places. His confidence had grown too. He had found a talent he did not know he had and though he was still shy with others and the quietest of the troupe, Mr Huskisson said he had really come out of himself on the tour. He would be sorry to see it end but it was time for another group of boys to have the chance to travel the land as Phil prepared to leave Barnardo's the following year for the world of work.

In the absence of a decent garden to look after at Dickies, when he wasn't practising his mandolin, Phil was happiest when he was scouting. The Captain had told them he had served under Baden-Powell in Africa and Phil was given a copy of the Chief Scout's Scouting For Boys as a present the last Christmas before his father had died. The Barnardo's homes took their scouting seriously and as well as their local sorties to Richmond Park many of the boys were given the chance to take part in a summer camp.

For many of the London boys this was their first exposure to life outdoors and they really took to camping under canvas.

When Phil was thirteen his scout pack were chosen to travel on the bus to the village of Warnham, deep in the West Sussex countryside for a memorable two-week camp in the spectacular grounds of Field Place, country house of the heir to the Mile End brewery fortune, Captain Guy Charrington and his sister Doris.

The Charringtons had made their fortune from brewing beer and buying pubs and the younger Charrington heir, Guy, had travelled the world after the Great War but always felt most at home in the English countryside and in his beautiful garden of his Sussex country house retreat.

As they travelled out of London in the DBH bus the Gaffer told the boy scouts that the Field Place mansion and farm in a lush green valley had been the birthplace of the poet Percy Shelley and was surrounded by acres of parkland – home of the largest herd of red deer in England and that the boys were allowed to explore, though they were to keep away from the Manor House and be really careful of the deer. The village, the sport-mad Gaffer said, was famous for its cricket. But Phil was more excited at the prospect of seeing the wild deer up close.

Phil loved seeing the deer in Richmond Park but the herd of red deer roaming the parkland near their Summer camp were somehow more thrilling to Phil as it felt to him like they were living as they had done through the ages, in the wild. Apart from one or two of the 'swedebashers', a term often given to Wiltshire farm boys, who had come to Barnardo's from small villages and taught the boys the skill of rabbiting, this was the first time most of the boys had experienced proper countryside. Phil loved to wake earlier than the other boys in the tent just to lie under canvas and listen to the dawn chorus over his fellow scouts' snores. In those summer mornings as the Sussex sun started to warm the tent a little before reveille and the bugle call to breakfast woke the other boys, Phil loved that feeling that the birdsong was just for him.

As much as he wanted to stay in the warmth of the tent this was his chance to explore the woods alone and stalk the deer. He would quietly untie the fastenings of the tent trying not to wake the others and run as quietly as he could towards the woods. If he was quiet enough not to disturb them he would catch a glimpse of the deer feeding nervously in the fields. This was a scouting job best done alone. The others just could not be trusted to be quiet. They would giggle at a fart or be startled by the crack of a fallen branch under their boots and frighten the deer off.

As the woods got warmer with the rising sun Phil knew it was time to head back to the tent before the Gaffer could work out he was AWOL. He was hungry anyway and however unappetizing, the thought of bread and scrape was enough to drive him back to the camp.

However cold he had been in the night in his broken sleep under his threadbare Barnardo's blanket this was soon forgotten as he cherished those brief moments alone with what felt like just nature to keep him company. Those August summer camps were the highlight of the year for Phil and were talked about by the Dickies boys for weeks before they happened. Though much of the routine was the same as it would be in Kingston, being outdoors made it much more fun for Phil. He even enjoyed the Sunday church parade in scout uniform to St Margaret's in the village when the boys were on display as the Barnardo's vicar, Reverend Snowdon Smith, preached a long and boring sermon that made the wooden pews feel even harder for the boys.

The group were treated to a day trip to the seaside at Worthing during the fortnight, though these trips were always fraught with problems as the local children and other holidaymakers often reacted to the 'banana boys' - conspicuous as they were in such a large group in their blazers on the beach.

The last time Phil got to visit Field Place was not in the warmth of the West Sussex summer but in the misty October of 1938, the month before his sixteenth birthday. As the country edged towards war with Germany and concern grew for the safety of children in London, Captain Charrington and his sister once more offered up Field Place as a safe haven for 150 of the Kingston Barnardo's boys, in the wet and sharp Autumnal weather asking their team of servants to prepare barns and outbuildings to provide better protection than living under canvas. Despite the extra work, the servants at Field Place loved having the poor boys around as they thought it brought some life to the sleepy village.

Phil was really looking forward to the visit. The Charringtons' posh house was almost as big as Dickies but unlike their Barnardo's home, did not look like a workhouse or feel like a prison. The beautiful gardens it was set in were like nothing Phil had seen before. Much nicer than at Woodford. More flowers than vegetables. He had befriended one of the young gardeners on the estate that summer, who introduced himself to Phil as Master Percy Scarland, when he noticed Phil was taking an interest in his glasshouse and potting sheds.

As Phil was helping him with the watering, Percy was a bit sniffy about 'Miss Charrington's war widows' as he called them, who were presumably the older ladies that Phil had seen pottering in the gardens when he first sneaked off from scout camp to explore the grounds. Percy said he thought they must have been married to young Captain Charrington's fellow soldiers in the Great War and the kindly Charringtons had taken them in to help fill the huge house as neither Miss Charrington nor the Captain had any charges of their own. He said the talk in the village pub was that the Captain preferred the company of young men but as far as Percy was concerned he had only ever shown him kindness and he would always stand up for him.

There was a lot of talk of War that year. Phil had read about the German dictator, Hitler, and how Germany had invaded what he called the Rhineland. The Gaffer said that he despaired that we had learnt nothing from the Great War though Phil remembered that the Captain had once said that the slaughter at the Somme was going to bring an end to all wars.

As the Scout group returned to Dickies, Phil knew that the scout camp was probably going to be his last one as a Barnardo's boy.

On reaching sixteen Phil was to be released from Barnardo's care, whether he felt prepared for the big wide world or not. It was with some trepidation that he said goodbye to Mr Gardiner and his life at Dickies as the DBH bus arrived to take him back across London to the Barnardo's Head Office and receiving home in Stepney.

The kindly Welfare Officer explained to the handful of boys making the journey that they would only be here for a week and were to be kitted out with the essentials they would need to start their working life.

They were to have a medical, be photographed by Barnardo's for the last time and provided with a suit as near to their size as they could manage, two shirts, two sets of underclothes, socks, overalls and working boots. Phil couldn't be sure what work he would be doing but he told the aftercare officer that he hoped it would be outdoors.

As the bus got near to Stepney Causeway, Phil was shocked at how noisy and crowded the place felt compared to leafy Kingston Hill. There were children everywhere on the streets and a large crowd of what looked like retired sailors who were lingering and smoking outside the building opposite. Phil felt he already knew the Barnardo's office as this was the place of legend in the Doctor Barnardo story. It was here they had been told in Church on Founders Sunday, that the good Doctor started his mission of saving poor London children like Fred and Phil and it was here that his body was returned on his death.

The grand entrance building with its 'No Destitute Child Ever Refused Admission' sign emblazoned across the front, was testament to that. Most of the children had moved out by now and the 'receiving home' as it was now called only provided a temporary stopping place for boys and girls of sixteen like Phil who were waiting to go to their work placements.

The welfare officer handed Phil over to a tall couple, who he introduced as Mr and Mrs Sandford and who were in charge of the home. They were friendly enough as they showed him to his noisy dorm, but Phil felt closer to Fred and Gert Berry who were, he was told, the caretakers of the building. Gert smiled a toothless smile as she introduced Phil to a boy of his age called Sid, who she said was the houseboy.

Looking around the tired old building he realized there probably was no need of a gardener here as the Stepney Causeway did not have much in the way of green space, much to Phil's disappointment, though if he was honest he thought he would prefer to be living somewhere a little greener than the East End of London.

After a restless night in the noisy dorm, the next morning Phil was sent to the resident Stepney tailor, Mr Maslin, or 'Maz the Snaz', as Sid had dubbed him on account of the snazzy suits he knocked up, who fitted him out as best he could with the suit and other clothes Barnardo's were to provide him with as he started his working life.

After a week in noisy Stepney, which reminded him a lot of his Lambeth childhood, Phil was feeling nervous as he was escorted by a different welfare officer on a train to leafy

Northwood, to the west of London, to the home of his new landlords and employers, Mr and Mrs Thomas. Phil was to be their chauffeur and gardener, though his driving duties would be minimal and most of his time, thankfully, was to be spent looking after their tidy lawns and colourful flower beds.

He looked out at the woodland and farm buildings as the train approached Northwood station en-route to his new temporary home, and it was hard to imagine that this was still London. It felt a world away from the Stepney and Lambeth he had known and was even quieter than Kingston Hill. Walking down the hill from the station past some grand houses and through a small wood, Phil struggled to believe that they were still in London.

Despite Mr Maslin's best efforts, Phil's Barnardo's issue suit was hanging off his thin frame and he felt a little shabby when he first saw the Thomas's as they were so immaculately dressed. Their tidy suburban home looked like something out of a posh magazine to Phil, with soft lighting creating a warm glow in their sitting room and classical music playing on a gramophone in the background as their Labrador, Rex, gently sniffed the nervous visitor. Mr Thomas informed Phil he was a textile designer, creating curtain ranges, and looking round the room Phil could see that he had brought his work home with him.

Mrs Thomas showed Phil to his box room that would be his digs for the duration and let Phil know the rules of their house. No smoking indoors, clean the bath after use, be home by nine thirty at night, and he was to help walk Rex, on occasion. A cycle was available to him for errands and the car was not for his personal use. Phil was relieved as his driving really was not up to scratch and he was surprised to have been told he had chauffeur duties. As it transpired, Barton Thomas liked to walk to the station on the way to work, and Mrs Thomas had most of her provisions delivered, unless she was shopping for clothes with her friends, so he was rarely called upon to drive them.

Phil could not believe his luck; he had been given a room of his own for the first time in his life! He would not be woken by another boy crying or pleasuring himself in the bed next to him in a dorm. He did not have to fear for his belongings or lock them away in a battered locker for fear of one of the thieving boys nicking them or destroying them just for fun. He could take as long as he needed in the bath, within reason, and the water would be clean and hot and not the freezing cold shower he was accustomed to. This is the life, he thought. He would make the most of it while it lasted.

He had barely settled in at Duck's Hill Road when Phil had the opportunity to be a movie extra. The Hollywood producers at MGM based at the Denham Film studios down the road from Northwood were looking for boys to volunteer as extras in a film they were making which was set in a fictional posh public school called Brookfield. They had built a complete set at the vast film studio buildings in Denham and needed schoolboys to take part in several of the school scenes, including a full school assembly. The garden work was less demanding in the winter, and the Thomas's agreed it was too good an opportunity to miss, so Phil jumped at the chance and soon found himself with a group of excited Barnardo's boys on a film set.

There was much excitement on set as the Director Sam Wood was making his first ever film in London, even though his most recent film 'Lord Jeff' – about a Barnardo's Boy, set in London– was filmed entirely in Hollywood. Phil glimpsed the tall American in the distance as they crowded into the vast warehouse full of lighting stacks and cameras, which had been turned into a made-up hall to shoot the school assembly scene, where the actor playing the Headmaster addresses the whole school. It was so thrilling to hear the American boom 'cut' the first time, though as the day went on and the scenes had to be reshot it did get a little wearing. There was a murmur of approval from the boys when the glamourous red headed Greer Garson arrived on set. She seemed to Phil to be a very friendly woman and not at all stand-offish like some of the cast. When they weren't shooting she would join the boys in making paper planes from the used production sheets that were lying around and her 'Garson Specials' took flight with ease.

In one scene the older boys, like Phil, were asked to wear army uniforms and march through the 'school grounds'. They were off to the front in the Great War. He stood taller in a military uniform even though he knew it was not the real thing. Phil wondered what the Captain would think of him being a 'Hollywood' soldier. The film world was an odd one for Phil. On his third visit to the set the boys had to engage in a snowball fight with fake snow even though it was snowing hard with real snow on the school buildings that had been constructed.

As the producer thanked the extras for their help, he told them that the film's working title was 'Goodbye Mister Chips' and would be released the following May. Though he was disappointed he did not have a speaking part he at least had plenty of stories to share with Mrs Thomas on his morning tea break.

Phil sensed a little sadness in Mrs T, as he cheekily called her once to her face, having got to know her better. She had no children of her own and he thought she might be lonely even with the boisterous Rex to keep her busy. She would often interrupt Phil while he was tending the gardens and offer him tea and ask if he had time for a chat. He always did, even in the busy times of the year when the beds needed the most work.

He loved getting his hands caked in mud as he lost himself in his thoughts as he worked. He was grateful to the Woodford Garden City superintendent for giving him the chance when he was younger to grow vegetables and help tend the rose beds. Mr and Mrs Thomas's gardens here at 42 Duck's Hill Road were on a much more manageable scale, thankfully, though they certainly kept the sixteen-year-old Phil busy.

The lively Rex had a habit of escaping from their garden when Mr Thomas was at work at the curtain factory, and Phil would often be despatched on his bicycle to retrieve him. Phil didn't really mind as it offered him the chance to put aside his shyness and pluck up courage to speak to the lovely

Marguerite next door, who Phil guessed was a few years older than him as she had told him she was an art student, to ask her whether she knew of Rex's whereabouts. He hadn't yet built up enough courage to speak to the elusive Helen from number 48, whom Mrs Thomas often spoke to in pleasant enough terms but privately was quite disparaging of on account of her profession as a masseuse.

Secretly Phil enjoyed what he called his 'Rexcue' missions as it gave him the chance to explore the nearby woods. Copse Woods which were a short walk from the Thomas's house, stretched from the reservoir to the centre of Northwood and was the biggest of the Ruislip Woods. Opposite their house were the Gravel Pits, a bowled wooded area which the locals had turned into a woodland to celebrate Queen Victoria's Diamond Jubilee with an abundance of sycamore, ash and common hawthorn trees. Phil's favourite woodland walk though, and not just because of its quirky name, was 'Mad Bess Wood'.

Mrs Thomas told Phil it was reputedly named after a local gamekeeper's wife and he loved to spot the different varieties of trees in the wood. He loved the sweet chestnut the best but he thought the hornbeam coppice had the best name and the oaks were the sturdiest, though it was the devil's own job keeping Rex away from gobbling up the acorns. Mrs Thomas liked to forage for fungi in the woods and loved the wild orchids, but Phil was a bit wary of the wild mushrooms. He joked that they were probably what drove Bess mad and, in any event, they could play havoc with his tummy.

It was on one of his Rex retrieval missions that Phil got to meet one of the residents of the Care Home for retired Actors, a few doors down from number 42. Denville Hall had caught Phil's eye earlier because it had such beautiful grounds surrounding its sweeping drive and imposing old building and he would often linger outside to speak to the elderly gardener Sid who kept the lawns so pristine and who had given Phil a passion for roses and lavender. Sid liked the young lad who showed so much genuine interest in the garden for one so young. He even clipped some of his treasured Holly at Christmas time to decorate the Thomas's table.

Sid could be quite grumpy about Rex spoiling his lawns, so Phil had to be careful when approaching him about the dog. One beautiful late summer's evening in September 1939 – Phil remembered it well because it was the day that he had heard on the wireless that Neville Chamberlain had announced that Britain was at war with Germany – Phil returned the smile from one of the retired actors who was enjoying his pipe in the gardens and seemed lost in his own thoughts.

Intrigued to know whether the retired thespian had been on the big screen Phil was delighted when Mr Cox introduced himself to the young garden boy. 'Cox, Charles Douglas Cox' dear boy, you may not have heard of me as you are too young, but I once had a career in film. Flicks like The Picture of Dorian Gray? '

Phil politely responded that he was not familiar with the works the aged Mr Cox had recounted but had recently been an extra in Goodbye Mister Chips. He was secretly impressed that he had actually met a real-life star of the silver screen. His Mum would be really impressed as she had loved it on that rare occasion when she had got to go to the pictures.

Before that the closest he had got, apart from admiring Greer Garson from afar at Denham, was when the striking young south London actress Diana Wynyard had visited the home earlier that year to meet the retired residents with the wife of the Prime Minister, Mr Chamberlain, and Phil had caught a glimpse of her from a distance as she posed for the newspaper photographers. Sid said he thought Mrs Chamberlain would make a darn sight better job of it than her hubby.

As Mr Cox puffed on his pipe on one of the garden benches and once again showed Phil his tattered scrapbook of newspaper reviews, he said that Wynyard was actually a cousin of his and her real name was actually Dorothy Cox. Phil did not know whether to believe him or put it down to his age. Sid had warned him that some of the residents had tall stories to tell. Once an actor always an actor and all that.

An avid reader of Mr Thomas's Times newspaper, that Mrs Thomas would let him take the day after her husband had finished with it and discovered the crossword clues he could not work out, Phil was anxious about the prospect of war and asked Sid what he remembered of the Great War. It was the only time that Sid had few words to say. Normally it was the devil's own job to shut him up. For now, he just looked sad as he put down his garden shears and quietly uttered 'shell shock'. Phil knew not to push it as he could see Sid's eyes welling up as he stared into the distance. He returned the subject to pruning, something Mr Cox said Sid could bore for Britain on, and left it there.

As the country started to prepare for what seemed like an inevitable war with Germany, Phil was relieved that the Thomas's were not going to need an Anderson shelter as their House had a cellar that could be used during air raids. He did not want to see their beautiful lawn that he had cared for so well dug up to accommodate an Anderson.

Phil was impressed with the wines stocked in the musty cellar and joked with Mr Thomas that he hoped he would not have to work his way through his collection during a bombing raid. Mr Thomas replied that these wines were for laying down and Phil thought that was a bit odd and that it would be a bit messy to drink that way.

When his twelve months with the Thomas's was coming to an end just after his seventeenth birthday the Barnardo's Welfare Officer paid him a visit and he could tell from the look on Mrs T's face that it was not good news for Phil. The couple had concluded that they could no longer afford to keep him on and though they were really pleased with his work and his demeanour, he could not stay on at Duck's Hill Road.

The welfare officer said that he would return the following week to take Phil back to Stepney for a few days until his new host family, Colonel and Mrs Watson, would be ready to receive him in their home in a small village in the Cotswolds called Southrop, pronounced Suvrup.

Phil was sad to be leaving and a little nervous about having to go back to Stepney, particularly now that the country was properly at war and the East End was so close to the London Docks. At least it was only to be for a few nights until he was to travel out of London completely and to what sounded like a posh house with a decent garden.

He volunteered to take Rex for walks through the woods for the last time and said his farewells to Sid and some of the residents of Denville Hall, before packing his small suitcase, leaving room for the lovely pair of secateurs that Mr and Mrs Thomas had given him as a leaving present and a thank you. He did not know what to say. It was the first time he had received a proper present for so long that he wanted to cry, but knew he had to be strong in front of the Welfare Officer who was waiting to escort him to the DBH bus.

As he left London later that week Phil felt an odd mix of emotions. He was excited about his new posting and the village life he was about to become part of. He was nervous about meeting the Watsons and could only hope that they were going to be as kind to him as the Thomas's had been. But he was also sad to be leaving the city he had known as home for all his childhood, however miserable much of that time had been.

As the bus to Paddington station made its way through the capital from Stepney, they briefly drove along the river bank and he could see across the river to Waterloo and the barrage balloons beyond and he imagined his childhood home lying just out of view. What had become of Ma and Henry? Henry was too old to be evacuated. He hoped they were somewhere safe and had not forgotten him or Fred.

He chuckled to himself when he saw a poster as he entered Paddington station. The poster depicted a figure of a soldier carrying a rifle talking to young boy wearing a helmet and carrying a toy sword and gun saying, 'Leave Hitler To Me Sonny – <u>You</u> Ought To be Out of London'. Don't worry, he thought, I soon will be.

As they waited for his Great Western Railway train to take him to the University city of Oxford where he was to change trains for the Fairford branch line and nearest village of Lechlade, the concourse at Paddington was filling up with noisy, excited schoolchildren carrying suitcases, many of them clutching their teddies tightly as they spoke to their tearful mothers.

It seemed he wasn't the only one being sent out of London to the safety of the country. He hoped this noisy lot weren't on his train. Looking at some of the labels on their luggage he could see they were also heading for Gloucestershire, though some were going as far as places he had never heard of in Cornwall. Maybe Southrop would not be as quiet as he had hoped.

As the train left London and slowly edged its way through the suburbs it was some time before Phil felt they were steaming through the real countryside and he could feel some relief that he was heading to a job in a country garden that he had hoped for since his Woodford Garden City days. He secretly hoped that Southrop would be untouched by the War and that he could live in peace there with his new host family. He felt bad that he was running away from his Ma and Henry but told himself that he didn't really have a choice.

Even though Ma's voice was less clear in his head he would never forget her and hopefully one day she would come and find him or at least let him know that she and Henry were happy. For now, he knew he had to think about the future and make a good impression with Colonel Watson and his family. He would keep his head down and hopefully stay out of this bloody War.

As the guard called 'next stop Oxford', Phil looked out at the ridge of rolling pastures in the distance and saw what looked like a giant tractor on the brow of a hill. As the train slowed further, he could see that it was actually a clump of trees forming that shape. He would need his wits about him in the countryside.

Arriving into Oxford Phil was surprised to see so many streets that looked identical with small brick houses and tiny gardens and as he pulled down his suitcase to leave the train he caught sight of some of the beautiful Oxford colleges the city was famed for. The porters had West Country accents he had not heard before, but he had to admit this was not quite the green and pleasant land he had expected.

Phil and his welfare officer had time for a warming cup of tea before boarding the Fairford train which seemed so much smaller and was full of uniformed young aircrew. As they pulled out of Oxford they were soon past the rows of streets he had seen from the train and passing villages that looked more like the ones in his imagination with small churches and farm cottages and village pubs.

At Brize Norton and Bampton station, a number of the RAF chaps left the train and Phil and the Welfare Officer virtually had the carriage to themselves for the rest of the journey to Lechlade.

A couple who Phil assumed to be Colonel and Mrs Watson were waiting for them as they stepped down from the train at the tiny Lechlade station with its honey-coloured stone ticket office. Phil could tell that they were well to do by their clothes and the way they spoke but he also felt that they were kind. Colonel Watson had agreed to become his legal guardian, so they weren't just looking for a cheap garden boy. The Colonel offered to carry Phil's suitcase, but he politely declined, nervous about offending him but wanting at the same time to show the couple that he was of age.

Colonel Watson slowed the car as they crossed the small bridge over what Mrs Watson pointed out was the River Thames and Phil could not believe that this narrow river could be the same as the dark wide water he played near to as a child in London. He was still pondering this whilst their car was stuck behind a tractor carrying what looked to Phil like precariously placed hay bales on a trailer, where two workmen eyed him as they clung onto the back as the tractor worked its way along the bumpy track. For the first time since his summer scout camps at Field Place, Phil could smell the country air and though it didn't exactly help his carsickness, he was glad of it.

The village of Southrop was exactly how Phil had pictured it. Surrounded by farmland, with its pub on the green, a small stone church with a tidy graveyard, a large Manor House with a stream running through it, a tiny village school and Cotswold stone cottages dotted along the roads. It looked like it had not changed much in hundreds of years. He would feel at home here. If it were not for the sight of uniformed aircrews and the occasional RAF training planes circling overhead before landing at the temporary airfield nearby, you would not know that this lovely part of England was at war.

As the car turned slowly onto the gravel drive of the grand Southrop Lodge Phil caught sight of a young lady he assumed was the Watsons' daughter as she got up from where she was seated on the lawns in front of the House to greet them. Phil straightened his Barnardo's issue tie and cursed the fact he had not got rid of the egg stain it had on it from the sandwich he had eaten on the journey from Paddington. He hoped Miss Watson would not notice.

Miss Watson introduced herself to the welfare officer and shook Phil's hand to welcome him to his new home. She said she hoped he would be very happy there and was looking forward to showing him around. Phil guessed she was perhaps a few years older than him but if was difficult to gauge without being seen to stare and he was anxious not to make the wrong impression. His time at Dickies had not exactly prepared him for adolescent exposure to the opposite sex. He felt his face reddening and was relieved when Mrs Watson interrupted them to offer to show Phil to his lodgings.

Lt Colonel Watson, Mrs Watson and their daughter Ina

Unlike in Northwood, Phil's lodgings were to be in a separate outbuilding in the yard and though he thought it might be nippy in the winter, he was sure to be able to make it cosy. Plus, it would be his very own space, close to the gardens. At first sight the garden looked like it would be harder work than the Thomas's, as Mrs Watson said he would also be in charge of keeping their grass tennis courts in tip top shape. Colonel Watson, though retired from the Army, was keen to keep fit and liked to play tennis with their daughter Ina, especially in the warmer months. Phil was struck by the Cedar of Lebanon tree that dominated the rear garden. He had seen them in books but never for real. Mrs Watson said she thought it was very old but should not give him too much trouble.

Phil smiled to himself. He knew he was going to be happy here and the secateurs that the Thomas's had given him as a leaving gift would come in handy, as the Lodge had some decent rose bushes to look after. After the paperwork had been dealt with, Colonel Watson took the welfare officer back to catch her train and Phil was free to settle himself into his room. He could not get used to how quiet the village was.

Southrop Lodge, circa 1939

The Lodge was next door to the Southrop Manor House and beyond that was a pathway through the graveyard to the church, but the road that ran past the window of his outbuilding barely saw a vehicle. It would take some getting used to after the noisy din of Stepney. The pub on the village green was barely a minutes' walk from the Lodge and he wondered if turning out time would be as rowdy as it was when they lived in Lambeth where, especially on Saturdays, they were often woken by a commotion in the street outside.

The Captain would often say that the magistrates would be busy come Monday morning. He need not have worried. There were rarely fights outside the Swan, just cheery young trainee aircrew cycling back to their base after one too many.

They didn't stop Phil sleeping, in any event. He was out for the count after long days working outside. If it wasn't too blowy, he would read by candlelight for a while but he was soon nodding off, being sure to snuff out the light before falling into a deep sleep under his rough blanket. He thought he would be happy here for as long as he could stay away from the war.

Chapter Six

Pinjarra

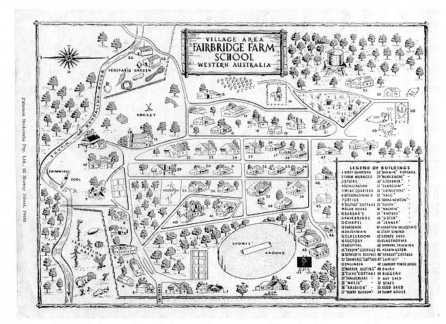

The deep blue sky felt so huge to Fred. He could not quite believe how far it seemed to stretch and thinking about that helped him stop thinking about the sickness in his tummy caused by the bumpy journey and the diesel fumes belching from the FFS bus.

The old bus kicked up more white sand as it pulled up outside the large tin-roofed building, that Fred would later come to know was the main Dining Hall for the Fairbridge residents. They were suddenly surrounded by children. This noisy, tanned rabble had no shoes on and were dressed not in smart suits and ties like Fred and his mates, but ill-fitting baggy shorts and shirts. Though they did not seem unfriendly, Fred felt slightly nervous about the reception he and the others were about to get as newcomers from England.

Their strict-looking school bus driver barked that there was no need for shoes here as he hurriedly collected them all in. Fred's feet were blistering and bleeding as he first explored the dusty, barren terrain without shoe leather to protect him. He knew not to moan. This was his permanent home now. He was being toughened up and drilled to become a fine citizen of the Empire and preserver of 'White Australia'. There was no time for tears. Fred fought them back as he had learnt to do since he was taken away from his Mum.

Fred was led, with a small group from his party, the Arnott brothers, Michael and Anthony, who were as close as Fred was to his Phil when they were at Kingston, Arthur Grenville (another boy about Phil's age whom Fred had struggled to beat at deck quoits onboard ship) George Tanner and Stanley Trigg, through the grounds of the Farm School to what was to become their new home. Newton Cottage, just one of a row of Australian-style bungalows that served as boys' cottages at Fairbridge.

Fred tried to show off to his mates with his knowledge that their new 'home' was named after Sir Isaac Newton who was a famous English scientist who was born on Christmas Day and made the laws of gravity. The others did not want to show Fred that they were impressed but he knew that they secretly were, even though he was glad they didn't ask him to explain gravity as he couldn't remember what the Captain had told him about it.

Despite being younger than the others by at least two years Fred could hold his own. He had the Captain's stockiness and, Ma had said, his dogged temperament. Having two older brothers to fight and argue with in the Old Country had toughened him up. It was just as well as Miss Brown could only do so much to protect him from their bullying if these bigger lads chose to turn against him.

Just like at 'Dickies' there was once again to be morning reveille here at Fairbridge, this time marked by the first bugle call of the day that made Fred think he had once more joined his father's army. Freezing cold showers with the freshest of water that came straight from the mountain streams of the nearby Darling range, gruel, bread and scrape were again a staple diet but only after the children had recited Grace. On Sundays at the cold brick built, but beautifully named, Church of the Holy Innocents, built from the profits of children's innocent pleasure gifted by the Wall's Ice cream king, Thomas Wall, they would pay homage to God and, perhaps more importantly, on Founder's Day, to Kingsley Fairbridge, the visionary with a heart for children like him, from the slums.

There were Cottage Mothers here too, just like at Woodford Garden City, this time overseen with military precision by Colonel Heath, whom the children dubbed 'Bonk'. Miss Brown, the boys were instructed to call her Miss, looked after Fred for the whole time he was to live at Newton cottage. Miss warned the boys that the Colonel was not afraid to use punishment if it was deemed necessary, but Fred never thought he was cruel.

For, Lt. Colonel Heath – 'Bonk' - was tough but fair. He took every opportunity, at dinner times at the top table in the vast Dining Hall and on Sundays in church to remind the children of the Fairbridge principles of 'unselfishness and consideration for others'. With his trimmed moustache and stiff-backed walk, Colonel Heath was very much still a military man and though he had lost an arm in the Great War he had clearly lost none of his authority.

The school at Fairbridge was also led by another 'survivor' of the Great War trenches, Mr Healy, who walked with a visible limp from an injury sustained at war. God had not blessed them nor their stern wives with blood children of their own but had charged them with the care of hundreds of 'lost' souls. But Fred wasn't lost. He knew exactly where he was from. He just was powerless to get back.

Fred settled in well in his new surroundings. Even though it was hard work he liked the routine of chores in the cottage, the smell of the polish they used on Saturdays to rub and redden the hard Jarrah wood dining table, which reminded him of his mother.

As he stood by his stripped bed for inspection by Miss before breakfast, he would pretend to be in the Army - doing his father proud as a young soldier he would have wanted him to become. He didn't even mind the food. It was little different to the Old Country although the dripping could be a lot harder to spread and here at least there was a little more jam than he had been used to in Dickies. Fairbridge had a fig orchard and Fred loved the taste of them even though they played havoc with his tummy.

Miss kept a rota for the boys to spread the chores out and Fred looked forward to being considered old enough to wield the axe to collect firewood for the wood burning stove that heated the cottage in winter. He liked the quiet times after bath time in the evening the best. Some nights Miss would allow the quieter boys to sit in her private room in the cottage and read comics or the West Australian newspaper or, when older, write letters.

Fred wanted so much to write a letter to his brother Phil. He had so much to tell him about his amazing voyage and the sights and sounds he had encountered. His young mind was racing with all the news he had to convey but for now he had to content himself with praying before bed that God would look after his brother and find a way to bring them back together. Fred didn't know what to say to God about his mother. He hoped she would write to him especially when some of the boys had heard from their families in England.

Saturday was set aside for cleaning the cottage thoroughly and for sports. Mr. Barrett was a popular sports master who, like the Captain, had been in the British Army, and loved to organize soccer, cricket or hockey tournaments, pitching cottages against each other. Newton was a good cottage for sports and Fred threw himself into the team games with much enthusiasm, if not so much skill.

On Sundays, just as they had at Woodford and Kingston, the boys would put on their best white shirts and corduroy trousers and walk to the Church for the morning service. The cold sandstone floor of the church was not much fun in the winter and competition for the crocheted prayer kneelers was intense ahead of the recital of the School prayer.

'O God, who by the inspiration of Thy servant Kingsley Fairbridge, who has so wonderfully made this School, and has set us to here to learn and do Thy will; teach us to live together in love, joy and peace; to check all bitterness, to disown discouragement, to practice thanksgiving and to leap with joy to any task for others. Strengthen the good thing thus begun, that with gallant and high-hearted happiness, we may strive to build according to Thy will. Direct the paths of those who have gone forth from this place. Inspire the hearts and minds of those in authority and fill us all with love towards Thee. To Thy honour and glory, through Jesus Christ our Lord,

Amen.

A month into his time at Fairbridge, his report noted 'Fred is a sturdily built boy – does not look quite so good a type as some of the other boys who came out with his party, but he may develop into a good solid chap. Has settled down well, and likes the country'.

In October 1934 in readiness for 1935, the year of King George V's silver jubilee, the Farm School received a Royal visit – from the Duke of Gloucester, the King's third son Henry. As the School bustled with the excitement of the visit and was decorated with bunting for the occasion, the eleven-year-old Fred was more impressed by the accompanying Band of the Grenadier Guards in their scarlet tunics and bearskins. As the children were lined up by the Bonk to form their own guard of honour for the Royal visitor, Fred imagined himself standing to attention as Colonel Heath would have the boys do so often, this time as a grown man in full uniform.

Later that week 'Miss' read out to the boys from the report in the West Australian, the account of the Duke's speech paying tribute to their Founder

He was, the Duke had said, 'a man after the Duke's own stamp'. Fairbridge had 'dedicated the whole force of his exceptionally powerful character to attainment of the ends he held in view – the removal of poor children from English orphanages and from slum areas in which hunger and neglect were their daily portions, to a brighter, ampler atmosphere in which their early miseries would vanish from their minds like the mists before the rising sun.'

Miss read on, proudly, 'Fairbridge, with a great love of England but an even greater love of children, believed that for many children England was not good enough, seeing that there they were denied their birthright. And therefore, he determined that they must be taken elsewhere. '

His vision was 'to take some at least of these little people before they were contaminated by their evil surroundings and to carry them off to a land of sunshine, there to be trained to be strong, sturdy and efficient citizens able to play their part in developing the vast resources of Australia – a land where the prizes of life are open to all.' Fairbridge is gone but the glory and the dream remain.'

Fred thought the Duke was certainly right about the land of sunshine. He guessed he himself, Frederick Alexander Wilson, was one of those little people. He just wished his brother Phil had been as well.

By December of that first year, the report from Miss Brown, his cottage mother in Newton Cottage noted 'a bright intelligent little fellow. Takes an interest in things in general and is really quite reliable'. His class teacher had promoted him twice in his first six months at the school.

It seemed that Barnardo's were right that Fairbridge would be good for Fred and he soon felt his homesickness receding, though in his gut he missed his Phil as much as ever. The bigger problem for Fred that first summer was the heat. At the end of his first Christmas at the Farm School, which was the heat of the Australian summer season, Fred contracted a fever which he could not shake off and the School doctor – Doctor Merritt diagnosed it as diphtheria. The whole farm school had been hit by an outbreak and Doctor Merritt had closed the School to visitors in an effort to contain it - news of such concern that it was reported in the West Australian Newspaper on the 25th January 1935.

The recent batch of Christmas arrivals from England – including one lad Fred Edwards, who was to become Fred's good friend, had been lucky to be held at the site of the school's holiday camp on the coast at Mandurah to prevent further spread. Fred remembered that his mother had said that it was this dreadful diphtheria that had killed his sister Mabel and was a little afraid to be told he had to spend two weeks in isolation to recover after his throat swab came back positive. Thankfully for Fred the rest helped him fight off the virus, but he was sorry he had lost two weeks of the summer swimming in the river which he loved.

He and his Newton Cottage housemates enjoyed listening to visiting speakers whom the Bonk had invited to Fairbridge to inspire the children in his care. Though sitting on the benches in the Dining Hall for any length of time could be painful, one particular visiting speaker, the famous English cricketer C B Fry, made a big impression on the youthful Fred as he had done so many different things in his life including playing English County cricket and soccer for his country. It was Fry, travelling across Australia with the English cricket team on their Ashes tour as a representative of the London Times, who advised the boys 'to 'make a fine art of whatever they did whether it be the playing of cricket or cleaning of a bucket. In that way they would make much of the unpleasantness of many of their tasks disappear.'

After giving the boys hints about batting and bowling he spoke to them about what he called the essence of these phases of the game. The young Fred was impressed that Fry had achieved so much in his life. This was a man who had interviewed the German National Socialist leader Adolf Hitler about his Youth movement in Berlin in 1934. He had played Test cricket for England and professional football at the highest level. The Bonk, who introduced him as a man of many parts, was delighted to invite him to speak at Fairbridge and Fred's 'fast' bowling felt like it took on a whole new speed after his speech in the Dining Hall.

1936 was a momentous year which started with the sad news reaching Fairbridge of the death of the King. Fred was moved when he read in the West Australian of the vigil of the Princes in Westminster Hall keeping watch over the King George's coffin– the King's three sons, including Henry, the Duke of Gloucester whose visit the previous year was still being talked about at the Farm School. Fred wished that he, Phil and Henry had stood vigil over Alfred's coffin before he was taken to Lambeth Cemetery. They were his princes and now, only five years after his death, the Captain was already beginning to fade from Fred's memory, which made him sad.

Later that same year, as the excitement built around the plans for the new King's coronation, Fairbridge received a special visitor – this time from the new Governor-General, Lord Gowrie. The children were roped in to hang red, white and blue bunting and flags around the main buildings and as his entourage arrived, the school brass band burst into the National Anthem. Thankfully, the rains held off until after the children had lined the roadside and the younger boys had run after the Governor-General's car with rousing cheers.

By this time, the Australian Spring of 1936, two years after his arrival in the country, Fred was really thriving. His school report of that year states he is 'imaginative and of nice fibre. He is pulling his weight in the cottage, and his schoolwork is exceptional. Fred is enjoying Manual Training and according to Mr Barrett is a keen sportsman. At thirteen his class teacher

Mr Elliot notes that 'he is promising and a very prominent member of the class.'

The young Canon Watson, who was to figure strongly in guiding Fred as he left Fairbridge as a young man, had Fred working with him at the rectory on a three-month traineeship, collecting wood, sweeping verandahs, raking paths, cutting lawns. Watson found him 'quite a good worker on routine jobs, honest and respectful but 'I don't think he has much initiative'. A further three months of manual work, digging culverts, weeding and cleaning and burning weeds on the compound, supervised this time by Mr McCormick who found him 'very satisfactory.' Fred still thought the gardening was more for his Phil as he used to really liked doing it. He hoped that Phil was getting to enjoy time outdoors, as he was.

The following year saw Fred join the rest of the school for a rare whole school trip out to Perth to mark the new King's Coronation. Two days after the official ceremony hundreds of children were hosted by the city and the Fairbridge orphans were given special treatment. In addition to seeing Shirley Temple in 'Poor Little Rich Girl' at the Capitol Theatre, which Fred thought was more for the young 'uns, he particularly enjoyed watching Gracie Fields in 'The Show Goes On' at the Regent Theatre, before joining some of the Fairbridge party who were warned to be on their best behaviour as they were being taken to lunch with the Lieutenant General Sir James Mitchell, at the Young Australia League Club.

Before they could tuck into their lunch, the Lieutenant General made a short speech 'We are glad to have you in West

Australia. I hope you will grow up to be good citizens, knowing the land in which you live. All the people of the State are very fond of children.' The School's new Principal, Mr. Patterson, who Fred wasn't too sure about since he had replaced the Bonk, gave what Fred thought he called 'a vote of thanks' though he was confused as no vote was taken.

Though some of Fred's friends found the lunch in the most formal of settings of the Club's memorial ballroom a bit boring, he was enchanted by the life size figure of Sir Galahad depicted on the room's central window surrounded by famous Australians. It made Fred feel part of something – his adopted country.

While the lunch and speeches went over some of the boys' heads, everyone was excited about their trip to Perth Zoological Gardens alongside the Swan River. As they travelled by bus through the city decorated and illuminated with faded flags and dingy streamers, and the shops still promoting 'Coronation Specials' the children felt excited about their new King, though some of the older boys were really more keen to find a way get to the special trotting meeting at Gloucester Park.

As some of the boys sheltered in the tennis shelter on the great lawn at the zoological gardens Fred remembered his trip to Colombo Zoo when they had stopped in Ceylon on the Ballarat. He could not believe that it was only three years since he had made that journey from London. He already felt a proud Australian and was a little torn as a result. Though these Coronation events were designed to make the

Commonwealth feel as one under the King, Fred felt a little odd about it.

Fred's school report in 1938 was a glowing one. He was 'a good patrol leader in scouts. A leader. Pleasant normal boy. Chosen for special holiday. Doing well.'

The month-long special Christmas holiday at Mandurah Camp was a memorable one for Fred. He joined in the singing in the back of the truck, a song passed down by Fairbridge children who had long left the farm school.

'There's a truck rattling back on the old Pinjarra track

Along the road to Fairbridge Farm

For the radiator's hissing – the sparking plugs are missing

Beneath the summer sky

For there's kero in the petrol and sand in the gears

And we haven't seen a garage for over forty years

There's a Reo rattling back on the old Pinjarra track

Along the road to Fairbridge Farm'

Fred loved Mandurah. He felt free there. He swam as often as he could in the sea to cool off from the searing sun. He could not believe that this was the same sun that he had drawn so often back in England. If it was, Fred concluded he must be so much closer to it here in Pinjarra as it really burnt his skin if he forgot to wear his Diggers hat. His cottage mother had warned him about playing out too long but there were days when Fred threw caution to the sun and let it burn him red raw. It was worth the strapping to feel the raw tingle on your freckly arms. He loved to swim. He had never had the nerve to dive into the Thames when he was a nipper. It was so grey and uninviting. And in any event Ma had scolded Henry for diving in once and Fred did not want to upset his mother.

What Fred loved more than anything was floating in the river ducking his head under and suffering the leeches so that the happy screams of his cottage mates were muffled enough for Fred to drift away in his own world. Fred's world. He felt safer there. No-one was going to take away anyone he loved anymore. He could live his own life, without early morning bugle reveille, scrubbing up duty, kitchen duty, polishing turns.

They said the heat messed with your head. His Head Teacher Mr Healey warned that he had seen men go 'over the edge' when, during the Great War, they had stayed out in the sun too long. But it seemed to Fred that Healey was suffering enough from his wartime escapades – hat or no hat. Come to think of it, Fred thought, all the teachers he had sat in front of at Fairbridge were a little bit disturbed by their misfortune. None of them had children of their own but joked that the Fairbridge family was more than enough for them.

Fred did not think of the school as his family. He knew well enough that he had been in a proper family once. He could vaguely recollect freezing in their London tenement when the Captain returned from his golf and Ma would laugh and joke while the Captain ruffled Fred's hair as he and Phil sat on his knee. It was Ma that gave them the cuddles that Fred missed most of all. He knew that Phil would miss them more than anyone as he was the quiet one, the Mummy's boy, who seemed to need Ma's attention more.

Sometimes, on polishing duty in the cottage, Fred would sniff the polish and once again be reminded of the whiff of Ma's cleaning coat when she returned home from her cleaning job at the War Office. The way it crackled as Fred touched it, or the comforting feeling of stroking Ma's hands through the material of her pocket as she tried to warm herself after her walk back home across Westminster Bridge. Things felt happy then, albeit briefly, before the Captain went to Jesus too soon. Fred even missed the shouting, as the house turned colder and so much quieter, almost overnight, after Captain Willson's heart attack on a tram. Ma only raised her voice once more. When Agnes came to claim his pension. She said that Ma and us kids were his 'dirty little secret'. We didn't feel that dirty. No dirtier than the mates we knocked around with outside Wellington Mills with its black soot and stinky smokes. Ma cried then. A different kind of crying. An angry and a sad cry. A cry to God for 'just is'. God didn't hear that one. It must be punishment for not marrying the Captain proper. That's why we kids had a different name to the Captain. Dropped an 'ell.

Fred was certain that Ma didn't even cry when the Barnardo's lady came and told her that he and Phil had to go into the home. She must have been keeping it all in, Fred reckoned.

Back at Fairbridge after the holiday Fred tried not to think too much about the life he had left behind or what might have been. It was brought home to him that September when Canon Watson read from the West Australian that their Prime Minister Menzies had pledged unstinting support to the mother country in their fight against Nazi aggression. Though the war in Europe seemed so far away he prayed that his family in England would be kept safe.

There were moments where he felt a pang when he caught a glimpse of life outside of the institution, of 'normal' family life. Moments like the Christmas of 1939 when he was allowed time out of the Farm School to spend his summer Christmas holidays with the family of his friend Noel Connop.

Perhaps it was the sense of togetherness that being at war gave to the Connops', or maybe it was just that Mrs Connop wanted her son to have some company of his own age for the holidays. Either way, Noel's mother, the widow Mrs Beth Connop, wrote to Canon Watson, by then the Principal at Fairbridge, to ask permission to take fifteen-year-old Fred in for a few days over the holidays in their home in West Leederville, a quiet suburb of Perth.

If the transport could be provided by the Farm school, then Mrs Connop was only too willing to offer free board for the boy whom her son Noel had befriended through the Scouts. Mrs Connop wrote that if Fred were able to bring a bike, 'the boys could have a marvellous time'. Ever mindful of their pastoral responsibilities, Fairbridge agreed once the District Commissioner's office had confirmed by telegram, a few days before Christmas, that the 'Noel Connop people and home' were 'highly recommended'.

Fred had a wonderful Christmas break with the Connops. Noel and his sisters Betty and Patricia made him feel part of their family. The first proper family that he could remember for a very long time. So much so that he wrote to Canon Watson in mid-January saying he was 'enjoying myself 'top-notch'. I have visited the Zoo, Kings Park, Crawley and Redlands. Yesterday I had a great time with Noel's sister. I am teaching her to swim. We go swimming every day at Crawley or City Beach.' Fortunately for Fred the telegram from Canon Watson asking him to return was sent to the wrong address prolonging his stay for a few more days.

It was a wrench for Fred as the Connops waved him off at Perth station after the holidays for his return to Pinjarra. Whilst he had missed his friends in Newton Cottage the taste of normal life in a family home and the freedom to have fun was something he had savoured. But he knew this was a big year for him as he was due to turn sixteen and leave the Farm school to take up work placements in farms hundreds of miles away from Pinjarra. He was ready for it. Canon Watson had said as much. His teachers were all pleased with his progress. They had made a fine young man of him.

One person in particular at the Farm School who understood Fred and had time for him was Fremantle-born Canon Walter Watson, a father of a daughter himself and the most popular of Fairbridge personnel He had started off as the Chaplain but was now Acting Principal. Charged with the spiritual wellbeing of the children in his charge, the Canon took his vocation seriously.

It was to Canon Watson Fred turned as his next of kin and guardian for advice on his career after he had left the school and begun working as a farmhand in May 1940 shortly before his sixteenth birthday.

Fred was happy working for Stephen Lundy on his wheat and sheep farm. Mr Lundy, Fred boasted of his new boss, was the chairman of the Mechering Road Board. In a letter back to Canon Watson on settling in at his digs in Cunderdin, Fred said 'he is a very good man to work with. He does his best to teach me all about the work I do. When I cleaned the tractor, he told me all the names and uses of all the parts'.

The small gold rush town of Cunderdin in the wheatbelt, 150 miles from Pinjarra had a smaller population than the Farm School. Crossed by the Number 2 Rabbit-Proof Fence, it was very much a farming township, and Mr Lundy was one of the most successful sheep and wheat farmers in the district.

Mr Lundy had applied for a boy for odd jobs and milking, feeding pigs etc in the Autumn of 1940 partly to help fill the gap left when his oldest son Jack had enlisted in the Australian Imperial Force as the War had been declared. Lundy himself knew how hard it would be to manage the farm on his own as he had taken on the management of it when his own father had answered the call in the Great War. It was good to have another young man around the farm to take his mind off Jack and his worries for his oldest son's wellbeing.

Fred was eager to impress the Canon and reported in his letter to him that 'at this morning's Empire Prayer Service, the church was over-flowed and one third of the congregation was outside. The minister, Fred said, is a good fellow too.' As the country had gone to war and so many of their young men and women were signing up to serve, the families left at home were running to the arms of the small-town church for comfort.

Fred felt the same pangs of fear and trepidation about the War. When the news of the London Blitz reached Australia in September, Fred wrote to Canon Watson for information about his family back in London as he really wanted to let them know that he was thinking of them at this difficult time. He had no idea where his mother or brothers were or whether they were safe from the German bombers.

Mr Lundy told Fred that the good people of Cunderdin, like the rest of the wheatbelt, were totally behind the war effort. It became very real to them when the RAAF identified land just north of Main Street to build an airstrip and temporary air base which was to become an Initial Training School shortly after Fred had left the town. On his Sunday off, after church, Fred would often walk to Cunderdin Hill among the pink and yellow everlastings and look out for kangaroos bounding through the bushland. From this vantage point Fred could see for miles and started to imagine the difference the airbase would make to the area. The war had come home and for the sixteen-year-old Fred, as Mr Lundy spoke proudly of his Jack standing tall with the AIF, it started to feel much more real. He knew he would be called to play his part, but he was torn between following the Captain into the Army or taking to the skies with the RAAF.

Two days after his sixteenth birthday, which he shared with the Lundy's middle son Arnold, the Lundys invited Fred to join them at a concert in Cunderdin School Hall in support of the Cunderdin Patriotic Fund, of which Mr. Lundy was the President, to support the war effort. He put on his best Fairbridge suit and tie as they walked into town and patiently waited to be seated in the Hall as the musicians were tuning up. Fred wasn't quite sure what to expect but was relieved when scouts from the local troop marched on the hastily erected stage in formation and provided a guard of honour for two overly sombre flag bearers.

The patrol leader in Fred wanted to inspect the group that included thirteen-year-old Harold Lundy and his brother Arnold, but he held back and when the whole Hall sang the National Anthem Fred was surprised when they also struck up the Marseillaise.

Such a striking anthem even though he and the Lundys struggled with the words. Mr. Lundy's daughter, Nancy, who was seated next to Fred, surprised him with the strength of her voice. At nineteen, after initially thinking she was aloof when Fred had first arrived to work on the farm, Nancy had become a good friend to Fred and they enjoyed playing tennis together with Arnold at the Cunderdin tennis club. Harold made a good ball boy. Things were a bit awkward with Nancy. Fred had to remember he was working for her father and so he kept his feelings for her to himself. Fred felt his face redden when the Cunderdin music teacher Mavis Carter sang 'Moonlight and Roses' and the line 'June's light discloses Love's golden dream'.

The audience were getting in the wartime spirit now and belted out 'They'll Always Be an England' which made Fred sad for a moment but his mood was lifted quickly as they sang 'It's a long way to Tipperary' and 'Pack Up Your Troubles'. England suddenly did not seem so far away as Nancy walked to the front and joined the small chorus to lead the Hall in the singing of Land of Hope and Glory.

Before they left the hall, Mr. Lundy stood up and spoke to the gathering to thank them for raising sixteen pounds and 8 shillings for the Cunderdin Patriotic Fund and for supporting the war effort. Fred felt a mix of emotions. He could see the strain on Mrs Lundy's face, and he knew the worry she felt for her firstborn son Jack. But at the same time, he knew he would respond to the call as soon as he was old enough if the war was not won by the time he had reached eighteen. Nancy too, she later confided in Fred, would be applying for the RAAF when she was 21 and they joked that might even end up in the same crew. If that were the case, Fred thought, he would have to work on his tennis game.

Fred had settled in well into his farm work and had even grown to like the weather board men's hut with its own bathroom that was his temporary home. His tennis game had improved though he still struggled to beat Arnie and the wily Nancy. He had been roped in from time to time to play cricket or football at the Cunderdin footy Oval with the Lundy boys and the farm work was hard, but it was keeping him fit.

He knew he would miss the Lundys and this quiet, small town when after eight months he travelled ninety-five miles northwest to start work at 'Corio', the family farm of George Purser, in the new, even smaller, township of Piawaning, at literally the end of the line of the extended railway. Fred was sent to Corio by Canon Watson to replace another Fairbridge boy, Len Henson, who had evidently been led astray by someone called Bish who had a bad effect on Henson and others who had worked at the farm. Writing to the Canon in March 1941, Fred informs him that the new job is 'all right or A1. I milk 3-5 cows then work with the boss. I have joined the local tennis club and soon felt at home in one short week.' He is a little over-familiar in his letter writing style for the Canon's liking signing off..'for your (sic) a jolly good fellow.'

George Purser confirmed to the Farm School in a written employment form of the same month that 'since this boy has been in charge of the cows there is already a noticeable improvement in the condition of the cows, and quantity and quality of milk.' The Pursers were a kindly family. Fred was aware that they had already provided work and lodgings for Violet Cox from Fairbridge and she had spoken well of her time there helping look after their new baby, young George junior.

After months at Cunderdin looking after Mr. Lundy's pigs and sheep, the early morning milking at Corio was a weirdly special time for Fred. Used to the early starts, wading through the paddock bare-legged and bootless, with a hurricane lantern swinging from his hands, trudging over wet grass or splashing knee-deep through ice-cold water, shivering as he looked for dark shapes that might be cows, was oddly thrilling. Lighting the copper fire in the milking shed, hosing down the floor and getting the milk churns and buckets ready for use became Fred's morning ritual and he grew to love it.

He remembered what CB Fry had said about taking pride in the everyday tasks. Mr. Purser was pleased with the increased yield that came from his happy cows after Fred's milking. He liked Fred's spirit and though he could be challenging at times, as many teenagers could, George liked having the young man around and not just for the extra pair of willing hands.

Happy though he was with working with the cows, and thankful to Mr. Purser for this opportunity, Fred was eager to move on with his life.

As Fred grew in confidence in his new employment he felt emboldened to ask Canon Watson to sanction the release of Ten Pounds of his Fairbridge Trust monies – monies that Fred now knew were rightfully his as he had earned them on the farm, for a course in 'Radio'. The course that the now seventeen-year-old Fred dreamed of. Col Watson implied that this was a youthful whim, and that Fred would be better off sticking to his correspondence course to improve his basic education. It was education, Watson insisted, that would bring Fred his life chances.

The pair crossed again in letters following Christmas when Fred again wanted another ten pounds of his money – this time to afford to be best man for his mate who was marrying on Christmas Day 1942.

Canon Watson pointedly refused and took issue, sternly though politely rebuking Fred for the tone of such a letter to a Principal of his former College. These youthful indiscretions were all forgiven later when Fred succeeded in gaining entry to the Royal Australian Air Force.

When Mr. Mansfield, the After Care officer from Fairbridge, filed his report as Fred reached the age of seventeen, he noted that Fred was using his free Sundays at Corio to work on a pre-enlistment course for the RAAF with help with the papers from his employer who was qualified in Agricultural Science.

Fred had asked Mr. Mansfield whether he could be transferred to a position near Guildford so that he might join the Air Training Corps, but Mansfield suggested to him that he was in an advantageous position where he was, with a sympathetic employer who was qualified to help him, and that in another position he might have less free time available for his preparation for the Air Force. Despite the demands of the farm and his own young family, George Purser was happy to help Fred with his interview preparations and pre-enrolment course work, as he could see the young lad was eager to play his part in the war effort.

Fred, like so many young men his age, was eager to do his duty and respond to the call. He had set his heart on taking to the skies with the Royal Australian Air Force.

George Purser did succeed in helping Fred attain a place with the Air Training Corps but mysteriously in April 1942, two months short of Fred's eighteenth birthday, and after a dispute with Purser over his demands for more pay, he absconded from the Farm to take up a better paid position with the Apple and Pear Board, 'opening boxes for the Inspector', leaving behind his bicycle and a few items of clothing. Mr. Purser could not hide his disappointment in his letter to Canon Watson, and both men agree that moody teenager Fred had been 'influenced' whilst visiting friends in Perth.

Chapter Seven

A Home Front

Kate knew she had to hold Henry, her one remaining child who was on the verge of becoming a man, close to her and try to rebuild her life without Alfred and the beloved children she had lost. She had never felt properly at home in noisy Lambeth and to her, even if she could afford to stay there, the rooms in the 77 Westminster Bridge Road house she had shared with the Captain would always hold painful memories. Too painful to bear for any length of time.

She thought about taking Henry back to Wiltshire and the Burbage village she had grown up in, but with her father dead her elderly stepmother was living alone and would not be able to take them in. There would be little work on the farm and though the new railway might be an option for him it would not be easy. In any event, she had taken the name Jones to turn her back on her Flippence family and the painful loss of her boy Cuthbert, and she was too proud to go back.

She had decided she would make a fresh start away from south London. Away from her debts and the ongoing feud with Agnes. A new identity. The widow Kate Jones. For Henry's health she decided they would move to the seaside and opted to look for lodgings and work in the small seaside town of Ramsgate, on the Kent coast. The sea air would do them both good and Kate needed to be somewhere where no one knew her past and hopefully her pain and shame of giving away her two young boys would not hang so heavily over her head. A seaside town with a constant stream of new visitors and temporary residents working the summer season would give her the cover she needed to get on with her life without busybodies judging her.

As soon as Henry had finished school at the age of 14, in July 1935, Kate packed up their meagre belongings in a couple of battered suitcases and they walked to Victoria Station for their train that would take them to the end of the line.

Kate was relieved to find lodgings in Ramsgate after a short walk from the station as she had not relished the prospect of sweatily lugging their bags around town on a warm and busy summer's afternoon. Number 20 Abbot's Hill was a real find. Just a short walk up from the Royal Harbour, across the promenade, the street was slightly tucked away from the front and as private as Kate would have hoped for somewhere in this bustling Town.

There would be plenty to amuse Henry and the busy High Street had all the shops Kate could possibly need. First though, she had to find some gainful employment as a domestic help and help Henry find a job too. Their small living room at number 20 felt a little musty at first but Kate was sure a good dose of sea air would soon sort that out. She scoured the shops on the High Street for job advertisements and in one newsagents' window among the cards offering piano lessons she found a neatly scrawled 'domestic worker wanted' ad in what looked like a lady's handwriting on a card and quickly called round to the large House in Ellington Street opposite the Park, having asked the friendly shopkeeper for directions.

The men in the shared house at number 66 were looking for a woman to clean their house for them and having been let down by two younger cleaners they were only too happy to employ the more mature Kate Jones, even before they had sought out a reference. Kate was guarded about her personal circumstances as she did not want to have to explain herself but she did tell them that she had Henry at home if they were in need of any garden work or odd jobs. The fourteen year old Henry was eager to find work of his own away from his Ma and quickly found work with the King's Street butchers, F Stockley and Son, as a delivery boy.

Mr. Stockley provided him with his first bike of his own which he was thrilled to maintain, even if the punctures were too frequent for his liking and some of the customers took a dislike to the packages being handled by oily hands. He tried to plan his routes to avoid the steeper hills up from the front but as he got used to the work, they were a little less exhausting for his bandy legs.

Henry in Ramsgate, 1935

On their Sundays off mother and son made the most of their new seaside home and never got bored of walking along the front. Kate warned Henry off the many fishermen's pubs near the Royal Harbour, as they could get very raucous and she did not want him being led astray. During the winter Henry was happy to watch the tug boats and the fishing steamers moored in the harbour, while the summer season brought so many characters into the Town they had a constant source of stories to share of frolics on the sands. Kate wasn't much of a beach person and the cleaner in her tried hard to keep the sand from getting everywhere in the House when they came home from their seafront walks.

In truth she preferred her new seaside hometown when the pleasure cruises had stopped and the cheery Londoners had stopped coming in large numbers at the end of the summer season. The sight of the younger children laughing with their mothers and fathers on the seafront, or hearing their raucous laughter in the Marina pool at the end of the slope down to the prom, made Kate sad for the family she had lost. Henry did not talk about them much. He kept his sadness to himself but from time to time, when they were both sat listening to the wireless of an evening, the pair would share a knowing look that Kate knew meant he was missing his brothers and mourning his sisters as much as she was.

Settled in Ramsgate, Kate wrote to Barnardo's requesting that Phil be allowed to join her and his brother Henry for a summer holiday. The sea air would be good for him. She prayed that they would allow her request and was heartbroken when it was declined.

Henry was happy in his own world. He would dream of sailing away to France in one of the old fishing boats tied up at the fisherman's dock or spend hours staring at the vast open skies out to sea as he sat on Marine Parade defending his bag of vinegar-sodden cold chips from the aggressive seagulls. He joked with Ma that they must be 'sarf' London seagulls as they were so noisy and their cries at times sounded as mad as the laughter that spilled out of the Rose and Crown on a Saturday night.

He didn't mind the quiet too much but he definitely preferred the busy season when the amusements were at their busiest and the pretty girls in their wide-brimmed sunhats on the sands were giggling as they self-consciously dipped their toes in the sea.

Henry's favourite was the Merrie England funfair with its tunnel World Service miniature railway that would transport you around the world from the snow-capped mountains of Switzerland to the Egyptian pyramids in a matter of minutes. He looked goggle eyed at the midget mansion with tiny people dancing, the stamp room and most bizarrely the monkey village with bicycle-riding chimpanzees. Kate joked that the chimps were steadier on two wheels than Henry was.

He was annoyed when the so-called 'Mad Mayor' of Ramsgate decided to permanently close down the miniature railway to create his spidery network of air raid shelters to protect the local residents from 'Jerry' attacks even though it did mean he would hopefully be able to venture underground without spending a penny.

Just as Kate and Henry were adjusting to their new life on the coast the mood of their neighbours in Ramsgate started to darken. As talk of war with Germany grew, Kate's retired next door neighbour, also called Mrs Jones, causing much confusion for their grumpy postie, was quick to curse just how exposed Ramsgate was being so close to France. The other Mrs Jones told them how she remembered the zeppelin attacks during the Great war and how the town had taken a right battering from the Hun. She urged Kate to teach Henry how to find the entrance to the cliff-side tunnels for shelter as she fully expected Mr. Hitler to have a go at them if he ever got the chance.

She needn't have worried. Henry had found the tunnels for himself while playing near the entrance at Townley Castle as he waited for Ma to finish at work one summer evening.

He had great fun descending the stone steps to explore the stinky tunnels though he wasn't sure Ma would approve of him being there in the semi-darkness on his own. He was never going to be one of the so-called tunnel rats who loved to spend more time underground. He preferred dodging the seagulls in the open skies and painting pictures in his head from the clouds hanging over the harbour. But the tunnels were thrilling to the young lad.

His boss had said that the Top Hat Mayor, the Mad Mayor as Ma called him, wanted to turn the tunnels into proper air raid shelters, with bunks and lights to protect Ramsgate from the Luftwaffe. It didn't sound so mad to Henry as he knew how deep those tunnels were and even the biggest bombs wouldn't be able to get you down there.

For now, the most fun you could have was on the World Service railway and if Henry was feeling flush, if Mrs Hawkins had tipped him generously as she sometimes did as he cycled round to Woodford Avenue with her favoured sausages, he would buy a ticket just for the thrill of the short journey underground. He didn't tell his Ma as he knew she would say that times were hard and his money should be saved for a rainy day. But that didn't make sense as there was little you could do on rainy days apart from sitting in the café on the front nursing a hot chocolate and watching people struggle with their brollies against the gusty sea winds.

The Mad Mayor got his way with the Government and Mr. Stockley told Henry he thought Ramsgate was as ready as they could be to take what Jerry could throw at them. Kate didn't want to let on, but she was fearful for Henry. She knew that war came with a heavy cost. Her Uncle Henry's son, her sweet cousin Bill, had answered Kitchener's call and left his job as a cowman in Pewsey to fight with the 5th Battalion of the Wiltshire Regiment.

His body lay somewhere in a grave in Mesopotamia and his poor widow, Minnie, was left to raise their two young children alone. Her cousin George had also died serving with the Wiltshires on Flanders Field, just months after the War had begun. As she could feel him getting caught up in the patriotic fervour sweeping the country, she did not want her Henry, or her other boys for that matter, rushing towards gunfire.

In her darker moments as she lay awake at night fretting about money or anxiously wondering what had become of her Bertie, Phil or Fred, Kate feared that God might take her Henry as a punishment for letting her other boys go. She could not bear that thought, but some of Rev Meyer's sermons from back in Lambeth had stuck in her mind. Those times when he would speak of a vengeful God. She prayed that she was wrong about that.

Though no angel, her Henry was the innocent one and she could not imagine her life without him. As she was in her fifties now and the Captain had all but put her off male company, Kate knew there would be no more babies for her. She would have to do all she could to keep her sole child safe but she knew that as he turned eighteen in 1939 he would want to stand on his own two feet and make his own way in the world and she braced herself for that day.

Kate had become friends with one of the gentlemen at Number 66, Joseph Saunders. He was slightly older than her and kept his room on the ground floor very tidy. She didn't mind cleaning for him as he was always grateful and very polite. He was on the road with his sales job a lot and often quite tired when Kate spoke to him, but he always made time for Henry which was important to her. When a room became available across the hallway from him, he suggested to Kate that she might like to take it on as it would make financial sense for her and Henry. He knew she was struggling to pay all the bills at Abbot's Hill. Ellington Road was a little closer to the shops and now Henry was older he was less obsessed with the seafront so being a little further away from the sands would not be a major issue. Kate took up Mr. Saunders' suggestion and he put in a good word to the landlord so they could move that summer.

The Ramsgate beaches were packed during the summer of 1939 as the London revellers made the most of the hot weather and the freedom they feared might soon be taken away, as war with Germany seemed more and more likely. Henry celebrated his eighteenth birthday with an ice cream on the front and Kate put aside her dislike for the sands to join him after she had finished work.

It felt like this was the last normal summer season for Ramsgate for some time to come. The town was filling up with naval ratings and squaddies and the RAF base up the road at Manston was busier than it had ever been since Kate and Henry had arrived at the coast.

Since Mr. Chamberlain's September declaration, that the two of them had listened to on the wireless that fateful Sunday afternoon, life in Ramsgate had largely carried on as before, though they were knocked back by an early air raid siren that turned out to be a false alarm but brought home the reality of what they might be facing next. Measuring up for gas masks, Kate tried not to let on to Henry that she was nervous and made a joke about the need to wear the mask in the House now that Henry had discovered the gassy effects of ale.

The war was getting close to home. Henry was disappointed that the navy had closed down Merrie England altogether, to make it the base for HMS Fervent to patrol the coast for German destroyers, and the midget mansion was now home to a group of young naval ratings with officers billeted in hotels on the seafront. A battery was set up at Wellington Crescent above the entrance to the caves.

As well as the influx of sailors in the town, on her shopping days in the High Street Kate noticed that there were more and more uniformed airmen from nearby RAF Manston passing through, and there was a lot more activity in the skies above them. Thankfully, the Mayor's plans to make the cliff tunnels a safe haven for local residents were well advanced. Henry badgered her to go with him to inspect the tunnels, but she was wary of the dark and damp underground and just could not understand what was so much fun about them.

Reluctantly she agreed to explore them with him over the Christmas holidays and they were in every way as unpleasant as she could have imagined. While she hoped they would provide some much-needed shelter from future attacks she would rather not be living in those conditions, thank you very much, and would certainly not be applying for a permit for a bunk, which is what Henry was hoping.

Kate might have tolerated joining her Westminster Bridge Road neighbours huddled on the platform of North Lambeth station opposite the room she had shared with the Captain, as they at least would be a little warm and not so smelly compared to the damp of the Mad Mayor's Ramsgate tunnels. Even if they did have barbers, greengrocers and even concert parties planned down there.

As they entered the new decade the 'phoney war' seemed more real to them when in January, the Dunbar Castle, a

10,000 ton liner bound for the Cape, was sunk by a German mine in the Channel, with many losses. After a brave rescue by Ramsgate lifeboat crews over a hundred of the passengers and crew were landed at Ramsgate and cared for on the front.

Whilst on one of his delivery rounds, cursing the fact he had left his Christmas woollen mitts at home in the bitterly cold wind, Henry was startled to see what appeared to be the body of an older man in uniform being swept onto the beach. He read later that a racehorse and two dogs had also perished alongside seven passengers and crew members bound for the Cape when the liner went down. It seemed no man nor animal was safe from the Germans in wartime.

Henry knew that now he was a man he should be doing more to help the new Prime Minister Mr. Churchill to defeat Hitler. As Ramsgate started to welcome refugees arriving from Belgium and Holland it didn't feel like Britain was on the winning side and the talk was of the BEF getting a drubbing. Jerry was edging closer to their Kent home, in the skies above and on the ground across the water in France. Kate had picked up their ration books and clothing coupons and Mr. Stockley warned Henry that he might struggle to keep him on as meat was going to be in short supply, so he may not be able to continue his home delivery service.

Kate was busier than ever. With Henry working now and learning as much as he could about the butchery business, she filled her time with the WVS and though some of Mrs Sutton's posher ladies sometimes seemed to look down at her and the way she spoke, Kate found the work with the refugees, preparing them meals and helping them to find somewhere to live, extremely rewarding.

Their work was to get even more demanding as Ramsgate was to be at the heart of Churchill's Operation Dynamo mission to rescue hundreds of thousands of BEF men from France at Dunkirk. As the weather turned brighter in May hundreds of small boats converged on the port as they prepared to attempt their audacious rescue. Henry had to give up counting these 'little ships' in the harbour that came from ports all along the south coast, some piloted by fishermen used to the channel's currents, others by volunteers answering the call. There were just too many to count. It was clear there were many thousands of men in need of being rescued.

All that Henry could do was watch and wait as boat after boat slowly left the harbour and headed for France. Kate would not allow him to even think about going on board one of the boats to help the rescue effort. She needed him here with her. He was to help her accumulate as much food as they could find from generous butchers like Mr. Stockley and so many of the other Ramsgate traders to feed the hungry soldiers on their return.

Fred Plummer, the colourful greengrocer with a handcart who they always saw plying the Ramsgate streets with his fruit and veg, helped Henry carry the provisions to the canteens across town.

As the exhausted and forlorn BEF Dunkirk survivors arrived in their thousands, Mrs Sutton's WVS ladies jumped into action supporting the relief effort with canteens at the fish market, the Pavilion and at the railway station. Some of the volunteers who had been trained as nurses treated the wounded in a building on the seafront, while Kate's group at the Railway Station helped provide loaves of bread, pots of jam, pats of butter and odd shoes, trousers, and other clothes for the hungry, bedraggled and unshaven men.

Kate was shocked by the physical state of the young men she saw as they dismounted slowly from the East Kent Road Car coaches that were ferrying them from the harbour to the Railway Station in the town. They looked crestfallen and utterly defeated. Many were clearly visibly shaken by their experience as they waited quietly for soup and coffee ahead of boarding Southern Railway trains out of the town.

The station concourse was already heaving as today was the day when all of Ramsgate's three thousand younger children were to be evacuated away from the threat of bombing to live with host families in Staffordshire. The Top Hat Mayor and a civic party were there to wave the children off and reassure upset mothers. The excited children were lifting the spirits of the soldiers as they clapped and cheered their arrival at the station. They did not expect to be greeted as heroes as many of them looked like they felt they had let their country down.

For a moment, seeing two young Ramsgate schoolboys struggling with their battered little suitcases and waving to their poor mother as they boarded a train, Kate's eyes filled with tears as she recalled that morning just eight years earlier when Phil and Fred were taken from her. Looking at some of the younger soldiers she was handing out bread to she could not help but think that by now her Phil would soon be old enough to be signed up for the Army and Fred would not be far behind him. She was already having to cope with Henry moving inland to Rochester to help build aircraft at the huge Short's factory. Losing all her boys forever was her greatest fear.

But for now, she had a job to do. It was oddly exhilarating for Kate to have a purpose beyond cleaning someone else's house and keeping her Henry on the straight and narrow. The lines of Dunkirk survivors were not getting any shorter as every departing train was quickly replaced with another ready to be filled with tired bodies heading home for much-needed leave. Henry said the station looked as busy as Waterloo Station in a rush hour. Their canteen was running low on bread, so Kate asked Henry to cycle round to King Street to pick up more and he soon returned with his basket brimming with on the turn loaves. That should see them through.

As they stood outside the station, Henry befriended a young boy who told him he was named Loic. He had good English. He was Belgian and only fourteen years old. He reminded Henry of his young brother Fred and he thought he was probably about the same age. Too young to be a soldier himself, he had arrived in Ramsgate with some tired French soldiers and was going to be sent to south London to be looked after by a kindly churchman. Henry said he hoped he would find his family again as he could only imagine how hard life would be for him away from his mother. Henry decided not to tell Kate about the boy as she seemed upset enough already.

As the line for the trains were at last getting shorter, Kate was relieved by another one of the WVS volunteers and was glad to get home to have a cup of tea and put up her throbbing feet.

As she rubbed her swollen ankles and struggled to stay awake, Kate was proud that Ramsgate had played its part in the rescue mission. It was shocking to see how defeated the BEF men had looked. While she trusted Mr. Churchill, it was clear that the war was far from over and that they might have to brace themselves to fight off an invasion.

As the Battle of Britain was due to start filling the skies above the Kent coast with dogfights, and nearby RAF Manston was pounded by German bombers, Henry moved inland to Gillingham to take up his job as a riveter's mate at the Short's Ministry of Aircraft Production factory near the Rochester airport, helping to turn out much-needed Stirlings.

Kate was afraid to let him go as she knew the factory on the Medway would be just as big a target as Ramsgate, and the airfield was very exposed to Jerry attacks, seated as it was in the 'bomb alley' to London. There was nothing she could do to stop him. Mr. Stockley had said he had to let him go as rationing had hit his home deliveries hard. He wanted to do his bit for the war effort and at least it would keep him in Kent rather than taking him away from her to the front.

For now, Kate would stay in Ramsgate despite the risks. Her friendship with their housemate, Mr. Saunders, Joe, had deepened and though he was away a lot with his work as a salesman, he was pleasant enough company when he was around and did not complain about Kate's cooking the way the Captain used to. She wanted to give Henry a chance to be independent in Gillingham without her intrusion.

He wasted no time. In his first week at Short's he fell for a pretty girl a few years older than him, Lily Smith, who worked in the canteen. Lily had been born in Staffordshire where her Dad was a miner but they had moved for work to Chatham when Joe Smith got a job in a sawmill and Lily's brother Harry drove a fire engine. He knew she was the girl for him. Lily was a very down to earth girl from the Black Country and Kate thought, she was a good foil for his sometimes-boyish ways.

It was hard for Kate because she didn't want to lose her Henry but she knew she couldn't hold on to him forever or hold him back. For now, she was just relieved that he had found someone who made him happy and could help take his mind off the war. She was a little surprised to learn that they were to wed after being together for so little time but Henry assured his mother that Lily was not pregnant, they just knew they wanted to marry and wartime was no time to hang about. He had asked Mr. Smith's permission and the Medway registry office in Chatham was booked for a September wedding.

Walking home mid-morning from a successful early shopping excursion in Ramsgate Town Centre in late August, to find an outfit for Henry's wedding, three weeks or so before the big day, Kate was alarmed to hear the wailing of the air raid siren as the sky above the town suddenly blackened with dozens of German bombers. She quickly calculated that she might not make it home, so she hurriedly descended the steps into the

Ellington Park Air Raid Shelter opposite the Park Keeper's Cottage.

As she stepped down, gripping her shopping bags tightly, she was shaken by a terrific explosion and stumbled to the ground, tearing her nylons. For a few moments everything seemed to tremble like mad and the whole of the shelter was turned pitch black. Kate could not see a thing in front of her eyes.

After what seemed like an age some oil lamps borne by air raid wardens and policemen brought light back to the packed shelter and Kate could see how everyone around her was equally shaken, with some staggering around, bleeding from cuts caused by flying glass. She knew she'd had a narrow escape, and in her head thanked Henry and their Mad Mayor for his damn tunnels.

When the sirens signalled the all clear, and the warden said it was safe to leave the shelter, Kate climbed out into the light to see the devastation that the bombings had caused to her adopted town. Thankfully her own Ellington Road home looked untouched by the 500 German bombs that had fallen in less than five minutes, but it was clear from the dust in the air that a lot of the town had been hit hard. The gasworks was aflame and Kate heard later that the popular greengrocer Fred Plummer, with his cart, who had been so helpful with the Dunkirk survivors, was among the 29 dead, as was friendly newsagent Mr. Lilley who had first helped Kate find her lodgings when she and Henry had arrived in the town.

The town's gas supplies had been hit hard by the attack on the Dacres Road gasworks so Kate couldn't cook any dinner for herself that night as Joe was out of town, but anyway she had already decided to join the WVS effort to help feed, what she later learned were, the 3000 or so Ramsgate folk made homeless by that morning's bombing. She walked past rows of devastated houses to the Old Constitutional Club where she knew the canteen would be under pressure to meet the demand for meals.

The WVS ladies managed to cook up hundreds of meals on six primus stoves and Kate was happy to help serve the teas to very grateful residents. As the Mayor toured the canteen in his Top Hat Kate resisted the urge to thank him for his tunnel shelters as she thought she might sound silly but quickly regretted not speaking to him as his party moved on.

The Mayor said that Ramsgate had received a heavy dose of the German medicine and it had left a very bitter taste, but the people had showed great resolve and would do so again if necessary. A few days later Kate watched with a group of WVS volunteers from across the pavement as the Mayor asked Winston Churchill, in the town to thank volunteers, to swap his top hat for a helmet and to stub out his beloved cigar before entering the air raid tunnel shelters. The Prime Minister urged one of the local wardens to 'keep his pecker up' and Kate thought that was pretty good advice for all of them in Ramsgate, as the Battle of Britain continued overhead.

The August bombing had convinced Kate that Ramsgate was probably not the safest of towns to be living in during this war and once the London blitz had started the following month, pounding her old neighbourhood, she was even more determined to find a safer place to be. Her relationship with Joe had come to a natural end and he had moved out of their Ellington Road lodgings and she was once more struggling with money.

Henry and Lily were eager for her to move with them as they were talking about relocating away from the war-ravaged South East to the relative peace of North Wales, once Lily and Henry, who were hoping for a baby, had started a family of their own. Lily's aunt and uncle had moved to work on a chicken farm there and her own parents were thinking of following them. They were sure the couple could find work there if Kate could help with their children. Kate needed an evacuation plan of her own.

Henry heard about the Ramsgate bombing while he was on a fag break at Short's. The work there was hard, with long hours on the production line at the beck and call of the riveter as his designated mate. He knew as the youngster he was at the bottom of the ladder but at least he was doing his bit. The job was secure and he was earning enough for he and Lily to pay their rent and have enough set aside to save a bit for the wedding, and children, if, as his Mum had said, they were to be blessed with them. He was also doing his bit for the war effort and the Stirlings they were turning out at Rochester were in big demand by the RAF, as the Battle of Britain was raging above them.

Henry was sorry he couldn't persuade Ma to move with them to Gillingham but now she had got used to the tunnels Ramsgate was safe enough for now, he thought. He remembered the advice of one of the BEF evacuees from Dunkirk who had told him that the Jerry bombs were all bark and no bite as long as you took cover you would be alright. Even when the news came through that a number of people had died in the attack on Ramsgate Henry felt in his gut that Ma was a survivor. He was sad to hear about Fred Plummer. He liked him a lot. He was a grafter and he always had time for the youngsters.

But Henry was to learn soon that nowhere was truly safe from the German attacks. Just ten days before his wedding, on the 4th September, and only eleven days after the Ramsgate bombings, Rochester and the Short's factory and airfield in particular were under attack from the Luftwaffe. The men knew they were a target and thankfully had drills in place to prepare for such an eventuality. More than anything they were frustrated to hear as they stood in the shelters, the direct hits on newly completed planes sitting exposed as easy targets on the tarmac of the airfield's runway.

Henry's resolve was greater than ever now. He would try to get Lily and Ma away from 'bomb alley' as quickly as he could after their wedding, and he would stay at Short's. The company was planning to literally drive production underground in a factory carved out of a series of tunnels in the chalk cliffs on the south bank of the river Medway, next to the existing MAP factory extension. Henry was going underground again. Lily joked that they would never get any colour in his skin at this rate, but she was quietly proud of their war efforts and at least the Short's Tunnels would provide some respite from the German bombers.

Chapter Eight

Joining Up

It was only a second war, a World War in the most tragic of senses, that gave Fred the chance to travel back to the country of his birth. Fred volunteered as soon as he was old enough (in fact some time before he was old enough, such was his eagerness to serve the Empire he had been brought up to build) to serve with the Royal Australian Air Force.

He could not have known, as a teenager bursting with Christian fervour and patriotic duty, that a journey starting with tests of his physical capacity and spatial awareness at the Clontarf Training School in Perth, would end with him astride a seat the size of a bike saddle, in a rear gunner's pod at the arse-end of a Lancaster, literally frozen to his seat, staring at the stars.

They weren't even the same stars. Not the Southern Cross he remembered seeing from his Fairbridge cottage dorm as he gazed with watery eyes through the chicken wire walls to the skies of the Southern hemisphere. They were arse-about-face.

When he signed up he could not be sure that Britain or the European Theatre beckoned. Completing his application form to be air crew at Airways House in Perth on 6th July 1942 – just ten days after his eighteenth birthday, three months later Fred was called for a medical examination at the No.4 Recruiting Centre in Perth.

He arrived as instructed with his cut lunch to sustain him through the selection process. He was relieved that the exercise involving catching a ruler before it hit the floor, to assess his hand-eye coordination, went well. When the instructor fitted an oxygen mask over Fred's nose to ensure he was a nose-breather, the perils of war started to feel a little more real.

On successful completion of the medical, and after reading three-dimensional diagrams of cogs and levers (something Mr. Purser had helped Fred to prepare for) he felt so proud as he was accepted into the Royal Australian Air Force as a trainee, and he read out the oath 'I swear that I will well and truly serve our Sovereign Lord the King in the Air Force of the Commonwealth of Australia for the term of the duration of the war and twelve months thereafter or until sooner lawfully discharged, dismissed or removed; and that I will resist His Majesty's enemies and cause His Majesty's peace to be kept and maintained; and that I will, in all matters appertaining to my service, faithfully discharge my duty according to law. So help me God.'

red was selected as part of the Australian dominion's contribution to the Empire Air Training Scheme, and was to travel across Australia completing his 36 weeks of training – firstly at Initial Training School in Clontarf, then two thousand miles away from Perth in Ballarat in Victoria (the very name conjuring up images of his earlier voyage already becoming a distant memory in this fast-changing wartime world) for the Wireless Air Gunners' School, then West Sale and Sabiaco and, achieving the rank of sergeant and position of Air Gunner Number 427967, in July 1943.

Fred Wilson, Air Gunner 427967

During the initial training at the former Roman Catholic boys home at Clontarf on the banks of the Canning River in the Perth suburb of Waterford, Fred was first billeted in mid-October on an iron bed in a large dorm, but then soon transferred as the summer approached to a shared tent with board floors and on a straw filled hessian bag called a palliasse. The bountiful apple jelly was used in the mess as a spread, 'opening medicine' for these trainees unused to the country diet.

Fred relished the spread and the training – the lectures, drill PT and sport though he found swotting for some of the exams a bore. He told Canon Watson as much when he wrote to proudly inform him that he was now A.C II Wilson FA, Number 427967 at Clontarf. He also informed Canon Watson that 'he liked it better than the Army, but censoring could not permit to tell him why.'

Fred had indeed had a brief six-week spell with the West Australian Field Troops (Signals Division) before applying for his beloved RAAF. When he wasn't swotting, he kept in touch with his Perth based pals, especially Pete Redfern, on his weekend leave every two weeks with transport provided. To his mates he might still be 'Willo' but he stood so much taller than his 5 foot nine and a half inches in his air force blue uniform.

On the 4th February 1943 Fred was transferred to 1 WAGS – Wireless Air Gunner School, 2000 miles across the continent at Ballarat in Victoria. It is here in mid-March, during training, that he learnt the sad news of his guardian Canon Watson's tragic death at the age of just 51 in his wife's home town of Mandurah from a heart attack, while sat in his car.

In sending his condolences to Watson's widow, Fred wrote, 'Good old Canon, we all had our ups and downs but all along he was a fine example to me. Such a loss and a big blow to such a fine school, which is plugging along under adverse conditions. I must tell you all the news which has stored up. I have been made a Wireless Air Gunner (WAG for short) and am half way thro' the course. The work here consists entirely with radio, in every aspect of it, in the military sense. We have to attain a speed of 20 words a minute in Morse Code and be able to maintain communications under any conditions.' Fred goes on. 'All aircrew want to be pilots and some are disappointed when made WAGs. After a time here, you realise that the WAG is as important as the pilot. For all the crew is a team, relying on each other to do the job efficiently.' Fred shares a poem 'The Air Gunner's Lament' which he hopes to be printed in the Old Fairbridgian Association magazine.

'If I must be a gunner, then, please God, give me grace

That I may leave this unit with a smile upon my face.

We all wanted to be pilots, to fly a P40-E

But if we all were pilots, what would the Air Force be?

And the pilot's just a chauffeur, who flies the carte the same;

And tho' we chaps do all the work he always gets the fame.

It takes pluck to be a gunner, and sit out in the tail,

When the Zeros start a-coming and slugs begin to wail.

But we're in this fight together and altho' we're nearly done

Let us put aside our quarrel and hop into it as one

And for a sporting gesture, let us make a sporting bet

That we'll be the best air gunners who have left this unit yet.'

'I find the place cold after the West and never seem to get warm. It is famed for its cold and wet weather. We just have to grin and take it and hope that we have no worse in action. About July I go to a gunnery school for a month and then become a Sergeant and get my wing. After a short leave, we are off to action, where depends on the service requirements.'

Fred's last contact with the Fairbridge Farm School in August 1943 before setting off for the even colder and wetter England was a call to say that he was now at RAAF Subiaco and leaving for the USA to do a specialist course in radio. He was, he had informed them, top of the wireless course at Ballarat and recommended for a commission at the completion of training.

His Fairbridge sporting days – no rugger here just soccer, English-style, and cricket, and being handy with the woodaxe, had set him in good physical shape for the endurance that war was to bring.

Not that it was necessarily a case of the survival of the fittest. It was all about chance. A dangerous vocation. Bomber Command, within which Fred's nominated squadrons were to play a critical supporting role, was notorious for its large-scale losses of craft and men. Kevin Wilson has noted that 'the likelihood of survival in the bomber war was so slim they were no more substantial than men of air, ghosts already, waiting to vanish this night or the next'.

Despite the obvious risks, Fred was itching to get stuck in, in defence of the realm. But first the waiting began. Melbourne's showgrounds, after graduating from the Initial Training School at Bradfield Park Embarkation Depot and his formal passing out dinner, was his embarkation point and on 30th August 1943 Fred received his first pay in English pounds and once again, barely ten years from his arrival from England, boarded an ocean-going liner. This time the exotically named Umtali, to set sail around the world on a six-week voyage that would ultimately take him back to the Old Country as part of a Pacific Convoy, via New York.

As he watched his adopted homeland disappear below the horizon Fred felt a mix of emotions. He was travelling as light as he had arrived as an innocent nine-year-old boy but his world had changed beyond recognition in the last decade. He had become a young man while the world was now at war and he and his fellow crewmates on this particular voyage had no idea what their future fate in the European theatre held for them.

All Fred knew was that he would suck out of his young life everything he could, every experience, new place visited, friendship made, while giving his all in this fight to save the Old Country. The nearness of war was brought home to the lads as their troop ship was accompanied by an Australian destroyer for the first leg of their journey until they berthed in Auckland.

After a day on shore exploring Auckland and taking in the amazing view from the extinct volcano at Mt. Eden, their troop ship was saluted at dusk by Hudson aircraft from the RNZAF. As the sun glowed red behind them, before it disappeared on the horizon, Fred now contemplated the long next stage of his voyage on the open sea, with the next stop being the Panama Canal and onwards to the land of the free and the home of the brave.

The time on this journey seemed to drag as all of the 97 Aussie airmen on board the SS Umtali were eager to get to work, though some might also admit to being a little excited about seeing New York first. In the absence of a billiards table on board Fred taught himself how to play poker though he resisted the urge to gamble his dollars or English money insisting on sticking to matchsticks instead, themselves a rare commodity.

After slowly navigating the Panama Canal, which Fred could not help but compare to the Suez Canal, as he recalled the heat and the smell of that memorable leg of his childhood journey from London, the men started planning their five-day New York itineraries.

They were advised to visit the Anzac Club and to stock up on goods that would be hard to come by in ration-ravaged England – chocolate, cigarettes, soap and nylon stockings. Fred joked that the stockings might come in handy as additional warmers for arse-end Charlies like him freezing in the rear of a Lancaster.

Approaching the American coast, the Manhattan skyline was everything the men thought it might be, and more, as it slowly revealed itself to them through the smoky mist. They had never seen such an impressive sight of skyscrapers and Fred could not work out quite how so many buildings could be jammed into such a small island. As they slowly passed the Statue of Liberty, Fred got goosebumps on his tanned arm as he thought about the meaning behind the monument. The land of the free. A freedom from tyranny that he and his mates on board and hundreds of thousands of other young men and women were prepared to put their lives on the line for.

This point was not lost on the people who saw them in uniform and smiled at their courage. Though New Yorkers had a reputation for being brash, the American people Fred met were so generous and interested in these Aussie aircrew and every Manhattan bar they went into it they were besieged with offers of free cold beer. When he told them they were bound for England, the barmen all joked about the warm ale they would have to put up with in that grey land but they all wished them well.

One of Fred's mates joked that New York could be their last hurrah. Fred did not want to believe that but, in any event, they packed a lot in to their five days in New York. From the oddly appealing breakfast mix of the sweet and the savoury, Fred particularly loved the jam with eggs, to the late night bars off Broadway. As Fred tried to say in a poor imitation of an American accent, 'they sure sucked life out of that Big Apple'.

By the time they boarded the Queen Elizabeth, 'Lizzie' to the Australian crewmen, for the last leg of their journey to war alongside hundreds of American soldiers, Fred had crossed through nearly all of the places he had hoped to see. He had waited in line and taken an elevator to the top of the Empire State Building. Walked through Central Park and tried not to mess up his uniform with ketchup dripping from a street-bought hot-dog. Fred's favourite place here though was the Rockefeller Center and the Radio City Music Hall. As a young lad his only real quarrel with Fairbridge's Canon Watson was over his guardian's refusal to allow Fred to spend his Fairbridge trust monies on a course on radio when as a teenager he had hoped to make the wireless his career. The Canon did not see it as a worthy career but looking round Radio City Fred could see a hundred people who would disagree with his guardian, as Fred had done as an ambitious teenager.

As he sat in the stunning art deco surroundings of Radio City, waiting to see whether he would get in to hear a recording of the NBC Abbott and Costello show, or later when he walked past what used to be the dazzling lights on Broadway before the wartime dim-up, to the Alvin Theatre to watch Ethel Murman star in a Cole Porter musical, Fred could only conclude that New York City was as far removed as it was possible to be from the Australian wheatbelt, where only two years ago he was happy in his world.

He wasn't sure he would ever get used to the noise here and the pace at which life was lived, but for the moment it seemed fitting that their five days of 'freedom' before properly joining the war effort should be here in a city bursting with so much life. Fred felt that energy so much here especially on the dance floor. The garish décor at the Hurricane Club reminded Fred of the tropical palms they had just glimpsed from the Umtali when they passed through Panama, and the exuberant Duke Ellington's band did not disappoint the sweaty crowd that had packed in to catch one of his last concerts in his six-month residency.

The young airmen knew they had to pack as much in as they could during their five-day leave as they had no idea what fate awaited them in the European theatre. As much as Fred would have liked nothing more than to brush up on his pool table skills in the comfortable surroundings of the Anzac Club, he pushed himself to do as much as he could during his visit. He knew that any tiredness could be soon recovered on the ship's passage to Scotland and in any event his nineteen-year-old self was bursting with energy, and New York was the one place where you needed it most.

Every evening they were in Manhattan the tired workers drinking in the bars and clubs that the Australian aircrew had sampled, had been excited that the Yankees were on the cusp of an historic World Series baseball final. Though he didn't really understand the rules of baseball Fred was enough of a sports nut to know that the Yankee Stadium – the 'House That Babe built' was worth a visit.

He was a little wary of venturing north of Manhattan as the kindly Anzac Club helpers had warned the men that tensions were still high in the negro neighbourhood of Harlem, but Fred figured that the trip out to the Bronx would be worth taking the risk now the riots were over.

He was not disappointed. Though the Yankees and their Chicago White Sox visitors team were depleted by war – Fred knew that the Yankees' Joe DiMaggio was one of a number of their hitters serving away in the US Army, and the evening crowd barely half-filled the huge stadium. Fred was still charmed by the ballgame and the glimpse of normal New York life it gave him. Sport could do that. Lift you out of your normal place and transport you to somewhere else as part of the crowd of spectators. The Yankee Stadium was definitely designed to do that, and Fred felt it. After just a few hours he was now a Yankees fan for life and would always follow their fortunes even if the ins and outs of the game would remain a mystery to the cricket player in him.

As Fred returned to the Anzac Club for one last afternoon tea to thank the volunteers for their help in making his visit so memorable, he knew that he would miss America. The sheer scale and confidence of New York was like nothing he had ever known. He could see now why they called it the Big Apple. So much of it felt like forbidden fruit that was there to tempt you into a life lived at the fastest of speeds. He would be glad of a few days respite at sea and just hoped that the Atlantic crossing would be as uneventful as the first leg of the voyage had been.

It was clear at the short arm parade that awaited the crew as they boarded the RMS Queen Elizabeth in New York harbour that some of Fred's fellow crewmen had gone way further in sampling what New York had to offer and were nervously worse for wear as they waited in line. Fred had enjoyed the company of the young women offered to escort the crew on evenings out in the big City, but had been quietly grateful that chaperones were in place to preserve his shyness.

There was one last surprise for the men from their American hosts before they set sail as warm doughnuts and chocolate were given out to cheer them through the rain as they raced to claim their hammocks onboard.

Fred caught up on sleep as the 'Lizzie' steered a zig zag course across the Atlantic as part of a 15-ship convoy. As the New York skyline disappeared below the horizon behind them he realised that these next few months were to be a very real test for him. The war was coming home to him in the Old Country.

He did not want to consider the odds for or against his survival. He was not much of a betting man anyway. All he could do now was train as well as he was able. Throw himself into everything that was asked of him, as C B Fry had taught his younger self. Stand tall and do his country and his Fairbridge teachers proud. Everything else would be down to the fates. In God's hands.

After a few days, on glimpsing the Irish coast Fred could tell from the faces of the men around him at breakfast that whilst they might try to hide it, they were all sensing the nearness of war as they approached British soil.

After the imposing scale of the New York and New Jersey ports they had left behind them, it was odd to see the Clyde port of Greenock looking so provincial in the rainy and grey winter light. The green banks of hedges running down from the vivid verdant hills beyond to the small harbour town with its proud civic buildings and austere churches looked out of place against the backdrop of the troopships packing the harbour.

It was a stark reminder to Fred that this green and pleasant land he had sung about in Church at Fairbridge and where he had been sent to defend, was a small island with a big love of freedom. It might not be the same energetic freedom they felt in New York. It would be gentler, less brash, less colourful. Grey mists rather than faded Broadway stars. But it was freedom, nonetheless.

The long slow train journey south from Greenock into England triggered memories for Fred as they passed small town after small town of tightknit brick houses. He desperately wanted to defend England's honour as some of his fellow crewmen were slating the greyness of their damp surroundings every time they approached another small town in between flashes of the soggy English countryside. As they fought off hunger tucking into the provisions they had been allocated for the lengthy journey, the noisy talk was of Brighton, on what they hoped would be a brighter south coast, where they were all heading.

Fred arrived in Brighton with 250 other service personnel, at the Personnel Despatch and Reception Centre on 10th October 1943. A further 400 personnel were to arrive the following week, so the bustling seaside town was awash with uniformed Aussies and New Zealand pilots and air gunners like Fred.

Fred joined the rest of the new intake the day after his arrival as the Station Commander gave an intake talk at Princes Hall, on the blustery seafront that he could see was littered with barbed wire and debris.

The nine days of training included three hours of navigation, 24 hours of signals training, gas talks and intelligence but also allowed for clay pigeon shooting, sports and cinema to lighten the load a little. The aptly named, Grand Hotel on the blustery seafront hosted table tennis club nights and Fred played badminton at Princes Hall. The wind played havoc with his plans to play golf at one of the three golf courses available to the crews. Having recovered from the long sea voyage Fred was ready for his first proper posting after his nine long days by the sea.

Fred was to be posted to the Operational Training Unit at RAF Desborough - a newly opened, somewhat nondescript base near a town called Kettering in the middle of England, for further training. The place may have felt dull to Fred, but the work certainly was not.

One Australian airman noted on seeing the coast of Ireland after a long voyage from his homeland 'Today seems to have started a new era for me by suddenly clicking me from a spirit of holiday to a known nearness of war.'

Even the four months of training flights as part of Number 5 Course with 60 other pupils on 'wimpy' Wellington Xs at RAF Desborough were hazardous as rookie pilots grappled with the reality of flying in real-time. Desborough, newly transferred from the US Airforce along with the satellite aerodrome at Harrington, was Fred's first real taste of English life, though the training regime was punishing and left little time for fun.

The physical fitness instruction included gym, boxing, soccer, synthetic parachute training, unarmed combat, cross-country running and Rugby sevens. Reverend Green of Desborough organized Church of England services on alternate Sundays in the gymnasium, a service that felt familiar to Fred from his chapel days.

When Fred arrived at the base in October 1943 the flying training was marred by persistent bad weather. He knew he needed to take to the skies. He had stood to attention when in early November, just after his brother Phil's 21st birthday, the leading US Lt General Eaker of USAAF had handed over

Harrington Aerodrome to the Royal Air Force and 'stressed the mutual objectives of the two forces, which was to bomb Hitler until his war machine collapsed.'

Air Officer C-I-C Arthur 'Bomber' Harris had driven the point home to the rookie aircrews. Their 'purpose to train skilled aircrew to break the enemy's means and will to war, to emasculate every centre of his production'. He warned the uniformed men and women gathered that 'whilst we are well on the way to achieve this, war was a race, victory the prize, but not to the man who eases up or looks over his shoulder during that race'. As he stood in salute to the strains of the two national anthems of the two nations, three Wellingtons roared by in formation, dipped in salute, and the Chaplain Squadron Leader Donald Knight read a benediction.

Fred prayed. But so much was down to luck. Or fate. They were superstitious times. But Fred was Boomerang Boy. He believed he would always come back. He'd proved it hadn't he? Shipped thousands of miles away to arrive at Fairbridge on his tenth birthday here he was just short of his twentieth back in Blighty. He held on to that copy of Pilgrim's Progress that he and Phil had cherished since their Woodford Garden City days. All the spiritual guidance that Barnardo's saw fit to leave the boys in one small, tattered book. Now it meant something. Being so close to the end of things made you cherish the life you had been given.

You had to live life to the full. Fred soaked it all up. All the ENSA shows. Even the cheesy 'Hot Spot Entertainers' variety show from nearby Kettering. A 48-hour weekend leave to

London where he dashed to the Boomerang Club, 'the Boomer', at Australia House opposite the bombed-through St Clement Danes Church, and caught up with news from home through the well-thumbed pages of the West Australian newspaper.

Fred particularly liked to played billiards. The Old Fairbridgians Club House had a marvellous billiards table gifted by an English writer, E V Lucas, and Fred had made much use of it on his return visits to Pinjarra. At the Boomer he tried to remember the trick shots he had been taught in the Billiards room at Dickies but wasn't good enough to chance any cash on a game. He wasn't a big drinker so he steered clear of the Codgers Inn on Fleet Street where so many of his Aussie compatriots signed in, though he did partake of the steak served by 'Dirty Mick' at his café on the Strand. Back on base Fred read his way through the Penguin books supplied to the Desborough library, when the fog curtailed training flights that winter. On New Year's Eve the men were treated to a play 'Gaslight' starring a beautiful young London stage and film actress, the newly married Diana Winyard.

The first few weeks of 1944 brought home to Fred how chancy his life now was. Although Group Captain Lowe had congratulated the crews on their thousand hours of flying in December 1943 with only one accident, he had clearly spooked things as three Wellingtons were downed within a month on training flights, killing eighteen of Fred's fellow pupil crewmen.

After completing 92 hours flying time training in the 'Wimpy' Wellington X Fred was promoted to the position of flight sergeant in February and posted out after a fortnight's paid leave from Desborough first to Methwold and Feltwell, on the Norfolk/Suffolk border, deep in the East Anglian countryside.

Here Fred joined the Heavy Conversion Unit notching up only 5.5 hours flying time due in part to the poor weather that winter. When the Lancasters arrived at Feltwell in March, Fred joined the No 3 Lancaster Finishing school to get accustomed with his crew to the heavier Avro Lancasters ways, managing over 10 hours of training flights.

Feeling more at home in the countryside, surrounded by forestry and family farms, Fred joined other trained farm hands in filling the long days of inactivity in between training sessions by helping out on the local dairy farm – the earliest of springtime starts were rewarded with the freshest of milk, still steaming from the milking and the occasional egg from Farmer Palmer's hens at Catsholm Farm. Fred proudly remembered how milk yields had soared under his stewardship at George Purser's 'Corio' farm back in WA. He told anyone of his crewmates who would listen.

Milk here was plentiful but fresh eggs were at a premium – reserved for the brave crews. Having sampled the horrors of powdered egg as a pairing with greasy spam, fresh eggs were a real treat. Offered before or after bombing missions the superstitious crews invariably opted to have a pre-flight full breakfast rather than chance it. Chancing it was part of their lives now. The odds stacked against them. Fred knew he had to seize life. As Kevin Wilson said, the crewman of Bomber Command 'lived as if there was no tomorrow, because for many there wasn't'.

For Fred there was no time to dwell on the past. His brother Phil was out there somewhere. In the air, at sea, or as Fred suspected, marching somewhere. Always was a marcher, despite his bandy legs, a physical reminder of having rickets as a boy.

His instinct was accurate. While Fred was preparing to fly many more than his requisite minimum of 25 sorties, first with 622 Squadron, flying in Lancasters out of the base that felt like it had been carved out of the Guinness magnate Lord Iveagh's sprawling Suffolk estate at RAF Mildenhall, and then, more at home at RAF Oulton as part of a ten man crew of a B-17 Flying Fortress, complete with top-secret radio-jamming devices dreamt up and operated by the youngest of Cambridge boffins.

Little did Fred know, but his brother Phil was one of Monty's men going through hell in Northern France and liberating Holland.

Chapter Nine

Phil's War

Just weeks before his younger brother Fred had signed up, as a rookie seventeen-year-old farm hand, to six weeks signals training with the West Australian Field Troops (proudly adopting the address as Pte W 78444) Philip Charles Wilson had been called up by the British Army, on the 19th March 1942 reporting to his English County town of Gloucester.

Unlike Fred, who had attempted to volunteer months before his 18th birthday and had undergone military training with the West Australian Field Troops with the express purpose of preparing for the war effort, Phil was in no hurry to join up. Not that he wasn't patriotic or didn't support the war effort. He was and he did.

It was just that, having just settled into a happy life in the beautifully quiet Gloucestershire village of Southrop, with a gardening job he took great pride in and that gave him the chance to use the skills he had learned all those years ago in the gardens at Woodford Garden City, he was reluctant to give all that up for a fate unknown.

Joey Iles, his mate who worked on the gardens of the Richardson's Manor House estate along the lane, a garden Phil envied, had already signed up and Phil could see from the face of his mother as he cycled passed her cottage on the way to Lechlade, that she was anxious for him. Phil daren't dream that Joey wouldn't come back, and he would walk into his boots, that was just too cruel and something that Colonel

Watson, Phil's kindly employer and owner of Southrop Lodge, would not tolerate.

Though his garden boy job didn't exactly pay a king's ransom, Phil could not complain. The Watsons were a lovely family. He had enough to get by and had a roof over his head. Best of all, he had a lovely garden and immaculate grass tennis courts to look after. The Lodge had once been the vicarage for St Peter's Church and the poet John Keble, the man who had an Oxford University college named after him, had once lived there. It had a beautiful Cedar of Lebanon tree and in spring the cherry blossom was so pretty, even if it did mess up Phil's attempts to keep the Colonel's lawn pristine in the Autumn.

Mrs Watson told Phil that Reverend Keble himself had sat under the very same tree to write many of his poems and hymns. Phil even memorized one of the verses from Mrs Watson's favourite of Keble's poems about Christ – 'But when he came the second time. He came in power and love. Softer than gale at morning prime. Hovered his holy Dove. '

Their garden may not have had weeping willow trees shadowing the river running through it like Southrop's Manor House next door, where Phil would sneak in with Joey when Captain Richardson was away in London to paddle in the shallow waters of the Leach, but it did give him the chance to make his mark and create a thing of beauty that he was sure his Mother would have been proud of.

Phil owed Colonel Watson too much to say or do anything to upset him. It was he and Mrs Watson who had offered Phil the chance to work in this most tranquil of Cotswold villages, to leave Barnardo's behind along with the noise and bustle of East London when the garden boy job he enjoyed, in Northwood, had ended and he was sent back to Stepney.

Though he knew he would be safer away from the bombs that were falling on the city of his birth, Phil was sad to leave London. Mr. and Mrs Thomas had been kind to Phil during his time in Northwood.

Phil missed those London times, but he missed his Mum more than anything. It was too painful to talk about to anyone else, not even to Maggie in the Swan or to Colonel and Mrs Watson's lovely daughter Ina. He just couldn't understand why his mother hadn't tried to find him and Fred. Of course, Fred was always going to be hard to find in Australia but Phil had only been in London. Why hadn't she wanted to seek him out and take him home to live with her and Henry wherever they were now?

Phil's best mate in Southrop, Coxy, George Cox to be precise, sadly no relation to Dorothy or Douglas, was becoming like a brother to Phil and that made him happy and sad at the same time. Coxy seemed to know how Phil ticked. He could tell when Phil was lost in his own thoughts while he was digging and would leave him to it. But Coxy was his friend and not his Fred. He was from a longstanding Southrop family, not a Cockney outsider with the gift of the gab. He could never replace Fred.

Phil thought about Fred all the time. Watching the children playing cricket in the playground at Southrop school opposite the Lodge, seeing the young cricketers practicing their bowling on the green outside the Swan, they all became his demon bowler Freddie.

Whenever the news on the wireless carried stories from Australia Phil wondered if he would ever save enough money to travel there to find Fred.

It seemed such a different country, despite speaking the same language and sharing the same King. When Phil heard that the so-called 'children of the Empire' were coming 'home' to Britain to help the war effort he secretly hoped that Fred would be one of them and find the letters he had sent to Barnardo's in case Fred showed up.

It was with mixed emotions that Phil enlisted in the Spring of 1942 at the age of just 19 years and 5 months.

He had seen the pain still etched on the faces of their neighbours, Bert and Laura Moulden, who had lost their oldest son Allan at Dunkirk barely a year after Phil had arrived in Southrop. The young Allan had gone away to the Gloucestershire Regiment as proud as punch in his regulation uniform and never returned from France. The previously jolly Mrs Moulden, who always had a smile for Phil when she passed him in the lane, never smiled again. I was as if the joy had been shot out of her.

But Phil also knew that his father - the Captain – as he still referred to Alfred (he could never quite forgive him for not marrying his mother and leaving her penniless when he died) would be quietly proud of seeing his son sign up for service. In a sense so much of what Phil had done since he was a child was trying to prove something to his late father. Even when still in short trousers in the Barnardo's cub pack, Phil took his duties seriously. Baden-Powell would be proud too. He was well-prepared.

There was only one thing he hadn't been prepared for. And that was losing his younger brother to Australia. When his sisters Mabel and Lavinia had died it was different. Phil knew from what his mother had told the boys that both girls were in a safe place. In heaven. Though he hadn't been allowed to go to Lambeth cemetery for his father's funeral or to say goodbye to the girls, Phil knew, from his secret trips to lay stones at the unmarked graves later, that they were in a better, quieter place. He couldn't say the same for Fred.

He just did not know for sure.

That was why Phil prayed hard for Fred. He tried to have a wager with Jesus. Bring back Fred and I will give the rest of my life to you Lord. He knew that things didn't work like that, otherwise the lovely, kindly Mrs Richardson would never have lost her brother to the Germans. And when Reverend Squire, whose own son had died in the Great War when he was barely two years older than Phil was now, preached in St Peter's Church about the Prodigal Son and killing the fatted calf to celebrate his return, Phil knew he would do exactly the same if Fred walked through the door of the Swan right now.

But it wasn't to be. So, despite his reticence perhaps going to war would be a good distraction. Take his mind of Fred. He would have to be focused now.

It wasn't as if sleepy Southrop had escaped the fatal impact of the war anyway. The newly created RAF Southrop, a small encampment and landing strip just outside the village on the road to the bigger base at Fairford, made sure of that. It was personal too. In the month before Phil joined up one of the young women who Phil knew drank in the Swan, Joan Jefferies, had been involved in a terrible accident on Valentine's Night when her fiancé's car was hit by an RAF Harvard training plane as the rookie pilot lost control on landing.

Though Joan escaped with terrible injuries after the kindly Welsh doctor Dr Morgan had taken her to hospital, her poor fiancé Len, a band leader in a popular local dance band, and her best friend Nancy Peachey from next door Eastleach, the band's talented pianist, were both killed.

Phil knew that nowhere was completely immune to the effects of this wretched war. In any event, Phil wanted to impress the frustratingly retired Colonel Watson and return his kindness by following him into the Army and do his legal guardian proud.

Colonel Watson, for all his kindly manner, still had the strong air of authority that came from being a cavalry man with many years of distinguished military service. Trim in his tweeds and his riding boots, relaxed with his pipe constantly in his left hand, the retired army colonel Evelyn Cyril Watson OBE had been a Lieutenant Captain in a Cavalry Regiment of the 7th (Princess Royals) Dragoon Guards when he married his beloved Dulce at St Jude's Church in South Kensington in

1908. After a posting in Sikandarabad, in India, he had fought at the Western Front, including at the Somme. On Armistice Day the Colonel regaled Phil with his experiences of riding ten miles to capture the Flanders town of Lessines on 11th November 1918 shortly before the armistice was declared.

With his bandy legs, a legacy of his childhood rickets, Phil joked with the Colonel that he had the build for horse riding but it wasn't something he would relish. Phil had always carried a fear of horses since he had seen the big beasts with mounted policemen charging unemployed protesters at St George's Fields when he was a young boy.

Despite his obvious disappointment that Phil was not cavalry material, the Colonel reassured the young man that he was a smart chap and offered to drive Phil to their County Town of Gloucester, and after performing well in the tests, the recruiting Sergeant concurred and recommended the Signals Corps for Phil.

He was to be Signalman Wilson – army number 5577383.

The initial training was tough. Just as Fred was to travel across Australia to pick up the skills he would need to become a wireless air gunner, so Phil had to make the, albeit more modest, journey north by train from Swindon to another great railway town of York, where his initial signals training commenced in earnest at Catterick camp. Completing the course was by no means a given.

Phil had to draw on the things he could remember from his time at Kingston school in order to get to grips with the technical details a signalman was required to understand. The 'Twelve Lectures on electricity and magnetism and their relation to wireless' may have seemed overly academic and theoretical to Phil but he knew he had to persevere to pass the course with flying colours. The exams were tough, but Phil got through. He particularly enjoyed practicing simulating morse code using spoons as it gave him a chance to show off his musical prowess in playing the spoons, as a bit of light relief in between lessons.

The practical elements of handling the various types of wireless handsets were much more interesting for Phil. As a regimental signaller to be based alongside the Wiltshire Regiment, Phil was to be most familiar with the bulky Number 18 wireless set with its 4-mile range.

In advance of what was to be Phil's and the Wiltshire's biggest test of the war to date, he was briefly billeted for further specific Signals Training at the imposing Golden Hill Fort on the Isle of Wight off the south coast of England.

Having recovered from seasickness, at first sight the Fort took Phil back to the small wooden fort that he and Fred had fought over when they were boarded out with foster parents in Woodford Bridge, on Phil's eleventh birthday. Even down to the sentries in their make-believe boxes. But this was not make-believe. As the sergeant-major boomed in the drill hall, this was the real thing. Soon all the months of preparation, the route marching and trench digging, would be put to the test.

For now, Phil was pleased to be able to at least see the sea. Even though every steamship that passed near the Isle of

Wight reminded him of that fateful morning ten years earlier when his younger brother had sailed out from Tilbury Docks and out of his life forever.

On completing his signals training Phil was posted to the Fifth Battalion of the Wiltshire Regiment who had recently moved inland from the cliff-side fort at Dover to their new tented camp base at the grand Waldershare Park on the North Downs.

Phil's love of the sea, from a distance at least, was soon to be put to the test. Allocated now to work alongside the Wiltshire Regiment, part of the 43rd Wessex Division, the Wyverns, led by the 'prickly' Major-General G I Thomas, the troops were gathering in large numbers in readiness for the start of Overlord.

Waldershare was the ancestral home of the Earl and Countess of Guilford but was in use as a temporary hospital for the wounded returning from the front. Regimental camp life was dull but at least in his bunk in the windowless tunnel shaped Nissen hut that was to be his home Phil could keep warm through the winter. The stove in the middle of the hut was constantly aglow, drying off the men's wet packs and fending off the effect of the icy winds. Phil kept himself to himself.

The infantrymen he was attached to were effectively two tribes – one of 'swedebashers' from Wiltshire farming stock and the other the 'cockney boys' with their London swagger and Phil didn't really feel at home in either. He told himself he had a foot in both camps and was better off with his own thoughts. He would join in when there was music to be made

– his spoons technique had been mastered at Catterick and the Barnardo's music master had said he had a decent musical ear - but otherwise he kept himself apart from a lot of the japes, and the trouble with the RSM that came with them.

When he had some leave, he would explore the Waldershare estate and offer to help out at Home Farm where the gardener Bert Sacre was happy to share his knowledge and his views of the war. He told Phil about the ancient Captain's Wood nearby and pointed out the famous Spanish chestnut trees. As they walked to the tiny All Saints Church on the estate, Bert told Phil that the yew trees in the churchyard were believed to be hundreds of years old.

Phil learnt to recognize the bluebells, wood anemone and the wild garlic, which Bert encouraged him to pick and take back to camp. As he admired the unusual architecture of an Oast House, Mr. Sacre said he would need to get used to those as they were everywhere in this part of Kent. Walking down the avenue of lime trees back towards the House, a man who Phil guessed must be the Earl, passed them on horseback with his young nine year old son and heir, Edward, struggling to keep up.

Though Waldershare was grand and he loved their walled kitchen garden, Phil still preferred the homely Lodge at Southrop. The grounds here would be a nightmare to maintain and he told Bert that he was never one for horses, so the busy Stud and Kennels here would really test his patience.

Phil missed Southrop. General Montgomery was making the lads work harder than ever and at least that meant the boring routines of drill and route marches were interrupted with other tactical exercises that saw them travelling around the south of England. For one, they were transported to the south coast at Selsey Bill and practiced landing from the sea. It brought home to Phil and the other lads the imminence of battle. After another of Monty's exercises, dubbed 'Spartan', Phil had to laugh when reports came in over the wireless that a bison had escaped from Whipsnade Zoo after one of the Wiltshire's tanks had broken the fence of the zoo. Proof that he never wanted to work with animals. Rounding him up would be a lot harder than coaxing the Thomas's Labrador Rex back to Duck's Hill Road.

After a long hot summer on camp at Waldershare, the battalion were on the move again and in the Autumn of 1943 the Regiment set up Battalion HQ further inland at the requisitioned Jacobean Tongswood House, in the Kent countryside, near the Sussex border at Hawkhurst.

Major Pearson was in charge and a tough training regime was instituted including rifle range, and simulated street fighting at St Margaret's Bay.

On 4th February the Regiment was addressed by General Sir Bernard Montgomery (Monty) at the Empire Cinema in the bustling Kent market town of Tenterden, ahead of a number of training manoeuvres designed to anticipate conditions they would be likely to face in Normandy, including river crossings of the Medway above Chatham and the formation of bridge heads.

The training was intense, and Phil was relieved to be granted a week's leave in the spring. He decided not to head back to Southrop but to stay locally and explore the Kent and Sussex countryside. On one of his visits to the Battalion Headquarters he discovered that Tongswood House had the most beautiful of gardens beyond the high wall that stretched along the Estate. He volunteered himself to help out in one of the thirteen glass houses and the gruff Yorkshireman Head Gardener Mr Hardcastle was happy to have an extra pair of hands, especially when Phil detailed his experience with the Thomas's and the Watsons.

As they worked potting out plants, one of the junior gardeners, Charlie, explained that Mrs Gunther who owned the House and was trying to sell it before the Army took it over at the start of the war, was really passionate about her garden which was why she had not sold it alongside the rest of the estate when her husband, the Oxo millionaire Mr. Gunther had died from a heart attack over decade ago. Her sons, James and William, known to everyone on the estate as Jimmy and Billy, were decent enough blokes but didn't want to take on the running of such a big place.

Jimmy Gunther had hit the newspapers when he married one of their housemaids, a real upstairs, downstairs love affair. Charlie didn't think it would last. Her old man was a gardener just like them. The older Lady G, as he called her, was according to Charlie, a lovely lady if a little potty.

She liked nothing more than pottering around the glass houses in her dressing gown late at night, so the lads were always careful to cough loudly as they approached so they didn't startle her. He may not have been formally schooled but Charlie knew his stuff when it came to gardening. In the Pelargonium House he explained that there were 280 different species of perennials, succulents and shrubs and before the war had started, Lady G was hoping to have as many as she could lay her hands on planted here in Tongswood.

They grew so many flowers that they gave some away to the local hospital and they were particularly proud of their Carnation House. Phil could not imagine ever working in gardens as great as these. He realized he had so much to learn and wished he had a teacher like Mr. Hardcastle to share some of his knowledge of plants and flowers with him. He spent time in the Fernery, and the Vinery and walked around the vast rockery that Mr. Gunther himself had ordered to be created. He marvelled at the peach house and the melon house but found the Hot House just too hot to spend any time in whilst in his heavy uniform.

On his last day in the walled gardens, Mr. Hardcastle took Phil aside as he said he wanted to show him something important on the estate. They walked in silence to a quiet spot where there had been created a rudimentary stone memorial to twelve young men from the Estate who had fallen in the Great War, including two of Mr. Gunther's sons from his first marriage.

'Norman Gunther', Mr H said, 'was about your age when he fell in France during a raid on enemy shell holes near Tool trench. He was awarded the Military Cross. His older brother

Charles was to die in action a year later just weeks before the end of the war.'

He looked Phil straight in the eyes and said, 'Make sure you look after yourself over there lad. Keep your head down and no heroics. I am sure your mother wants to see you home safe and sound.' Phil didn't know what to say, merely mumbling, 'Thanks Mr. Hardcastle' as he shook his hand on parting, 'and thank you for showing me your incredible gardens.'

On the eve of entering the fray, in May, the Battalion were addressed by their Brigadier Mole at their Tongswood House HQ before the 800 plus men took part in a recreation day, complete with fairground, tug of war and an ENSA show and open air dance. It was a rousing address but Phil, like many of his comrades in arms had his mind elsewhere. He had written his 'last letter' to Colonel and Mrs Watson, asking them to look out for Fred if he, Phil, was one of the fallen. He trusted the Colonel to inform his mother if she were still alive and do the right thing by Fred, if he could find him. He handed the letter to the padre and had a brief walk around the fairground trying to take his mind off what was to come.

For all the training and the months of drill in all weathers, this was now the real thing. The moment when Phil would be tested like never before. He consoled himself remembering that his father, the Captain, had survived postings in the Cape, Sierra Leone and the Great War. Their mother had briefly cherished his seven medals to prove it. It didn't stop Phil feeling as nervous as hell in the pit of his stomach.

The 43rd did not go in on the first wave on 6th June 1944. It was to be twelve days later, on a Sunday, 18th June that Phil's contingent left their tented camp at Ditchey and Newhaven harbour, a place that in other circumstances would have been a lovely early summer holiday camp where the fields and woodland fell away to the sea, after a 'last supper' that was cynically described by one of his mates as them being 'fatted up for the kill'. They were full of fear and trepidation.

Chapter Ten

Bellamus Noctu

Fred's new 622 Squadron's motto was 'Bellamus Noctu' – we wage war by night. Their badge a long-eared owl just to emphasise the point. Unlike their 'Memphis Belle' American comrades of the air, Butch Harris's Bomber Boys were nocturnal creatures. In all, Fred completed a 'lucky for him' 13 sorties with 622 squadron. The rear gunner of an Avro Lancaster.

The instructions given to the Tail End Charlies like Fred were very clear.

- Search the sky before take-off and landing when your a/c is most vulnerable.
- If you perceive gun fire, search for fighters, and ask for evasive action.
- Always watch your own tail
- Conserve your ammunition: if you're fired upon from long range, instruct pilot to use evasive action.
- Use good teamwork with the rest of the crew
- If using tracer at night, remember it leads to momentarily destroy your night vision: hold your fire until necessary
- The aim of an enemy fighter is to destroy; the aim of the bomber air gunner is to get safely to target and back to base.
- Never fire until fired upon. Again: never fire until fired upon.

- All aircraft approaching are considered to be enemy until unmistakably identified otherwise.
- Remember: to be surprised is to be dead.

Arriving on the sprawling RAF base at Mildenhall on the 12th April 1944, Fred was thrown straight into the preparatory attacks ahead of Overlord, the campaign that unbeknown to him, his brother Philip was to be deeply involved with on the ground.

Earning ten shillings a day, with leave every six weeks and extra rations when you came back safely from a sortie, this was what Fred had signed up for as an earnest young Australian and spent so long training for in his homeland.

Kevin Wilson describes the atmosphere of the ops room well. 'the callow and the cultured, the novice and the knowledgeable, the profound and the profane; all waiting for their immediate futures to be revealed. Cigarettes passed around. Chatter rose. Bursts of nervous laughter as a crewman recalls a raucous incident in the pub, a bumpy landing or a lucky escape on ops the night before.'

There was a definite theatricality about airmen's lives in Bomber Command from the histrionic lifting of the curtain to reveal the target to the crimson ribbon marking the proposed route as COs handed over to section leaders for times on target, bomb loads, wireless frequencies and airfield marshalling procedures. Now all the crews could do was wait all alone with their thoughts.

But this was no performance for the entertainment of others. This was the serious work for which all of Fred's 80-odd flying hours in training had prepared him. But nothing could properly prepare him for the gruelling experience he faced as an 'arse-end Charlie or rear gunner. It was, as Kevin Wilson has noted, 'an unglamorous, pitiless war in which they pitched themselves against barrages of flak, and other young enemy flyers, in the dark and freezing cold, as searching eyes grew heavy-lidded and limbs ached for rest'.

On 17th April – just five days after Fred joined Bomber Command's Number Three Group: 622 squadron at Mildenhall, a directive was issued to the US Eight Air Force commander Spaatz and the RAF's Bomber Harris 'Our re-entry on the continent constitutes the supreme operation for 1944. All possible support must be afforded to the Allied Armies by our Air Forces to assist them in establishing themselves in the lodgment area.' Eisenhower saw Tedder's transportation plan as essential to the success of Overlord. Bomber Harris's reputation as a team player was on the line on the ground as much as the arses of his men were in the air.

To Harris's credit, immediately Bomber Command set to work with attacks on the French railway system. On 18/19th April, the marshalling yards at Juvisy near Paris were disabled. Whole marshalling yards were pulverised into rubble. 'Yellow flashes on the ground where bombs were landing. Red and green indicators cascading in rapid succession. The bombers were in and out in ten minutes. These sorties – shorter than normal at 2- and three-quarter hours may have seemed to crews used to longer sorties in German airspace like 'cake walks'.

The following night, 20th April, saw Fred's first mission with his adopted eight-man crew led by Wing Commander Ian Clifford Kirby Swales and Flight Sergeant Fenwick. The four-hour sortie saw the crew as part of a 17-bomber raid attack Koln, with the crew reporting a very successful bombardment.

There was little rest for Fred as the next night he joined a different crew under Flight Sergeant Clarke as part of a bombing raid on Dusseldorf. The Clarke crew report notes that 'they bombed red TIs from 23000 feet at 0121 hours. The built-up area and the river were seen, and the bombing was concentrated on the target.'

After a week's respite, Fred re-joined Flight Sergeant Fenwick's crew on a 'rather scattered raid' by 10 of their aircraft against the German-held Nantes airfield in Northern France on 7th May. The target was obscured, and the bombing scattered, though all of the 10 bombers were able to shed their load.

Twelve days later as the build up to Overlord intensified Fred's Fenwick crew were one of 15 bombers from 622 attacking the Le Mans marshalling yards. The attack was successful with large explosions being seen bursting across the lines. Hampered by bad weather the next day, the crew returned to the skies on the 21st May successfully attacking marshalling yards at Duisburg.

For the most part 622 were very successful in their campaign. However heavy losses were sustained in May with 12 Lancasters shot down over Lille on 10/11th May and 5 further lost at Bourg Leopold in Belgium two nights later.

On 24th May, Fred's crew had to abandon their mission against Aachen due to very severe icing and their bombs were jettisoned at 8000 feet.

They were not disheartened though as three nights later when they carried out a four-hour sortie and a very successful raid as part of a 20-bomber attack on Boulogne and the Gironde area of France, with all crews returning safely. The next night, despite his exhaustion the crew were very successful in their bombing of Angers. They bombed red TI at 0002 from 8500 feet. Fires were burning in an oblong area approximately 700 yards by 400 yards. One very large explosion was seen at 0012. The logbook recorded that 'Bombing was very accurate'.

Fred now had a five day respite from the nervous exhaustion of a flap, and a chance for him to sample some of the local ales, reputedly dubbed Suffolk Punch as they knocked you out; though Fenwick's theory was that they were so-called because they tasted like horse piss. Fred's crew were in action once more on 2nd June as 10 Lancasters attacked Wissant. This time Fenwick's crew were less successful in their mission as heavy cloud prevented them from seeing their target and bombing was scattered with some falling in the sea.

By 3rd June the British bombers had attacked every one of their allotted targets. In the final days before D-Day 54,869 tons of bombs were dropped, 33,090 of them from Lancasters like the one Fred was allotted to. A railway desert was successfully created. 1700 sorties in 30 separate attacks on gun emplacements and batteries added further to Bomber Harris's reputation as a leader who made things happen.

Not that the airmen like Fred knew precisely what was planned below. After the crews for the night's battle order were posted on the blackboard by mid-morning, their intelligence briefings before a flap in those smoke-filled, nerve-ends-charged briefing rooms at Mildenhall, merely told them their own target for that mission and for the next few hours that was their precise focus.

Indeed, coming back on the night before D-Day in the early morning light after a moderately successful attack at the French port of Ouistreham, to weaken Nazi defences ahead of the subsequent allied landings at nearby 'Sword' beach, crews were startled to see what at first were feathers in the water that proved to be this massive array of ships. Hospital ships with a big red cross, cruisers bursting with nervous squaddies and battleships. It looked like an armada with ships as far as the eye could see, thousands of them.

Overlord had started. Fred was not to know, looking down at this impressive sight, that his brother Phil was to be part of it.

Chapter Eleven

March of the Wyverns

As the Sussex cliffs disappeared from view Phil prayed that he would live to see the England he loved again. After sixteen hours of buffeting in choppy waters – with their helmets taken off their newly shaven heads and in turn serving as soup bowls and sick buckets, the men arrived off Arromanches at the carefully constructed 'Mulberry Harbour' in the Seine Bay.

The ramps connecting to the harbour were unstable in the storm that was blowing up, so Phil had to jump into the surf. It was a long march up the hill in damp, steaming khaki gear, inland to the village of Sommervieu and the woods nearby. He had that sick feeling in his stomach that might be hunger but was more likely driven by fear. His mouth tasted of metal as the grumbling of guns and the nearness of battle forced the jesting and the singing among the men to cease.

It seemed a bit surreal to Phil to see a French café open for business in the thick of a war. Tired from their journey to their dismay the men found that the vehicles carrying their greatcoats and blankets had not arrived. But soon they were at least able to dry off properly as they opened their tinned 48-hour rations, broke bread, set up a concert party and broadcasting van and dug-in safely for a few days.

Compared to their comrades who had faced the hostile fire of the first few days of the Normandy campaign this was a relatively soft landing. For all the build-up, in fact, a bit of an anti-climax. It was just as well. As the next few days and weeks were going to test their endurance to the limit.

By the 23rd of June (the day before what Phil always remembered as his brother Fred's birthday – this year he would be 20) when the transport vehicles finally arrived, the troops of the 43rd were ready for battle. Three days later the fighting for them began. In the villages of St Mauvieu and La Gaule near Cheux, the dead from both sides of earlier battles were still on the streets. There hadn't been a pause in the battles to find time to bury them. The stench was intolerable. There were bursts of gunfire all around. It was a shock to the young men's senses, this first taste of real warfare. Phil savoured the taste of his ration pack cigarettes to try to take away the smell of rotting human and horse flesh.

The 43rd Wessex Division had the task of relieving the Scottish Division attacking the enemy towards the River Orne, south west of Caen.

After a successful reconnaissance trip to Carpiquet Aerodrome on 27th June, two days later, the 5th Wiltshires were tasked with clearing the woods and orchards between Tourville and Baron. The woods spelt danger. They were real death-traps with Jerry well and truly dug in. Here Phil's big ears were assaulted with the multi-barrelled mortars of the 'sobbin sisters' – German bombs fired six at a time in the air.

For a signaller like Phil, always on the move backwards and forwards, constantly exposed, often only escaping bombardment by flinging himself into ditches, this a testing time. Whether on line-laying ops or struggling to get the unreliable wireless sets to kick into action, he was constantly on the go. It was vital that the Major was informed of the Colonel's intentions or directions and keeping Battalion HQ informed of progress.

There was much to occupy Phil's mind as the Wiltshires, now led by Lt-Col. 'Pop' Pearson reached the Caen-Tourville road and fought their way through the woods over River Odon and up into Baron. They were in the 'Odon Box'. They were to hold their exposed positions here for ten gruelling days, facing heavy shelling, as they prepared to attack Hill 112.

It was widely believed by the German military planners that 'he who holds Hill 112, holds Normandy'. For the Allies, then, this was a critical Hill to take. The job of the 43rd was to capture the high ground from Eternville to Hill 112 including the village of Maltot.

After recces through the swishing cornfields for the soon to be executed Operation Jupiter, with mines and booby traps laid, the Battalion HQ moved on the 8/9th July to La Rue St Martin in Baron, in readiness for the testing battle to commence.

The following morning of the 10th July, supported by Churchill Tanks, the 5th Wiltshires moved against the fearless SS 10th Panzer Division and their Tiger tanks. The Germans were lying in wait in pits in the corn and attacked with their cruelly effective Spandau automatic machine guns. They were a formidable enemy and the losses on both sides were great. 26 men of Phil's regiment were killed, 68 wounded and 21 were missing in action. The tiger tanks were strong in number and the reverse slopes of the hill were a significant challenge.

After five days of fierce fighting, on the 15th July, beer was issued to the men, one bottle per head, and Phil was at last able to toast his brother's 20th birthday properly. Even three weeks late and without Fred at his side, the celebratory ale was like a nectar for the Gods.

After a few days of relative inactivity, and a chance for Phil to wash his stinking underpants, on the 22nd July the Wiltshires attacked Maltot. With fierce fighting around the wood and chateau, again up against the tiger Tanks, this time the Wiltshires took 400 German prisoners. After a brief rest in the hot Normandy sunshine the Wiltshires were again engaged with the enemy, this time in bocage country around the village of Caumont – hilly, an area with wooded and sunken lanes and high hedges that restricted visibility.

A further battle ensued as August approached at Bois du Homme, another treacherous wooded hill, six miles south of Caumont. It was here that the Germans struck at the Wiltshire's' morale capturing their parcels from home and smoking all their cigarettes. Phil, a relatively new and fervent smoker, reckoned he would have swapped taking the hill at Bois du Homme for a seven-fag ration pack.

The men made up ground over the next two days travelling on tanks to Montcharivel ahead of the launch of their attack, on Mont Pincon. August 5th dawned misty and grey and the Regiment sustained heavy casualties, including their CO Major Thomas, as they fought successfully to capture the bridge at Duval. Not only had Major Thomas fallen, so had the popular man of God whom Phil and all the men admired, Irish padre Reverend Jimmy Douglas.

It somehow didn't seem right that a man of the cloth would be slaughtered in this way. The kindly celtic Padre was a man apart. He had almost floated above battle like an angel. Now his angel's wings had been irreparably torn like the helpless damaged swan Phil had once seen trapped in a lock on the Thames at Lechlade.

This was the saddest of days of Phil's war so far. Even the wild pink roses growing in the Norman hedges or straggling round cottage doorways could not cheer Phil nor take away the sweet stench of dead cattle laying bloated or decomposing in the fields. The Regiment was now down to half the strength it had been when Overlord began. They had paid a heavy price for the ground they had won.

The Wiltshires had been driven down to just two companies. Only sixty-three men were left standing to fight by late afternoon of the 6th August. Phil was not one of them. Shells were flying in both direction as the force of one knocked him to the ground and stunned him. He knew he had to try to get back to the medical station but with so many other men more seriously wounded he would need to get there unaided.

He crawled slowly to the first-aid station dragging his rifle and his wireless set, fearing for his life as the shells continued to rain down and angry splinters of steel whined around his head. As he reached the field hospital through the blasting crack of mortars and black plumes of smoke, Phil could see the full extent of the damage wreaked by the bombardment.

He had a narrow escape. He would not be shipped home to Waldershare Hospital just yet.

He was almost one of those fallen. Suffering from severe shell shock he was being cared for at the 129 Field Hospital where he was to remain for the next five days. As he was laid up in a makeshift bed and tended by overstretched medics Phil looked around at the groaning men around him and it seemed to him that the fire had almost been completely taken out of the Wessex Wyverns by Jerry's defence of Mont Pincon. Hitler's 'stomach boys' had thrown everything at them and knocked them for six.

Phil wondered how much more of this he could take. He knew he had to get back to the front to be with his adopted Regiment but in his heart, he just wanted to be back in Southrop enjoying an English summer.

As he returned to his position it felt like everything had changed for Phil. He had faced the most horrendous attacks in one of the hardest fought battles he could have imagined. And it wasn't over yet. The next day the Wiltshires were pinned down by heavy enemy fire in the village of La Variniere. 'Pop' Pearson, that most eccentric of CO's with a red rose in his steel helmet, was shot dead by a sniper. Now the Wiltshires' fighting strength was down to 5 officers and only 70 men. They had to stay and try and hold the crossroads at la Variniere until they were relieved the next morning by reinforcements from the Berkshire regiment.

They were soon on the move again through valleys dotted with old grey farmhouses and lovely church spires. The chime of the church bells on a Sunday took Phil back to Southrop. On the 20th August Phil made a special effort to take part in the church service in the village of St Honorine led by the new Padre Reverend Hewis. He may be no match for Jimmy Douglas, but Phil felt there was so much to pray for. So many of his mates had fallen. They had lost Pop Pearson who had Phil's respect. Pearson had led from the front, his red rose bringing a flash of colour and old-fashioned chivalry to the campaign.

Five days later, the Wiltshires crossed the Seine at Vernon, though despite Phil's constant radioing ahead only one of the eight expected storm boats survived the enemy machine gun barrage to carry the men across. To make things worse, Major Milne was missing. They had difficulty landing as they had been given the wrong information on the whereabouts of the enemy by their intelligence officers. Over half of the company were ferried across the Seine by one brave Sapper officer and fought to get a footing on the outskirts of Vernonnet.

Under sustained attack from the enemy the Wiltshire lost an entire company – 'A' Company, as they were exposed to relentless machine gun fire. It was a tough battle as the 129th brigade fought to make this most important of river crossings.

The relentless overnight rain had made the riverbanks as muddy as the Somme and the heavier vehicles struggled to make it down the bank. As August ended, the 5th were now dug in on the edge of the woods to the west of La Chapelle St Ouen. Phil was part of the Battalion HQ in the forest.

After such a testing time, respite came two days later as the men were greeted by cheering French crowds and thrown pink Normandy roses to twine into the netting of their muddy helmets, on arrival in the small town of Gasny, for what was to be two weeks of much-needed recuperation and regrouping. Phil's signallers' office was located in the village bakery and he really savoured the smell of freshly-baked bread every morning they were there.

Proffered ripe fruit and kisses from the locals with equal lavishness, the figs played havoc with Phil's stomach, the torrential summer rain did not dampen the spirits of the men as they recharged their batteries among the prettiest of towns, with its Benedictine Priory ruins. A Vernon tomato grower had shared a huge crop with the men and Phil savoured these like they were grown by his own fair hand. He had never tasted a sweeter tomato.

After a couple of days rest and proper sleep, disturbed only by his nightmares of mortar fire and the white lightning of muzzle flashes that made him twitch and left him waking in a sweat, Phil decided to walk back the few miles along the banks of the narrow River Epte to the village of Giverny, where the 4th Wiltshires were camped, to see the famous artist Monet's garden. Joey Iles, Phil's mate the gardener on Captain Richardson's estate, had tried to emulate the waterlily effect back home in Southrop and as he walked in the rain Phil was hoping to see the real thing up close.

When he was first out of Barnardo's and working as a shy sixteen-year-old garden boy for Mr and Mrs Thomas in

Northwood, kindly Mrs Thomas had shown Phil some of Monet's paintings and he was captivated by the ones where the Frenchman had painted the flowers in his garden. The Thomas's were an artistic family. Mr. Thomas worked as a textile designer and their house was full of beautiful things.

Phil had shared his enthusiasm for the garden paintings with Sid Bates the gardener at the actor's retirement home a few doors down the road where he and Phil would sit in the shade of Denville's Rose Garden on quieter, warmer days. Bates had a wealth of knowledge about the ageing thespians living at the House of Rest at Denville Hall – Phil's fascinating West London neighbours. If Bates was to be believed there was much scandal in the lives of the now sleepy actors and actresses counting down their days. Phil hoped the Thomas's lovely home and Denville Hall had survived the Blitz.

Here in Giverny, Phil was disappointed to see that the war and neglect following Monet's death had left the faded Pink House with its green shutters and huge Garden, created after the Great War, largely looking unloved. Monet's widow had offered lodgings to soldiers from the Worcestershire Regiment so Phil was relieved to see fellow English soldiers resting in the grounds. They too were recovering from the punishing assault on Vernon and the tough crossing of the Seine.

As he peered into the former cider farmhouse and grounds Phil dreamt of working there to restore the Garden to its former glory. In the midst of the wreckage – there were even trees growing in what looked like the artists' former studio – Phil was sure that the beauty of nature was fighting back - just as the scarred and pitted trees on the battlefields were growing fresh leaves.

The greenhouse panes may have been shattered by allied bombs but Phil knew that he could bring these grounds back to life with water and tender care. The pond was overgrown, and the Japanese bridge was clearly rotting and unsafe to cross but Phil could imagine how the late summer light could transform the waterlilies that once flourished in the pond. Nothing could put mother nature down for ever, not even Hitler.

Once more Phil was dreaming about Southrop and the beautiful Cedar of Lebanon he was missing at home. He hoped that Colonel and Mrs Watson had found another garden boy to look after the Lodge, though guiltily prayed that whoever had the task wasn't up to the job so that Phil would have a job waiting for him if he got through this blasted war in one piece. The Colonel and Mrs Watson had promised him as much, but he wondered whether even they had faith enough to believe that he would make it back from France. It was the quiet Phil missed more than anything.

He longed for it all. The bubble of the Leach, barely more than a brook, running through the Manor House gardens where sometimes it was so quiet you could hear the splosh of the water voles as they dived into the stream. The cold peace of St Peter's on a frosty Sunday morning before the congregation arrived, where your breath broke the air like incense, or the warming crackle of the bonfires he would light in the back garden of the Lodge as Autumn was moving into winter and he struggled to keep the place tidy.

The slow and gentle pulse of the Cotswold village routines with the comforting cacophony of children's voices at playtime in the school opposite, silenced only by the Headmaster's bell. The village was quiet most days of the year, apart from a brief few weeks in the summertime when everything and everyone in the village seemed to burst into life and colour, and when drunken revellers at the Swan danced without a care on the green, before Harvest heralded a peaceful Autumn and a long frosty winter and peace descended once more.

The only trouble now was that in those quiet moments Phil's head would be filled not with music from his 'Notes of Happiness' tour days, but with the horrific sounds of battle and images of blood-soaked bodies that were so far removed from the peace of his Cotswold village and would never leave him.

Inspired by his short Giverny excursion, Phil told himself that if he made it through this bloody war he would draw and teach himself to paint in those long Winter evenings when he was safely back in his lodgings in the quiet of Southrop. For now, after searching for Monet's family grave in the churchyard of the pretty village church in Giverny he had to return along the riverbank to reach the camp at Gasny before lights out.

The camp was full of excitement as an ENSA troupe had arrived and were planning to put on a big show for the men.

Initially sceptical of the 'Every Night Something Awful' troupe, a feeling not disabused by the mediocre Florence Desmond with her impressions of American screen sirens, Phil found he loved the comedian Mr Pastry with his walrus moustache, black suit and bowler hat, and really enjoyed the headliners 'Flanagan and Allan' as they were the voice of the London he had known as a child. When they linked arms and sang one of Phil's favourites from his childhood, 'Underneath The Arches', Phil, having drunk a little too much of the local Calvados cider brandy, drifted off into a dream that saw him and his brother Fred linking arms, performing their own bandy-legged dance routine underneath the darkened arches of Waterloo station where they had spent so much of their childhood on the streets.

He remembered now the coffins stacked under the arches that prompted one of Henry's ghost stories. They were neatly stored there before being transported on the Necropolis Railway to Brookwood Cemetery in the plush Surrey countryside for what his Mum had said was a 'posh send-off'. He didn't want a posh send off. For now, Phil just wanted to be back in Southrop, and to know that his Mum and his brothers were still alive.

This was a proper rest. The longest Phil had known without work to do since he was a child back at the Scout camp at Field Place. His aching body started to feel a little more human again. Though his nightmares continued, even Chalky's snoring didn't stir him from the deepest of sleeps. He had time for a proper shave. He didn't fancy going on the hour's drive to 'gay Paree' on a '48 like some of the cockney boys. Like the swedebashers, he was happiest in the relative quiet of the Normandy countryside away from the front line, flirting with the milk maids and feasting on fruit and bread with the yellowest of freshly made butter.

As they moved into the second week of their sojourn in mid-September, Phil couldn't help thinking that this extended break was in readiness for a return to hostilities as the Allies advanced into the occupied Netherlands and across the Rhine.

Phil's instincts were right. On the 14th September Phil's company joined the convoy of men transported 190 miles across the site of the historic battlefield of Waterloo, to Longreuee in Belgium. As they travelled, grateful locals pleaded for cigarettes and sweets and bombarded the troops with fruit and flowers until the placed looked like the very Market Garden that Monty had dubbed this most audacious of next campaigns.

Back in Britain, Phil's brother Fred's bomber support squadron was gearing up to provide the aerial cover for the 'Market' element of Monty's plan. The skies of Fred's temporarily adopted East Anglian home were filled with Horsa gliders preparing to fly fearless hardened paratroopers into enemy-occupied Nijmegen and Arnhem.

Here on the Dutch soil, surrounded by the tallest and loveliest of Dutch girls and their younger brothers and sisters hurling flowers and slowing their progress, what was left of the Wessex Wyverns were trying to make their way overland to repulse the expected enemy attacks, but were held up on the heavily congested road. To relieve the boredom and the hunger Phil joined his colleagues in picking mushrooms from the fields. Even raw, their earthiness was a rare treat though he wished he had the wild garlic he had found at Waldershare to flavour them. His need for energy had helped him lose the earlier reticence for picking them that he had when foraging as a teenager with Mrs Thomas in Ruislip Woods.

Delayed for days on the congested road, when the Wiltshires did eventually reach Nijmegen a carrier exploded with many casualties. The following day in Lent, troops were dug in within only 50 yards of the enemy, and the capture of the enemy ration dump provided some additional nutritional relief, though Phil was one of the few who actually appreciated Jerry's tinned black pudding, the honey - set like butter, and caraway seed biscuits.

The Wessex Wyverns were now on the place they called 'the Island' an area enclosed by the Waal and the Lower Rhine. Progress was too slow. Operation Market garden was judged a humiliating failure for Monty with the remaining men of British Airborne evacuated on 27th September. After two weeks of heavy fighting north of Elst, where the Division had met the most ferocious German opposition imaginable, the Wiltshires were relieved by the brash guys of the 101st US airborne Division. At least the tall Dutch houses with cellars provided some protection from the freezing winter weather and the sporadic shelling.

By this stage the number of 'old hands' including Phil, did not exceed twenty in any of the rifle companies. The last month of Phil's 21st year on earth was spent dug in on the Siegfried Line, as heavy losses were sustained facing enemy troops in the boggy, rain-soaked Reichswald Forest. They were once more up against the so-called 'stomach-boys' – the remnants of a German division populated with men with stomach complaints. Phil's mate Chalky joked that after quaffing all their black pudding Phil might have to join their ranks soon. But he was fine, he laughed, so long as kept away from 'les figues'.

Chapter Twelve

Oulton

On D-Day itself, as part of an Allied offensive of nearly 15,000 sorties, 35 Lancasters from 15 and 622 squadrons struck coastal battery targets along Hitler's Atlantic Wall. This was the first daylight bombing raid by 622 squadron, mostly through cloud. The owl had stayed up during the day to surprise his prey. The next day 33 Lancasters, including Fred's Fenwick crew and 15 others from 622 squadron, attacked targets near Lisieux. All returned safely.

In the Lancaster, as Miles Tripp has noted, 'fear was the eighth passenger'. Rear gunners like Fred had a sense of detachment. It was often joked in the mess, 'Never fear, rear gunner, never fear, the Lord is with us' to which the rear gunner replied 'he might be at your fucking end but there's no sign of him down here.' He was subject to what Leo Mckinstry has described as a 'cruel symphony of shell-bursts and blinding lights'.

Rear gunners like Fred had it tough. The tail turret on a Lancaster was only accessible through two small sliding doors. It was very tight squeeze in there and there was no room for Fred to don his parachute, which would be clipped inside the turret. Holding on to the handrails above his head, Fred would swing himself into the turret and onto a small bench seat. Once the doors were closed before take-off, the rear gunner would be separated from the rest of the crew.

Alone with his thoughts, Fred worked his way through his routines as the crew prepared to start their mission. Switching on the gunsight, he would then unlock the turret by pulling up a knob and test the power controls. His four Browning guns and ammunition feeds would now need priming. Using a wire with a loop on the end, Fred pulled the first round of the belt into the breeches and shut the covers. Using another wire tool, he would pull back the bolts and cock the Brownings. Fred had to be sure to slide the metal slider to the right to prevent the guns from firing on the ground, set the guns to safety and check the cranking handle.

It was a fiddly procedure and one Fred had mastered wearing four pairs of gloves he would need to prevent frostbite mid-air. The cold was something you never quite got used to especially if, like Fred, you had grown up in the heat of Western Australia.

Often the Lancaster had to resort to 'corkscrewing' – a sudden dive to one side followed by a twisting spiral in the opposite direction. The entire fuselage shuddering, rivets screaming. Plunging at over 300 miles per hour for 1000 feet and then wrenched into a steep climb. Being 'coned' by searchlights or experiencing St Elmo's fire – static electricity in a storm or the Schrage musik of enemy fire. This was no job for the faint hearted. Fred knew that every flap could well be his last.

Fred had survived his Mildenhall posting. A 'lucky for Fred' thirteen sorties in a lucky thirteen weeks. He had lived to return to base from the pub singing with steaming breath 'They say there's a Lancaster leaving Berlin. Bound for old Blighty's shore. Heavily laden with terrified men. Bound for the land they adore.' He had also avoided the legendary 'chop blonde', the Mildenhall WAAF of whom it was rumoured every man she had shown an interest in had been killed in a bombing raid.

Fred had found a 'family' in the Fenwick crew. In addition to Flight Sergeant Fenwick, their Navigator 'Red' Redshaw, Signaller Jim Pearcey, Bomb Aimer 'hanky' Hankison, Mid Gunner Bob Higgins, and Haynesy the engineer, were now brothers who had put their lives on the line for each other. To them he was Willo, their arse-end Ozzie Charlie. The Boomerang Boy who kept coming back.

Of all the Fenwick crew, Fred got on best with JP. He was a farm boy like Fred. His Dad was a shepherd on a small Hampshire farm in the Itchen Valley and lived in a cottage in the brilliantly named village of Martyr Worthy. When JP spoke about his home and the farm it reminded Fred of Cunderdin back home, with its village hall and tiny church and everybody knowing your business.

Fred celebrated his 20th birthday on his last sortie with them, some cause for a boozy double celebration in the mess on his return. The following month, after a couple of weeks' leave, which gave Fred the chance to properly explore Cambridge and walk along the river at Ely, down the hill from its beautiful old Cathedral and a few customary visits to Tilley's pantry for tea in the small Suffolk town of Mildenhall, on the 27th July Fred was transferred to Bomber Command's 100 Group: 214 Squadron (Federated Malay States) based up towards the North Norfolk coast at RAF Oulton.

Riding on the crew bus through the Elveden estate in Thetford Forest conjured up memories for Fred of the Jarrah trees so prevalent in the shadows of the Darling Range around the Fairbridge farm of his youth. The same green and sun-dappled woods. With important differences. No kookaburras here to mock you with their curious laughter. No bursts of colour from the parrots. And young muntjac deer taking the place of the 'roos. They seemed to be staring at Fred and his crewmates as the truck trundled through the forest, wishing them a safe passage or, more likely Fred thought, hoping they were too distracted by the job in hand to consider the thrill of a roadkill.

The journey through to North Norfolk took no time at all. Fred had barely got forty winks when the truck was screeching to a halt outside what seemed to him to be some kind of small palace. What a place to lay your head? A long gravel drive with manicured lawns on either side leading to what seemed to be a Jacobean house.

To sleep, even alongside nine other men, packed in a Nissen hut around the lake in the grounds of Blickling Hall felt like another world for Fred. Like something out of the Fairbridge School's History lessons that old Mr. Healy took such pride in. This most stately of ancestral homes, with its uneasy relationship with the British Royal family, had itself already played more than its part in the war effort.

Just as the Hall's first owner, Sir Thomas Boleyn, had sold his daughter Anne's soul to Henry Eighth, claimed by the locals to have caused both father and daughter's souls to walk abroad on a midsummer's night, so had its current owner, Philip Kerr, the Marquess of Lothian, prompted by Winston Churchill, as Britain's ambassador to the United States, prostituted the historic English charms of Blickling to sweet talk the Americans into supporting the Allied war effort.

There was no sense of the house as a whore when Fred and his crewmates bathed in the estate's lake to cool off on an idyllic summer's afternoon. Listening to records in the station record club in the beautifully-panelled main room of the Hall. A pint or three in the Buckinghamshire Arms, known to the men as 'The Buck', conveniently located a short stagger from their Nissen huts on the estate. Or cycling to a dance in Aylsham Town Hall after evensong at the estate's St Andrew's church.

Staggering back after one too many Bullards in the Black Swan pub (dubbed the Dirty Duck by the crews). Boring Chalky and Slim silly about the real 'black boys' back home on the farm. Cycling back with mates after another night of losing at darts against the friendly locals, singing the customised 'Bloody Hell' RAF ditty, 'this bloody town's a bloody cuss. No bloody trains, no bloody bus. And nobody cares for bloody us. Bloody Oulton.'.

To tell you the truth there was little bloody about Blickling. It was a kind of dreamland for Fred. One of the Aylsham pub landladies, Ena Spink, could even be relied upon to cook up a brace of locally caught pheasant or Hungarian partridges if the lads were quick-witted enough to catch them. Ena also kept a separate room in the Anchor at the entrance to her cellar with an old phonograph and a pile of Bing Crosby records if you fancied a sing along with the American crews.

But the singing and the dreaming had to stop and the praying start when you were on a flap. However boring the lengthy flights could become, especially when his crew were flying above the serious action to form unbroken Mandrel screens off the enemy coast, Fred could not afford to drift off. His life, and those of his crewmates, literally depended on it. As a fellow Australian crew member put it, '(I had) the feeling upon me that death itself could be nothing more than the breaking of the thin shell that bound us.' (Don Charlwood)

214 squadron was a new formation led by the highly respected Wing Commander D J McGlinn and Squadron Leader Bill Day – they formed part of the critical 100 Bomber Support Group. Based as they were in a series of airfields within fifteen minutes reach of their new Headquarters, Bylaugh Hall in Swanton Morley near Norwich, 100 Group brought together the potentially toxic mix of the bomber boys and the boffins.

214 Squadron, Oulton, 1944 - SR 386. BU-N

This highly-secret operation led by Air Vice Marshall Edward Barker Addison was the clandestine side of bomber command. Their 'trade' was electronic warfare through the targeted deployment of radio countermeasures, radar jamming and night-fighter activities. Their principal purpose was to reduce the effectiveness of the Luftwaffe night-fighters and ground defences, through 'spoof' sorties all over Germany and the deployment of electronic countermeasures (ECM).

The B-17 Flying Fortress that became Fred's new crew's home for the remainder of his campaign, was modified with its deep bomb bay stripped of ammunition and instead filled with ECM equipment. By the time Fred arrived at Oulton 'the airborne grocer' system had already been superseded by the JOSTLE IV jamming device, designed by exuberant young Cambridge dons and undergraduates, to jam enemy communications with its multi-directional radiations jamming wavelengths of German fighter control.

The Fortresses had larger ten-man crews and so Fred was relieved of his arse-end moniker and instead took his position as a wing gunner as part of Flight Officer Bayliss's crew. This new crew was truly a Commonwealth crew with two Canadians, Crerar and Hoffman, with Fred flying the flag for his adopted Australia.

For now, Fred's task, with the rest of the crew was to dump 'window', sheets of metal foil, as fast as they could, at the rate of 10 bundles per minute, to disrupt German airwaves at key moments during August raids to Kiel, Stetin and Bremen.

Six flying fortresses, with two waist gunners ferociously windowing, could produce the same effect as a force of 200 to 300 bombers. On one mission the windowing force would form up behind the Mandreek screen and fly to Heliogoland, 50 miles off the north of the Elbe.

There were missions where Fred's crew took huge amounts of flak. On 16th August on a mission to Kiel with Main Force of 348 heavy bombers, 214 faced considerable attack as they approached and flew over the target.

The following week the Oulton crews were frustrated by bad weather but pleasantly surprised to receive a visit from 'Boom' Trenchard, Marshal of the RAF, whose motto 'You Work Hard; You Play Hard' was legendary and taken on board by so many of the young crewmen. Fred had mixed feelings about Trenchard. His brother Henry had once told him that it was he who was in the charge of the Metropolitan Police when the hunger marchers were charged by police on horseback in St George's Fields near their Lambeth home just before Fred and Phil were sent to Barnardo's. As a child Henry's loyalties were with the marchers as he and his brothers knew what hunger felt like. To Fred the rear gunner, 'Boom' was the legendary founder and defender of the Royal Air Force and he was happy to judge him for that now.

After a few quiet night flying tests, the crew were once more in serious action as the Squadron took part in the Main Force attack on the Baltic port of Stettin. For Fred, these missions were oddly exhilarating. You had to stay alert as the tension built on board as you drew large numbers of enemy fighters into your immediate area.

Often it was the foul weather that was your worst enemy and the squadron seemed to lose a crew on most sorties during October and November. But Aussie Fred, Willo to his crew, was the boomerang boy and for some of them he was becoming something of a lucky talisman – not a role he relished. It was too much responsibility to carry the fate of your brothers in your hands. He was just always relieved to sip his rum-infused coffee at the end of a sortie.

A new piece of kit, in classic Cambridge don style named Piperack, was later installed and tested by the boffins, to replace the unsophisticated jammer code-named Mandrel. Piperack was a rearward facing airborne jammer protecting Bomber Command from German airborne interception. Fred's crew were under strict instruction not to discuss these strange machines with the Special operators. These German-speaking new additions to crews raised the odd eyebrow in the mess. These wireless operators, often German or Austrian-born, could never be wholly trusted by the original crew. Men like Hoffman in Fred's crew had been trained in verbal jamming in their course at Stradishall. Fred took great pride in cleaning his Piperack aerials in between sorties.

The crew were your life, your whole world for the duration of your war. You worked together and, following Boom's advice without really needing it, played hard together too. Sure, in true British fashion, the pilots were set apart. Billeted in the attic of the old hall they at least had the warmth of Blickling's spirits to warm them through the chill winter of December 1944, even if the cold baths felt ten degrees cooler than the North Sea. Fred preferred the banter of the huts even if the smells at times left a lot to be desired, especially when the water was too bloody freezing for regular showers, as it was that very cold winter of 1944.

It was a very English Christmas Fred had there too. Not like the previous Christmas when he had taken advantage of his '48' hour pass out and travelled to the Boomerang Club in London, that very Australian of institutions designed to make you feel less home-sick, but that ended up reminding you of just what you were missing so far away on the other side of the world.

It was ironic that when the BBC World Service broadcast live to Australia Newsreel from the Boomerang Club in Australia House during that Christmas Eve concert and dinner dance of 1943, where the Club cooked 22 turkeys and 11 hams for Fred and over 800 of his colleagues, it was less than a mile from Fred's actual place of birth. Just one short Number 33 tram ride away across the River Thames to Westminster Bridge Road.

Of course, by then, like the bombed-out St Clement Danes Church next door, it was now just rubble, Jerry having destroyed the home of his childhood during the 1940 blitz that had so mobilised Churchill's beloved Cockneys to invoke that Dunkirk spirit. Only the Lincoln Tower was still standing – a fitting symbol of Anglo-American alliance that was undefeated.

The '44 Christmas had the Norfolk-based airmen literally snowed in their huts for a while. At least it brought some respite for the rest of the crew, fearful of the next flap. No doubt there was the odd scrub too – where flaps were cancelled or called off at the last minute. As Charlwood put it you learnt 'never (to) curse a scrub..it might have been the op you were to go missing on'.

For Fred, though, after 30 sorties with 214 squadron and 138.5 hours of flying time, as he looked back on the year, he knew that, for him at least, the war was over. No more comparing chop rates. It was now just a matter of waiting for confirmation of his despatch back home to Australia.

No more of the post-op routines of throwing your flying clothing into wooden lockers, the parachutes into the drying rooms. Sitting on stiff-backed chairs to be interrogated by the intelligence officers in the de-briefing as you sipped rum-infused coffee before the return to the fuggy billet. No more would he hear the 'sonorous song of the engines'. He was no longer going to be one of those 'who waited in the night across the flat fields of bomber country' as Kevin Wilson put it so well.

Thinking as he might that this would be his last taste of British life, he savoured every moment. Even the overcooked Brussel sprouts and the cloying plum pudding on the Christmas Menu.

Leaving the snowy splendour of Blickling Hall after the New Year's Day festivities, Fred had to then wait a month, first in a wet and bitterly cold north of Scotland near the shores of Moray Firth at RAF Blackla, next to the (sadly closed) Royal Blackla distillery on the Cawdor estate (where Fred explored the haunted Cawdor Castle nearby and thought of his green-fingered brother Phil when he stumbled across the wonders of the Tibetan Gardens created by the eccentric Scottish laird). He was then sent down south back at the Reception Centre in Brighton, watching 'worldly-wise' in the requisitioned Grand Hotel on the seafront as the dwindling number of new recruits arriving daily went through the nervous trepidation he had long put behind him.

The war had changed him. Returning to the Old Country in these circumstances had made a man of him. Fred knew that the Boomerang Boy mantle was well-deserved, he had done incredibly well to survive this much action. The fact that there were only 17 other sergeant WAGs arriving with him in Brighton that cold January morning, the bitter frost so hard that the RAF's beloved rugger had to be postponed, the restrooms full of chattering crewmen thwacking dominoes or playing cribbage, a game Fred never really took to, proved to Fred that he was a rare survivor in this particular numbers game. He may be a man, but he was still the 'boomerang boy'. He kept coming back.

Though there was no shortage of invitations for the crewmen to party hard in Brighton, including a YMCA organized dance in the Ballroom of the aptly-named Grand Hotel on the front, Fred felt it was wrong to go overboard with the celebrations.

He knew that though his work was done here, that for many, he hoped including his brother Phil, the war was far from over. He allowed himself some frolics on the skating rink and the odd dance at Princes Hall while he waited to sail back home, on a long six-week voyage, retracing the journey he had first made as a nine year old boy.

Fred's train was to leave Brighton at 2307 and the OC draft informed him that the train would stop at Sheffield at 0620 for twenty minutes only before proceeding to Liverpool, arriving at 0945, where a bus would transport him to the troop ship waiting for him at the Docks.

After a good sleep, helped by the few pints he had downed in a number of the Brighton pubs on the last night of his tour-expired leave, he hopped out at a freezing Sheffield station for a cup of hot tea before quickly returning to his seat. As the train pulled in to Aintree station on the outskirts of Liverpool, Fred thought it was fitting that for his last ever morning in England it was just as cold and cloudy as it had been when he had arrived in Greenock less than two years ago.

The English weather may not have changed in all this time, but the young Australian rear gunner Fred Wilson certainly had. Working alongside English pilots and crew members had made him realise how much of a proud Australian he had become. He had little time for so much of the stuffiness he had witnessed in the RAF. It wasn't just his Aussie humour that set him apart. He knew that at the Boomer you could mix with any bloke regardless of rank because you were all Aussies together and, as their tragically now dead former Prime

Minister John Curtin had said in the year that Fred joined up, they were 'all-in' for the battle for Australia in this war effort.

It didn't matter that he was a child of the slums who had been schooled in an orphanage. His class didn't matter. Somehow for the English 'what your Daddy did' was what defined you. He had given up trying to explain that his late dad was an English Army Captain as it made it hard to explain how he had ended up milking cows in Pinjarra. For his Oz and New Zealand crew mates 'good on ya' was enough of a reassuring response for Fred to know it didn't matter to them.

Fred had travelled a long way to find this out for himself. Now it was time to go home.

Chapter Thirteen

A Fight To The Finish

November 1944 was a tough month for Phil. After spending his 22nd birthday hauled up in the Dutch town of Groesbeck, the Wiltshires advanced into Germany, arriving in Stahe on the 12th. Two days later the Regiment's respected Brigadier Gerald Mole was killed from wounds sustained as a mine dump of 700 mines exploded. He was buried back across the border in the Dutch mining town of Brunnsum.

Having fought for almost every mile of the way across France and Holland into Germany, the bloody battle for the Geilenkirchen sector was to add further to the Wiltshires' casualties. They were entrenched in the sodden, gloomy Hoven Wood, where the mud and water were so deep in the trenches it reminded Phil of the tales the Captain would tell the boys about the Somme. Knowing what he did now about the captain, Phil wasn't sure what to believe of his tall tales but the medals they lost to his other 'real' family at least must have been awarded for a reason.

The Anglo-American battle for the Geilenkirchen salient in November 1944 was infantry warfare at its most fierce. Ken Ford vividly describes how the onset of winter saw the Allied advance from the Normandy beaches forced to a halt on Germany's doorstep. The clock had been put back to the days of the Great War, the Allies had arrived at the Reichswald Forest at the Siegfried Line and were forced to attack the fortifications from the hell of the trenches. Geilenkirchen was the first battle on German soil to be fought by the British since

Minden in 1759. Neither side was victorious, both lost more men than they could afford and paid a heavy price in young lives for a few miles of ground.

Operation Clipper was planned as an assault on the small town of Geilenkirchen, situated astride the River Wurn. It had been incorporated into the Siegfried Line and was heavily fortified. The US 84th Division were allocated a section of high ground that stretched up to a large fairly flat plateau, whilst Phil's 43rd Division were on the left side of the river on flat farmland studded with occasional dense wood. The open countryside, thick with crops of sugar beet and cabbage, offered very few means of concealment for the attacking troops. As Phil and the other line-laying signallers got on with their job they could be seen coming from miles away.

Despite the isolated village of Tripsath being under constant bombardment, the 5th cleared its northern end and fifty-five of the German 'Stomach Boys' were taken prisoner.

Phil was relieved that following the grueling stand-off at Geilenkirchen, the Wiltshires went back off the front line and into reserve in Holland. In the middle of December the Division started to head north for training in the Eindhoven area as they prepared for the Allied breakthrough to the Rhine. However as two German Panzer units attacked the Americans through the Ardennes, the British units about turned and Phil's Regiment were now concentrated north of Liege.

As Christmas approached, the Wiltshires once more loaded into their trucks and passed through Belgian towns and villages that had been devastated by fire from both sides. The houses with Christmas wreaths on their doors with candles aglow felt like defiant acts of the season. They were to be regrouping in the small Belgian town of Tongres in the Maas Valley and as the Germans were driven back Phil and his comrades were able to have a restful Christmas break away from the front line. It was such a relief to be sleeping in a warm barn loft after melting snow in their helmets to wash themselves properly for the first time in days.

On the dark cold night that was Christmas Eve 1944, and the men huddled together in their greatcoats to keep warm, Phil dug out his harmonica from the bottom of his kitbag and started to play Silent Night. He had tears in his eyes as he remembered his first Christmas in Southrop and the frosty breath on the cold parishioners faces as they sang carols in church. Even as a child in Barnardo's, Christmas had felt a special time for the boys but it was always tinged with sadness that their Ma was not with them. He thought about her now, and Henry and Fred, and prayed that they were safe wherever they were.

He had saved opening his parcel from the Watsons for Christmas morning and was thrilled to find neatly wrapped fruitcake, tartan socks, hankies, soap and, a lovely touch from the Colonel, an expensive cigar. Not much of a cigar smoker, he would eke that one out. Never had a Christmas present been so much appreciated even if the letter from Mrs Watson updating him on the village news, made him feel so homesick for Southrop and longing for this war to be over.

Three days after Christmas the Battalion were on the move again and the Headquarters moved nearer to the German border in the grounds of a pretty stone castle in the Dutch village of Wijnandsrade. Thankfully, they had a fairly quiet few days. On the 6th January, a Twelfth Night still resting in reserve, Phil typed a letter from the temporary HQ to be sent to the Fairbridge School in an effort to trace his brother Fred in Australia.

Phil had no idea where Fred might be but hoped that the letter would find him if sent to the Fairbridge Farm School authorities who were looking after his younger brother.

5577383 Pte P.C.Wilson
"HQ" Company Signals
5th Bn Wiltshire Regt
B.L.A

6/I/45

Dear Sir ,
            I was hopeing you might be able to
help me to trace my brother Fred Wilson who
was under your care a year or so ago .
            I have tried many ways to find him
but each time have met with no success . The
last time I heard from him he was quite well
and although I wrote many letters to him I
never received a reply .
            So if you could help me in any way
I would be very grateful indeed.
            HE often used to talk about way
you live out there and I was always sorry
that I could not join because of my health
            Well sir there is not a lot I can
say and hope you can help me

                    Yours Faithfully

KINGSLEY FAIRBRIDGE FARM SCHOOL. PINJARRA
LETTER No.   RECEIVED   OPENED BY
Mr.2.9.1   12 MAR 1945 Cy
REPLY SIGNED BY.............................
DATE POSTED.............................

Phil's letter took two months to reach the Kingsley Farm School in Pinjarra on the 12th March 1945 and C.P. Grant, the Acting Principal replied two days later.

Dear Private Wilson

Your letter reached me two days ago, and I have pleasure in informing you that your brother Fred is at present stationed in England. He is a member of the R.A.A.F. We do not know just whereabouts in England he is stationed, but if you apply to RAAF records branch, Kodak House, Kingsway, London, they will probably put you in touch with him, particularly if you explain the circumstances of your case. Fred has done very well in the Air Force, and he is a Flight Sergeant. I think he is a wireless airgunner, his number is Aus 427967. I shall write to Fred by this mail, and tell him of your inquiry.

Yours sincerely

CP Grant

A/Principal

Mr. Grant did write to Fred who by now was already on his way back to Australia having completed many more than his requisite sorties as part of the RAAF serving in Bomber Command. Mr. Grant wrote again to Phil on the 10th April 1945 to inform him that Fred had recently arrived in Australia. He promised to tell Fred of Phil's enquiry 'when he comes on leave' in the hope that Fred 'will probably write to you then'.

Sadly, no contact was made, and Phil was left for the rest of the war, or at least when he could snatch private moments, homesick and searching for the younger brother he had lost over thirteen years ago.

For now, though, after that brief Christmas respite in Belgium and the Netherlands, by mid-January Phil's focus was back on the front line in the Geilenkirchen sector as the 43rd moved to pierce the Siegfried line. The ground was frozen hard, ideal for the use of tanks and other tracked vehicles, except for the danger of undisclosed minefields under the snow.

On 24th January the 5th Wiltshires advanced from Breberen on Uetterath, a village over five miles away. Over 100 armoured vehicles moved in deployed formation. One tank struck a mine, and there was a little shell fire as the Battalion passed north of the 4th in Straeten. The wireless net would not work at a critical moment when the Commanding officer was set to order to assault near Uetterath so the orders had to be given verbally.

Eighty prisoners were taken during the successful assault and Phil was relieved to see an enemy horse drawn ration wagon that had driven into Straeten by mistake with hot soup, sardines and coffee that the Tommys were quick to tuck into.

With their latest operation complete the Division were on the move back to a rest area at Westmeerbeek in Belgium as they prepared for their next encounter with the enemy which was to take place in early February in the Cleve area of Germany. Their Divisional task was to clear the Germans from the ground between the Maas and the Rhine as far south as Wesel.

As darkness fell on the 8th February the Wiltshires were riding on their supporting tanks and other tracked vehicles alongside the Somersets on the only usable road from Nijmegen to Cleve. Cleve contained a German Divisional Headquarters, numerous other troops and tanks, all of whom were taken by surprise when the entire British brigade descended on the Town. Phil was engaged in a key battle as the 5th Wiltshire Headquarters came to the aid of the Brigade HQ in beating off a group of Germans and two tanks at dawn on the 11th February.

That afternoon, the 15th Scottish Division took over the defence of Cleve and the Wiltshires had a rest after fighting for thirty six hours.

The respite was short-lived for Phil and his colleagues. The two Wiltshire Battalions were quickly drawn into battle on the vital ridge at Bedburg and were under violent shell fire and enemy counterattack from Panzer Divisions for two days. Tracer bullets fired overhead as Phil scurried along the lines. Both Battalions had heavy casualties, 300 in all, and their Medical Officers and stretcher bearers saved many lives.

In early March, as the allied forces fought fierce German opposition to the west of the Rhine, the 43rd Division were given the task of clearing the area held by two panzer Divisions who had personal orders from Hitler to fight to the last man. When the 5th Wiltshires attacked Luttingen from the village of Wardt, about 1500 yards to the north west of it, the company's wireless set was put out of action, but a foothold was gained in the German trenches. Fifty German dead were counted in the trenches when the battle was over.

As the Allies broke the German bridgehead and the Wiltshires returned to Gennep over the Dutch border, it felt to Phil like his war would soon be over but he tried not to get his hopes up, as he knew from bitter experience that the enemy would fight to the bloody end. As they were resting in the wrecked Dutch houses in what Phil thought might once have been a pretty town of Gennep, the lads in HQ celebrated Major Pope's birthday on St Patrick's Day with a bottle of beer.

By the 27th March the whole 43rd Division were across the Rhine and the 5th carried out mopping up operations in Holland before advancing back across the German border. Mid-April was spent clearing a network of roads, villages and woods in the Lindern area of Germany as they prepared to attack Bremen. The remnants of the German parachute army had withdrawn inside the Town to augment its considerable garrison.

This was to be the Division's last major action of the war, with the two Wiltshire Battalions leading. The 5th Battalion on the right cleared the racecourse before encountering heavy fire from houses around a cross-roads. After dealing with many pockets of resistance, both Battalions converged on the large and fashionable Burgher park, which was strongly held by the enemy. By the next evening Bremen had fallen.

Phil's Battalion were in the Lower Saxony town of Tarmstedt when news of the German surrender came through that evening. The 4th and 5th Battalions were still alongside each other after nearly six years of war, fighting together proudly under Phil's adopted West Country 'yellow devils' Wessex Division. Phil was proud to wear the golden winged Wyvern badge and was looking forward to taking it back to his adopted Cotswolds' garden now that his war was finally over.

It was hard to feel triumphant. They had witnessed too much bloodshed and agony to feel anything other than relief that it was all over. So much had changed for Phil since he had enlisted just over three years ago. He may be physically fitter and have muscles in places he did not know he could from carrying his pack and his signals equipment every day for two years, but mentally he was scarred.

He had seen things he could never unsee. Experienced the hell of mortar attacks and sobbin' sisters at the front line. Dived for cover from aerial bombardments and the deadly spray of lethal shrapnel. He had been forced to lay among dead and dying comrades, powerless to help them, praying frantically for his own life to be spared.

His adopted Wiltshire Regiment had suffered so much loss and he had witnessed much of it, whilst having to coolly report all of it back to HQ and carry through orders that he knew would push those tired and brave infantrymen back into the fray.

If he had ever thought that signals company would be a breeze in this war that thought was far behind him now. He had played his part. It was now, he hoped, time to try to return to England and some semblance of normality for the rest of his life. To cherish the small things. The beauty of the countryside.

The clean air of the rolling hills. The babble of the brook. Swapping the normal tiredness after a hard day's graft in the Southrop gardens for the exhaustion that had him sleeping standing up at times in Normandy.

Maybe in time he would save enough to rent a home with a lovely garden of his own. For now, he just wanted to go home, to resume his search for his own family, hoping among hope that they had all survived this bloody War.

Chapter Fourteen

Home Again

It was time for Fred to go 'home'. To head to Pinjarra and pay his personal respects to Canon Watson's widow at Fairbridge, his legal guardian, the man who came closest to a father figure to him, and reassure Mrs Watson that Fred's name would not be carved on the Old Fairbridgians memorial of the fallen. To play one more game of billiards in the OFA clubhouse. To venture into Perth where it had all started with his RAAF medical and, who knows, initially at least after he had completed his RAAF commission, start again in Western Australia with a life of farming.

Even before he left Britain, as he had sipped his warming Christmas brandy, Fred knew in his heart that farming, however much he loved the early morning communion with the cows at milking time, might not be enough for the man he had become. Though outwardly he still possessed the cheeky youthful looks that charmed the WAAFs, his brief time in Bomber Command had aged him inside.

It had made a man of him.

The long days on the deck of the Clyde-built Canadian Pacific steamship 'Empress of Scotland' as it made its way from Liverpool as part of a Convoy of fifteen troop ships and destroyers before charting its own course towards the Panama Canal, gave Fred plenty of time to reflect. Sitting decked in his life preserver, carrying a torch and a tin of emergency rations, Fred caught one last glimpse of the old country through a smokey haze as their convoy headed into open water. Of course, this last journey was not without its risks. The sister ship of the Empress, the Duchess of York, had been sunk in Spain after a German air attack the previous Summer had taken it out of action.

Fred knew that he had tested his luck as the Boomerang Boy in a crate. He was not one of the 3500 Australians who had lost their lives in Bomber Command. Once this long voyage back to Australia was over it was time to get his feet safely back on terra firma. He had done with freezing in the rear of a Lancaster or a Flying Fortress. Of being de-frosted from the saddle before being lifted out of the cockpit. He was glad to be heading back to the warm and to the rest of his life.

His fate surely rested in following his father, the Captain, into the regular Army. The Australian Army of course. For Australia, he knew now, was his home. Still part of the Empire. Still, for him at least, loyal to King and country. Dominion, not colony. Strangely, he felt little blood ties to the old country. Despite a number of visits to London on his '48 weekend leave, and to the Child Emigration Society offices in Notting Hill, he had not managed to find nor make contact with his mother or his older brothers, Phil or Henry.

As he viewed the bombed-out ruins of the site on Westminster Bridge Road where number 77 had once stood, he could not be sure whether this most bloody of wars had claimed them. He imagined his brothers were, like him, away at war and prayed that his mother was not mourning their loss as she had their father and sisters.

It was time for Fred to accept his future life was without them and to get on with living, back in the warmth of sunlit Australia. If, as Canon Watson had often recited in the Church of the Holy Innocents back in Fairbridge, death has no dominion, then Fred was going to grab life after the War. Find a different way to serve his country.

For now, though, he was going to enjoy the journey home. As a child, his voyage to Australia had taken him through the Straits of Gibraltar, the Bay of Biscay, Mediterranean Sea, the Red Sea and the wonders of the Suez Canal and Indian Ocean. Now returning to Australia as a man he was to travel the Pacific Ocean, see the Panama Canal again and have the boyish enthusiasm at the workings of the locks that would take the Empress of Scotland slowly past the lush greenery of Panama as they docked at Christobel and traversed the Gaton Locks.

As the troopship slowly sailed passed the pretty town of Gamboa, Fred caught sight of herons as he marvelled at the palm trees beyond and reflected on the contrast between this peaceful tropical idyll and the grey and damp of much of the England and Scotland he was leaving behind. How much easier was it for those majestic herons to take flight and soar gracefully in this rich blue sky. No bumpy take-offs and uncertain clearances for them.

The long last leg of the journey home made Fred only too aware of how far Australia was from his European birthplace. He had to reconcile himself with never returning to England again. A few days from Sydney it hit home to him that he might never see his Ma or his brothers again. His hopes of being reunited with them while he was serving in England had been dashed.

He had searched in vain when granted leave and the officers of the Child Emigration Society had also assured him they would forward on any correspondence and inform his relatives of his forwarding address if a family member were to contact them. The best he could do now was to visit Mr. Grant at Fairbridge on his return to look up what had become of some of his old Newton Cottage pals and leave the School with a forwarding address.

From now on he was on his own and he would make of his life what he could.

And so it was that Airman 427967 after 47 successful sorties in the European theatre with Bomber Command, became, after a brief two years respite back on the ground with the RAAF reserve, Army Number 5/487 of the Australian Regular Army.

Fred enlisted in the Australian Army on 8th September 1947 at the age of 23. His friends told him that they thought he had seen enough wartime experience to last a lifetime, but Fred told them he was a patriot and ready to serve whenever his country called.

Posted to the Second Recruit Training Battalion at Barnia Barracks at the World War Two military camp at Ingleburn, a suburb of Sydney, Fred threw himself into the training and within nine months had been promoted to the rank of corporal. Adjusting to camp life was not hard for the former

Fairbridge boy and he quickly realized that answering the call of the bugle was the right decision for him. Transferred to 1 RTB staff the following year, Fred was soon to be transferred to 1RAR – now a regular soldier in the Australian Army.

With Japan entering the Second World War and the fall of Singapore, and closer to home the upheaval in Papua New Guinea, the Australian military effort was turning to the growing threats from the East. Fred had even felt a bit of that when on his return from the Europe Theatre in 1945 some of his neighbours were questioning why Australia made so many sacrifices for England and the protection of Europe when their 'real enemy' was much closer to their shores.

Nothing brought this home harder than the emerging conflict on the Korean peninsula. Fred did not have to wait very long for that call to be made as Australia raced to out-do the old Country in their support for the South Korean people against the China-backed Communists of the North.

While Fred was transferred to RAR First Battalion in May 1950, and undertook specialist weapons training which at one point resulted in him being hospitalized, less than a year later he was ordered to move again, this time to the RAR Third Battalion as changes in the command structure and a clear out of the 'old regime' following the first year of hostilities in Korea, led to Fred's new Battalion being called up to play their part in the Korean campaign. China had launched their massive attack in April 1951 with a 250,000 strong army. Australian forces were to form part of the Commonwealth response to this Communist threat to South Korea.

With their jungle greens and kitbags slung over their shoulders the men of the newly-enhanced 3RAR were transferred to the Leave and Transit Depot at the Sydney suburb of Marrickville where the diggers enjoyed the hospitality of the town's bars and hotels while they waited for their flights out.

Fred kept a little distance from some of the younger lads. He had become something of a loner. He put it down to his childhood journey and his rear gunner life which found him apart from the rest of the crew. He had learned to be happy in his own skin. On the truck ride to Mascot Airport Fred had the same trepidation his comrades were feeling, the same sickness from fear in the pit of his stomach, but his experience had taught him to keep a lid on it.

The flight to Japan took the men through Darwin, a Manila overlay and onto Guam. Their brief stopover in Manila and their 24-hour leave was like the Wild West with palm trees, and some of the younger guys really went for it there. Fred kept away from the trouble, soaking up the tropical climate. As their Qantas Skymaster plane landed in Guam, Fred smiled when he saw a Flying Fortress parked at the USAF terminal. It was great to see the old girl was still in action. He had a lot of time for the American B-17 crews he had encountered at Oulton. They had so much swagger and lived life to the full.

On the last leg of the journey to Japan the men were handed 'King Neptune' certificates as they flew over the Equator for the first time and Fred had to politely decline the offer as he admitted this was not his first crossing of the line. He smiled at how much he had changed since that first voyage to his adopted home of Australia as a frightened and lonely nine-year-old boy. Now at twenty-seven he felt he had seen so much in his short life. Travelled so far, physically, and mentally.

Yet at times that nine-year-old boy's sadness at losing his whole family and being torn from his dear brother Phil came straight back as though it were yesterday. He always felt that pang of sadness when he had to update his will before a major action, because he knew that his passing would not be marked by his loved ones as they had no idea where he was or the ordeals he was about to encounter. He could only hope that they had lived through the Second World War unscathed.

Looking down at the beautiful terraced paddy fields of Shikoku Island as they made their descent to Iwakuni air base, Fred thought how much his brother Phil would love the uniformity and neatness of the Japanese gardens and was astonished at the ancient Buddhist temples they could see in the distance.

As they waited to board a ferry to Kure Docks Fred pointed out the Short Sunderland flying boats in the harbour and remembered what he had been told about the underground factory in the south east of England where they had been built to protect them from German bombers. He wasn't to know that his own older brother, Henry, had worked there during the war, sweating with the effort of driving rivets into the very Stirlings that Fred had flown in training.

Arriving at the Reinforcement Holding Unit Camp in Hiro the men were again granted a few days leave, assaulted on all sides by Japanese girls eager to please at a price. The Japanese Dance Halls were something to behold and Fred was happy to be a voyeur as he cradled his Asahi at the bar. At least the Japs knew how to serve cold beer, not like the good old English with their warm ale that Fred never really took to.

He took his army duties seriously and was ready for their posting to the British Commonwealth Battle school at Haramura to start putting his three years of drill training to the test. The three weeks training in full battledress with a heavy Vickers rifle slung across his shoulders was viewed as necessary to pull the soldiers into shape as a coherent fighting unit, fit to face the onslaught they were expecting from the chows.

The monocled English colonel in charge of Fred's unit ran around flogging the men with a short swagger stick if they were deemed to be slow. Fred was more grateful than ever for the physical fitness bestowed on him by the Barnardo's and Fairbridge drilling and his RAAF training. Fairbridge's PE instructor Mr. Barrett would barely recognize the fit young soldier he had become.

As they flew from Japan to the south of the Korean peninsula, their flight was diverted via Nagasaki and they had a bird's eye view of what was left of the city after the atomic bombings. This current war had left its own devastation in its wake. Circling over Taegu airfield before landing, Fred could see what was left of the airfield with mustangs splattered all over the mountains around them. As the DC3 thudded to a halt on the pierced steel runway Fred could see why the Yanks were anxious to lay concrete to replace the damaged landing strip.

After such a hairy flight Fred was relieved to be on the ground in one piece and reassured a little by the strong US Airforce presence at what they called K-2. They were soon on the road north to Seoul to join the rest of the battalion under the leadership of Frank Hassett.

In a preliminary operation named Mindon, Fred and his comrades in arms experienced the tension of coming under enemy fire to prepare them for the testing battles they were due to face.

Both sides were dug in close to the 38th parallel.

There were 90 men in each of the four RAR companies, 15 below their full strength. The rifle companies like Fred's had undertaken three weeks training in full battle dress to develop the cohesion and stamina for what was dubbed Operation Commando. They were as ready as they ever could be for the fight that was to come.

Ten miles to the north of the 38th, just west of the Imjin River, were two dominant hills, Hill 355 (the Commonwealth forces knew it as Little Gibraltar , the locals Kowang San) and Hill 317 (Maryang San) which were, the men were told, a vital part of the enemy's main winter defence line.

In a two-phase approach, 3RAR were to support on the right as Hill 355 was attacked, and in the second phase 3RAR would take Hill 317.

D Day for phase one was scheduled for 3rd October. It was to be Fred's first significant battle. The day before the action commenced a makeshift stage was constructed in the forming-up place and Australia's legendary 'Queen of Song' Gladys Moncrief stepped up to perform accompanied by a pianist to cheer the troops with her musical comedy routine and distract them from any nervous thoughts. Now in her sixties, when Our Glad sang the waltz song 'Love Will Find a Way', for some of the younger lads it was as if their mothers were singing them a reassuring lullaby. Many had fear in their wet eyes. They knew they faced a fearful oppo.

The assembly area was west of the Imjin. B company led by Captain 'Wings Nicholls of Melbourne moved to Hills 159/199 north west of Hill 355 to provide fire support to the King's Own Scottish Borderers, The Kosbies. They moved off at first light at 0600 hours and under enemy artillery shelling, made contact with an enemy patrol.

The five-day battle of Maryang San, Hill 317, was to be the toughest test of the war for Fred and his Digger comrades. Two American battalions had previously tried to take this highly strategic vantage point held by the Chinese but had been brutally repulsed. The hill was now swarming with two Chinese regiments of some 6000 men. It was decided that the Diggers were going to attempt to run the wooded ridge that ran from the eastern flank to the summit of Hill 317.

Attacking through a blanket of thick mist at dawn on 5th October, B and D companies launched their assault on Hill 317 from the front and on the flanks. At 10am the mist began to lift, exposing the Australian advance. The communists briefly hesitated before firing which allowed 3RAR to capture the first line of defences in a fierce burst of fighting.

The attack continued all day until Fred and his fellow soldiers were exhausted. The men from B and D companies were facing massive resistance and so C company was pushed through them to capture Baldy, a feature immediately to the east of Hill 317, and then take Maryang San itself. While artillery hammered the Chinese positions, C company led by Fred's fellow West Australian, Jack Gerke, advanced three hundred metres across a scrub-covered saddle to Hill 317. The Diggers had to climb up on their hands and knees to surprise the retreating Chinese. The Aussies now commanded a panoramic view of the surrounding hills and valleys in three directions.

The Chinese were not going to surrender such a strategic spot without a massive counterattack. The Diggers were soon to be subject to a ferocious bombardment that grew in intensity until by dawn the next day it was almost continuous. 3RAR, despite some modest reinforcements flown in to support them, was seriously understrength and the force that would face hundreds of Chinese attackers on a wooded knoll dubbed The Hinge numbered fewer than one hundred men.

After intense bombardment and hours of, at times, hand to hand combat 3RAR saw off the Chinese in what was later described as the most significant Australian battle of the entire Korean campaign.

The trenches abandoned by the Chinese were only chest high on the taller Australians, with shallow fighting pits in front in which to fire their weapons. Fred had to dig out the trenches to get some much-needed cover. The men worked quickly to dig foxholes and set up trip fares and booby traps before the gloomy autumn mist descended.

There was a brief lull in hostilities but Fred and the other tired men in his platoon knew that this would not last long. A few nights later white phosphorous flares lit up the sky as the Chinese gunners searched for targets before mortar bombs began to rain down on the hillside where the men were dug in.

For weeks to come the men were subject to Chinese counter-attacks. Bugles and Whistles were deployed alongside a crescendo of Chinese artillery fire as the Diggers' senses were assaulted from all sides. The men were angry when they learnt that as they were withdrawn from the front to recuperate on 5th November, Maryang San was recaptured by the Chinese.

Late November saw the first snow of the winter to come with 16 degrees of frost, but the wide Imjin River had not yet frozen over. When it was flowing, and not full of decomposing bodies, the men could bathe in it. For the last week of November, B Company's main duty was to send patrols across the river into a vast valley that ran directly north to investigate the enemy. You lived on your nerves during the ambush patrols.

Charlie was a respected and fierce enemy and booby traps were potentially everywhere. You had to have your wits about you. There was a lot to give thanks for when on Thanksgiving Day the men were given a roast turkey meal and ice cream. The American rations gave some respite, but it was Christmas Fred was really looking forward to, if they could hold out till then in these grim conditions.

Christmas 1951 saw Fred's Regiment reunited and under canvas at Castle Hill on the route that Genghis Khan had taken to Seoul. Icy winds sweeping across the mountains brought snowstorms in their wake, but this wasn't the kind of White Christmas that Fred might have dreamed of. The bone-searing cold of this Korean winter made Fred's snow-bound Norfolk Christmas of 1944 in a freezing Nissen hut back in England seem like warm respite. Fred's fellow soldiers were feeling the strain of months of battle this particular festive season.

In an effort to boost morale and show political support for the Australian military effort, the battalion was visited by the Australian Minister for the Army and Navy, Josiah Francis. On Christmas Day, Fred was chosen to take part in a photocall as the Minister presented him with a Christmas Parcel which had been purchased by the Australian Returned Soldiers and newspaper firms and packed into wooden boxes in Japan by the Australian Army canteens service. The boxes contained stout, beer, tobacco, canned goods, sweets, writing material and other handy items. Fred smiled for the camera, but Minister Francis looked less than comfortable in the shot that found its way onto all the Australian newspapers in early January. Boomerang Boy was now a media star!

While the battalion stood to attention on the freezing parade ground on Christmas Day, Minister Francis took his place on the reviewing stand with an oversized army parka covering his suit, white shirt and tie. The minister then made, what to many of the lads was an excruciating speech, which started with the words, 'I have come a long way to see you. I left Australia quite some time ago to be here with you today.' At the end he said one of his purposes was to listen to any grievances the men might have and called for comments. The parade ended in disarray when one member of D company piped up, 'Sir, before we left for Australia you promised that we would lack for nothing. Well that's what we bloody well got – nothing.'

Spirits were lifted a little by a Christmas dinner of roast turkey and all the trimmings, washed down with copious quantities of beer and followed by diced banana and custard, all served to a thousand men in large marquee tents. The bottle of whisky set aside for the Minister was taken by one of the men and the culprit was later identified as he was heard mocking the hapless Minister, 'I've come a long way to see you bastards!' The Minister was lucky to come out unscathed as another soldier smashed his plateful of bananas and custard in the face of the Company's Commanding Officer, mistaking him for the politician.

After Fred had enjoyed a week's leave back in Japan, exploring downtown Tokyo and making the most of the Ebisu Leave Hotel, staffed by smiling obliging young Japanese waitresses. In early January more snowstorms heralded the New Year of 1952 and 3RAR trudged back to the Jamestown Line, the Commonwealth Division's section of the Main Line of Resistance that stretched across the Korean peninsula, and started digging again.

The temperature frequently dropped to minus twenty degrees Centigrade. Fred's slight frame had to be bulked out with many layers of clothes, a string vest, fleecy-lined underpants, a shirt and several woolly jumpers under his Army issue hooded jacket. Three pairs of thick woollen socks helped fight off frostbite and the men took extra care wearing gloves to avoid metal burn.

Their daily ration of Asahi beer never needed chilling and the American combat rations, ham and lima beans, baked beans or pork and baked beans were the three main meals, alongside salt biscuits, jam coffee and sugar in a small cardboard container that also held much-needed toilet paper.

Fred lived in an eight-foot square hutchie lined with sandbags and covered with a tarpaulin to make it as waterproof as possible. He heated his food by placing the can on a little three-legged stand and lighting a fuel pellet underneath it. Eggs had to be thawed out before they could be cooked. Fred kept his water bottle close to his chest to prevent the water from turning to ice. He slept with his boots on and kept his gun inside his sleeping bag to keep it in working order. A petrol burner heated the hutchie if he was lucky enough to source fuel. He thought he had known freezing conditions in the arse end of a Lancaster but this took freezing to a whole new level.

On top of the enemy and the cold, the toughest challenge was lice. There were no washing facilities and lice drove many of the men mad. Every man was given a rubber bombe of DDT with a nozzle to squirt the poison powder over his body; heads and armpits were shaved. Rats and mice too sought out foodstuffs in the hutchie. After a battle, rats would feast on dead bodies and come into the bunkers for warmth. Fred knew that they carried a flea that caused the deadly Manchurian fever and he hated them more for it.

After a further four months of this living hell, the weather warmed in April and after a memorable Anzac Day commemoration where the men laid wreaths and held a two minute silence in memory of their fallen mates, they were later treated to a concert party with Albert Sheballe and the English star Joan Mann. Fred had earned three weeks leave in Japan.

He was flown to the Japanese capital, Tokyo, to Ebisu Camp and the Leave Hotel where he was so relieved to disrobe and shower and have his clothes taken away to be burned. Freshened up with a new uniform and some local currency Fred once more enjoyed a cold Asahi beer in the Koohaburra Club and in the Japanese beerhalls and savoured the attention of the pretty petite Japanese girls, resisting the advances from the pimps proffering their girls' services. He was fascinated by the Geisha Girls but in truth he preferred the Aussie girls with a bit of spirit.

It was a troubled time for Tokyo. The San Francisco Treaty signed a few days before had formally ended enemy occupation of Japan but the day before Fred flew in on May 2nd, Communist-organised May day demonstrations with 350,000 students and workers had turned violent and there had been a series of attacks on American and Commonwealth personnel. Fred was warned on the flight from Korea that he may need to confine himself to barracks in Tokyo for his own safety and should certainly avoid venturing out in uniform if he could possibly do so as 'foreign troops out of Japan' was one of the protestors' calling cards.

The Ebisu barracks had been spruced up ahead of a visit from the Chief of the General Staff and Fred had a chance to speak briefly to General Rowell as the troops were presented to him for inspection. One of the Diggers in the mess was full of tales of how his jeep had been stoned by the hordes of protestors and beaten with poles on the day of the demonstrations. He warned Fred off visiting Meiji Park where the protest organisers were gathering.

Later that week, as he tentatively ventured out to see more of the city after things had calmed down, there was still a strong police and army presence in the city's parks and in front of the Imperial Palace. American troops with fixed bayonets and machine guns were still visibly guarding American residential areas. Things quickly appeared to be getting back to normal and Fred saw as much of the city as he could by tram, taking tea at Buddhist temples and enjoying the city's parks. He did not relish a return to battle after a decent break like that.

On his return to the front in late May, the troops' boredom was relieved a little by another Australian Concert Party 'Keep 'Em Smiling' with some of the Aussie radio and stage favourites, the glamorous Lester Sisters, Ray (Waca) Davies, Reg Redgrave and Gus Mercy. The guys needed a laugh after so many months in the trenches.

In July 3RAR moved into the forward line again. A Monsoon downpour saw many of the hutchies collapse burying Diggers alive before they could be frantically dug out. The Imjin was rising six inches an hour at one point, to a depth of more than 12 feet, flooding the paddy fields around them. Torrents of water pouring down the hillsides were running through the trenches like rivers and made them impassable without the use of helping ropes.

The Summer saw continued enemy activity and Fred's Battalion were on regular reconnaissance duty in efforts to entrap the enemy and defuse booby traps laid by the Chinese, while other fighting patrols were despatched at night in the Samichon Valley.

The enemy shells continued to rain down on the diggers and Fred was hospitalised briefly on August 11th 1952 after a heavy bout of shelling. Knocked to the sodden ground and rendered unconscious, he was woken by a kindly turban-wearing Sikh medic in an Indian Field Ambulance offering him curry.

He would have welcomed a longer rest, but he was quickly back on duty in advance of Operation Buffalo to attack Hill 75. The troops crossed the Samichon valley through the burnt-out village of Song-gok to reach the forming-up area at the bottom of the hill they were due to assault.

With artillery and mortars from tanks from their own side and Chinese mortars returning fire, the deadly phosphorous was burning into the scalp and legs of some of Fred's comrades. As stretcher bearers arrived to carry the men off, Fred later learnt that they had lost 'Clever' Trevor Dick and Racer Hill who had both died from their wounds. From the crackle of automatic fire, Fred knew he had to keep his head down. He was nearly at the end of his year's posting.

When his year was up on 6th September 1952 Fred felt relief to be leaving Korea. He was glad that this hellish war was over for him, but just as he had in 1945 when he left Brighton before victory in Europe had been secured, he felt guilty at leaving the front while the battle was still being fought by his comrades.

He had served his time on the front line and had been part of something that felt like it was making a difference. He had been tested physically and emotionally in a way that was only matched by his early sorties with Bomber Command. It may only have been twelve months, but it had changed him as a man.

His time in Korea had hardened him and taught him how much he needed the mateship of the Army. They were his family, and he couldn't see what else he could do in his life, professionally, that would match up to serving his country in this way.

He had made his mark, kept his head down and survived the tough months of the war. It was time for him to pass on his experience to a younger cadre of Australian soldiers. Fred was to be transferred to a new role at Army Headquarters overseeing cadets in the 32 Cadet Battalion back in Australia.

Chapter Fifteen

Honouring His New Queen

Fred might have hoped that a return from Korea would be a chance to take it easy for a while, but he was much mistaken. In January 1953 Fred was to once more be in the media spotlight. This time in the Perth Sunday Times under the headline 'beribboned W A Men for Coronation', it was announced that 'the first 2 Western Australians selected by Western Command to go to London with the Australian Coronation contingent have imposing World War II records'. They are Sgt. F A Wilson (28) of the Royal Australian Infantry and Sgt W H Jones. The two Sergeants are members of the ARA.

Sgt. Wilson wears the ribbons of the 1939-45 Star, France and Germany Star, Defence Medal, War Medal, Australian Service Medal, Korea Star, British General Service Medal and the United Nations Medal.

He was an air gunner with RAF Bomber Command during World War II and made 47 operational flights over France and Germany. He saw the war out, and when the war in Korea began, enlisted with the ARA. Since returning from Korea in Sept. last he has been instructing Army recruits and cadets.'

Fred was honoured to have been selected to supervise a group of the cadets who were to form part of the ANZAC Commonwealth Contingent. It would mean a long journey back to the Old Country, retracing the steps he had taken to travel to Australia nearly twenty years earlier and again ten years from then when he had answered the call to defend King and Country.

The Commonwealth was something Fred treasured deeply. His childhood experiences at Barnardo's and Fairbridge had infused him with images of King and Empire and his military service in the Old Country, and as part of the Commonwealth Division in Korea, had shown him the enduring importance of the Commonwealth.

Now the RAR had a new Commander in Chief in the soon to be Queen Elizabeth Second, Fred was honoured to be chosen to play his part in celebrating this transition, back in the City of his birth. It was a responsibility he felt he had been trained for since childhood. The Captain would have been so proud.

For now there was a lot of planning to be done as the rest of the Australian contingent were recruited to form part of the 240 strong RAAF, Army and Navy grouping from Australia and New Zealand which was to sail around the world on this momentous five month long voyage. Though Fred has made this journey before, this one still felt like a huge honour.

Under the Command of Captain Buchanan, the contingent was to sail on HMAS Sydney leaving Australian shores at the end of March and arriving in England a month before the June Coronation. Fred had a fondness for the hulking aircraft carrier Sydney. It was fighters from the carrier that provided aerial cover for Fred and his digger mates when they were battling it out in Korea and had made it easier on the ground, just as Fred had done for the boys ahead of D-Day.

As Fred and his ten West Australian Army colleagues made the news as they travelled by trans-Australian train from Kalgoorlie for the Eastern States, he tried to calculate just how many miles he had travelled in his short life so far. This boomerang boy just kept coming back.

Fred was granted two weeks leave before boarding HMAS Sydney at Garden Island. On the 23rd March HMAS Sydney berthed at Princes Park, Melbourne where 130 New Zealand squaddies joined them from the cruiser HMNZS Black Prince, which was to sail with them in convoy. Now the Anzac contingent was complete and after a night in Melbourne they sailed for Fred's home town, or the nearest port to it, of Fremantle. 125 miles south of Cape Paisley in Western Australia, a 40-gun salute was fired by both ships in honour of the late Queen Mary as their flags were lowered at half-mast.

Fred was happy to see 817 Squadron carry out formation flying practice in preparation for the forthcoming Spithead review.

As the HMAS Sydney tied up at North Wharf in Fremantle Harbour on the 29th March watched by a large cheering crowd, Fred could not quite fathom how far he had travelled since he first made this journey nearly twenty years earlier, when his welcome from the out of work dockworkers had been so much less warm.

Canon Watson would have been so proud to know that the young Cockney urchin with no shoes and an attitude had grown into Sergeant F A Wilson helping to lead Australia's military tribute to their new Queen. Perhaps even Captain Alfred, Fred's father, would be nodding with approval from Heaven. Certainly, his brother Phil, if he had survived the War, would be so proud of what his younger brother had achieved.

This really was a march down memory lane for Fred as the following day the Contingent marched through Perth from the Railway Station to Anzac House where the Governor Sir Charles Gardiner took the salute. Fred remembered fondly how Perth had rolled out the red carpet for the Fairbridge children and other orphans for the 1937 Coronation of King George. His visit to the Perth Zoo. He remembered too the Christmas he had spent with the Connops and wondered what had happened to his friend Noel and his lovely family. They made him feel so much at home back then, so much so that he was reluctant to return to Fairbridge. He was sorry they had lost touch, but the War had done that so often.

Back on board at Fremantle and they were on their way for the long journey to England and the world's biggest pageant. The ten day stretch on the Indian Ocean to Ceylon and a stopover at Colombo passed fairly uneventfully with a routine of rifle drill, marching and sword drill on deck, apart from a 'bump' caused by the Gunnery Party just after they Crossed the Equator by dropping two hand grenades over the forecastle which exploded under the hull of the ship. Fred thought this must be the most memorable of all his Equator crossings so far.

A two-day stopover in Colombo brought back more childhood memories for Fred as shore leave gave him the chance to visit Colombo Zoo, just as he had as part of the excitable Fairbridge party twenty years earlier. The bright colours at the zoo had faded somewhat, though the bird life was as exotic as Fred remembered and the snakes only marginally less scary now that he had encountered them in the wild in Korea.

At Aden and Port Said, Fred recalled the British soldiers who he had seen there 'protectoring' – he had been in awe of the uniformed young men and was only sorry that the area was still unstable twenty years later. The flies and the smells and sights along the Suez canal, with the show boats trading and the noisy traders calling up to the flight deck of the vast carrier Sydney, brought back memories for Fred of the brown boys diving for coins at port Said. They seemed so free to him, despite their lack of money. He had yearned then for the freedom to swim.

On St George's Day the crew docked at Tobruk where an Anzac Day memorial service was held at the Cemetery. Four Aussie VC winners had their photograph taken behind the grave of Corporal J H Edmondson who was posthumously awarded the VC in 1941.

Two days later, after entering the Mediterranean Sea, the HMAS Sydney was once more in the media spotlight as the Pathe News cameraman recorded the ANZAC Day inspection of the crew by Earl Mountbatten, while they were anchored at the pretty port town of Valletta in Malta. Fred joked that the

Digger Hats would hide their good looks from the viewing public. He enjoyed exploring the small harbour town and started to feel even more excited about returning to London.

Fred wondered whether any of the old boys were still around. What had become of his brothers? Had they survived the Blitz? His previous attempts to contact them through the Child Emigration Society had come to nothing. He would love them to know he was doing so well.

As the Sydney slowly left the Grand Harbour at Malta, Fred started to feel the sense of scale of the Coronation celebrations to come as their two Anzac ships were joined by 18 ships of Mountbatten's British Mediterranean fleet and their large flotilla undertook intensive exercises as they headed towards Gibraltar.

On May Day, the crew left Gibraltar after a day's shore leave where they had been entertained by dancing girls in this strangely English outpost in the Med. After a smooth crossing of the Bay of Biscay and some fruitless whale watching they docked to some fanfare in the southern English port of Portsmouth on 5th May.

The welcoming party was a grand affair. As the men assembled on deck of the Sydney, Admiral Hubbock welcomed them to England. Lieutenant -general Sir Edmund Herring, the leader of the contingent, said they had arrived on a lovely day and it was good augury for the future.' Fred remembered his previous time in wartime England and knew only too well that the English weather could change as quick as a flash.

Herring said that the Queen is terribly interested in all her subjects, and when she is crowned, she binds us all together. We are all bound together in a way we really don't understand but we must try to understand. Fred knew he understood this more than most. He was bound to England through his family, even if he had lost touch with them, he would always have that connection to the old country.

The Australian High Commissioner in London Sir Thomas White welcomed the men on behalf of the Australian Dominion and the Australian people living in England. When he said that 'many of you have been here before' Fred allowed himself a wry smile under his Diggers slouch hat. 'You know how warm-hearted the people are without being demonstrative. They will be just as warm-hearted again.'

You will, he said, be taking part in the greatest pageant of the Twentieth Century. When Sir Thomas described them as 'a blend of old serving men and young men' Fred knew he would have those words played back to him in jest by the younger lads.

As the High Commissioner finished his speech the men cheered as he joked 'you will find a rival contingent in England, the Australian cricket team. They are already commanding great respect and capturing a lot of wickets. They are smaller in number but are making their presence felt.'

They had nearly a month to prepare for their role in the Changing of the Guard at Buckingham Palace and the Coronation Day Parade. As they bundled onto a train at

Portsmouth, Fred recalled the cold and grey of the 1945 January when he was last in England, stationed in Brighton waiting for his ship back to Australia.

As the old, creaky and damp smelling train trundled through Hampshire towards their temporary home in Surrey, the countryside looked greener than he had remembered and as they disembarked at Brookwood station the local area felt a lot leafier than the Lambeth he remembered as a child.

Brookwood itself conjured up memories for this was the final stop of the now defunct Necropolis Railway that took the bodies that were once stacked under the arches at Waterloo near the home of Fred's birth, via the Westminster Bridge Road station to Brookwood Cemetery.

The Cemetery was bigger than anything Fred had seen before. Rows and rows of pristine white military gravestones lovingly maintained by the Commonwealth War Graves Commission reminded the men just how many of their fellow soldiers had been lost in the two world wars this continent had started. He was hopeful that the new Queen would mark a better chapter in the world's history which, once the Korean armistice was finally achieved would mean a long period of peace.

Thanks to his older brother's ghost stories, the young Fred had been haunted by the thought of bodies on the train rattling their way to their very own final destination. He knew that neither his father, the Captain, nor his poorly younger sisters, Louisa and Mabel had been bought a ticket for that particular journey. Theirs was a humble pauper's burial in Lambeth cemetery in an unmarked spot his Mum said was hard to find.

Judging by the size of Brookwood there was no shortage of dead ticket holders from London.

For now, Brookwood was an entry point for the living, an exhausting three weeks camp of drill preparations at Pirbright Military base for the Commonwealth contingents as they prepared themselves for the biggest honour of their professional lives.

As they set up in their tented camp at Stoney Castle the Aussies were disappointed that the facilities here in the old country did not match what they were used to at home. It took some deft Aussie plumbing to fix the boilers to sort out hot water but at least, unlike on board the Sydney, the food rations were decent, with the meat ration increased from 3 ounces to 5 ounces per man per day. For their first day's, Fred's younger colleagues paid their first visit to London by train to Waterloo, and Fred took a trip to Sandown Races and lost a few bob in the process.

While back on duty the men knew they were in the public eye. A BBC crew arrived on the 8th May alongside a number of newspaper photographers as public interest grew in the presence of the Coronation companies.

The Canadian contingent marched into camp on the 8th May upstaging their Aussie counterparts for the first and not the last time as the cameras rolled. The Papua New Guinea delegation, dubbed Fuzzy Wuzzies by the British press, followed suit as the camp took on a more international flavour.

For his first weekend leave Fred headed into London and walked across the River to the Oval to watch the touring Australian team thrash Surrey in the cricket with his mates. They had been warned by the senior officers not to barrack at the Oval as this would not be tolerated in England. Beered-up shouts of 'Have a go' would not be appreciated by their Surrey hosts. It made the Aussie lads laugh as the Oval crowds were heard to shout 'have a go, you mug', as the Australian team trounced Surrey.

Ashes fever had hit London and Lindsey Hassett's Australian team were on good form as they prepared for the First Ashes Test set for June. After Aussie bowler Ron Archer had taken 6 Surrey wickets for just 26 runs, and Surrey were all out for a mere 58 runs after just 26 overs, and Australia had a commanding lead, Fred took the opportunity to walk along the River from Kennington to Westminster Bridge Road to show off to his mates where he had started his life.

The old place had taken a bit of a pounding in the Blitz and had still not quite recovered but the Church spire of the Lincoln Tower next door to what had been the Oakey and Sons Wellington Mills factory was still standing tall. It was hard for Fred to see again the knocks his family home had taken.

Even though life after the war was getting back to normal after eight years the old country still felt like it was in the middle of rebuilding and in need of cheering up. Perhaps the Coronation of the new young Queen would help lift their spirits. It didn't look like the Ashes tour would.

On 11th May Fred's senior officers were nervously awaiting the visit and inspection by Sir Edmund Herring, the leader of the delegation. He gathered the men on the Parade Ground to drill home to them the importance of their mission.

He stressed 'how much energy and effort all concerned with the Coronation, from Her Majesty downwards, were putting into their training and preparations' and he emphasized 'the necessity of the Contingent to do the same'. Sir Edmund remained on camp all that day and observed Fred and his mates as they undertook their palace guard training, and later when the whole Contingent nervously drilled together.

The Australian soldiers in the contingent under their Captain, Ron Taylor, had to be taught how to undertake the staccato stomp drill, the British way. Four Guards instructors were sent to Pirbright from the English, Welsh, Scottish and Irish Guards to drill the men in their way of marching.

The training at Pirbright was hard work and the men knew that only 42 of them would be selected to stand guard outside Buckingham Palace and St James Palace when the time came. At first some of Fred's younger colleagues, who had not travelled outside Australia before, struggled with the accents of the instructors especially the Scottish drill sergeant Hamilton who had the thickest Glaswegian accent.

It was Sergeant Hamilton who provided a brief comic respite during training, at his own expense. He was adamant that Fred and the lads were not hitting their rifle butts hard enough on the ground during drill. Grabbing a rifle from one of the men he rammed it to the ground only to find that the magazine had split in the process. His face reddened as he realized the reason the soldiers facing him had broken out in broad grins.

The instructor in Fred felt for him. The guard drill training was intense as the guarding of the Palace required a particular skill set that the men had to be taught. Sign language was used by the Palace guards to ensure the synchronization required to execute the about-turns, salutes and halts, without verbal orders.

They learnt that working in pairs, one guard always acts as the timekeeper and leader. If they are standing at ease outside their sentry boxes and wish to start patrolling, the leader gives one sharp tap of his rifle butt on the pavement. Two taps for a butt salute. Three taps for present arms if the Queen or a member of the Royal family goes past.

Fred knew that a lot was at stake. The eyes of the world would be on the Australian men as taking over the guard as the first Commonwealth contingent to do this was a great honour and an awesome responsibility. They could not mess this up.

Later that week, Fred again took the bus and train to London, but on this occasion there was no time to walk the short way from Waterloo through the Cut to Westminster Bridge Road as he and his mates were to observe the Changing of the Guard, and then walked down the Mall, through Trafalgar Square and up the Strand to Australia House to a reception in their honour.

As Fred arrived at Wellington Barracks he remembered as a child how he and his brothers had spent what seemed like hours watching the guards outside the Palace with their polished boots, scarlet tunics and bearskins that made their heads look so long as they peered through the Buckingham Palace railings. All he had wanted for his sixth birthday or as a Christmas present that year was a set of model Grenadier Guardsmen to guard his toy fort.

As a man he wasn't feeling the same thrill he felt when a band of the Grenadiers marched into Fairbridge Farm School with the Duke of Gloucester nearly twenty years earlier. He was a soldier himself now and he knew that the glamour and the pageantry came at a price. Bloody hard work.

Fred was certainly no stranger to Australia House but back here in his best blues he had never seen the opulent Marble Hall looking so grand before nor been treated quite as five star as they were now. The stand-up tea party was a High Society occasion with Sir Thomas and his wife Vera hosting a room full of dignitaries as well as the men of the Contingent. Fred had a lot of time for Tommo. He may have been a politician for most of his career, but he was a heroic military man before that and like Fred had been in the Australian army and also flown with distinction too, in the Great War.

Fred had been taught by him briefly in Melbourne during his training, though Fred doubted Tommo would remember him. Lady White was the daughter of one of Australia's Prime Ministers, Alf Deakin, and had spent her much of the Great War helping wounded Australian soldiers at Gallipoli.

Fred was charmed at the reception by the High Commissioner's daughter Miss Judith White who was working the Marble Hall helping her mother with introductions alongside lady Herring, Sir Edwin's wife, and Una the daughter of Field Marshall Slim.

Fred took great pride in telling Miss Judith and some of the younger Army cadets about his childhood briefings at Australia House before leaving for Fremantle, his trips to the Boomerang Club, during the war and how airmen like him could catch up on news from home at the Boomer. Reading the West Australian in between games of billiards. He told them how that whole part of London had been a mini-Australia during the war. With Kodak House around the corner and the Strand Palace Hotel on the nearby Strand the residence of choice for Aussie servicemen, and the Codgers Inn their pub of preference, Fred joked that's what was meant by Aussie Rules! He wasn't sure Miss White got the joke and, in any event, she seemed more interested in the smiling Papuan soldiers entertaining their hosts with their pidgin English on the other side of the Marble Hall.

It was fun seeing London as a tourist even though the ravages of the Blitz were still all too visible in places and the place felt a bit grey. Fred accompanied a group of the cadet lads as they enjoyed a day at the Royal Naval College in Greenwich. Sitting on the hill in Greenwich Park near the Observatory and looking down across the smoky city gave Fred a strange feeling like he had been there before as a child. Perhaps his Mum had taken him and Phil to row in the boats in the tiny lake there?

It was odd for Fred to be back in a place that should feel like home but didn't. He loved the old country but didn't really feel part of it. They had sent him away after all. He had no idea that the church spire he could see in the distance to his left was where his father Alfred, the Captain, had married his only legal wife, Agnes, more than fifty years before.

There was little time for reflection though as Fred and the others chosen for guard duty were back in London on 23rd May for a dress rehearsal of the Coronation March and the changing of the Palace Guard. The rehearsal went well, and the men were stood down at midday with orders to return for Palace Guard training on the Bank holiday Monday 25th ahead of the Changing proper on 26th.

When the 26th May came, the streets around Buckingham Palace and Westminster Abbey were already crowded with tourists. The police struggled to contain the crowds as they mobbed the new Queen Elizabeth and Prince Philip, as their car arrived at Westminster Abbey for the rehearsal of the Coronation service. Though the cheering crowds were in no way hostile, mounted policemen were called in to allow the royal couple to proceed to the church.

Fred felt so proud as he and the other Australian soldiers stopped the traffic in the summer sunshine, as they marched out of Wellington Barracks, down Birdcage Walk overlooking St James Park, led by the Coldstream Guards army band, playing Waltzing Matilda in their honour, and on through the archway in front of Buckingham Palace.

As they presented arms in salute to the Horse Guards clattering down Constitution Hill to the Mall, running down from the Palace, the Horse Guards trumpeter blew a long call returning the salute. This was what Fred had trained for. To be part of this timeless pageantry that only the English can do.

It was hard to comprehend that he was here representing Australia. This boy that was shooed away from the front of the Palace gates by a friendly policeman as a bedraggled south London street urchin, was now standing guard for the new Queen in front of the Australian Prime Minister. He had travelled so far, and he had come 'home' again, but in place of the dirt and holes in his clothes, Boomerang Boy had medals on his chest. A chest that was swollen with pride.

Fred, in his smart uniform with his Australian shoulder flash, held guard in the Buckingham Palace sentry post in front of the Australian Prime Minister Robert Menzies and the High Commissioner who were stood alongside Sir Edmund Herring and Lord Brice of Melbourne in the Buckingham Palace forecourt. Taking over from the Grenadier guards at the required 1030 time, the Australian Military Force soldiers mounted guard at both Buckingham Palace and nearby St James Palace for a 24-hour period.

Fred was delighted afterwards that Sir Edmund remarked that 'All guard members carried out their duties with distinction to the great credit of the AMF.' After a cocktail reception at the Palace Guard Room, where Fred regaled the

Sgt F A Wilson, standing guard outside Buckingham Palace

group with tales of his childhood love of the Grenadiers and their visit to Fairbridge, he and his colleagues were delighted to return to Pirbright to catch up on sleep.

There was no time to dwell on their successes though as the following day the Camp received a visit from their Colonel-In-Chief, the young Duke of Edinburgh, just a few years older than Fred, who arrived at Pirbright by helicopter, the first time one had ever landed on the Buckingham Palace lawn and enjoyed inspecting the Contingent. After a group photograph the following day, Fred and the rest of the group were on the move into London to their temporary home for the five days before the Coronation Day Parade, which was at Earl's Court Camp, along with 9000 other men. There were some grumblings as the men had to queue for hours to get into their new camp which again lacked hot water, but a trip to a Magic Circle Show and the general air of anticipation of the big day carried them through to the 2nd June.

The 1st of June was a 'drying out day' as the men were instructed to lay off the beer and prepare themselves for the arduous 17-mile march around London that was to follow. Fred didn't sleep too well on his palliasse that night and was up early to shower and put on his khaki uniform and slouch hat. The Contingent marched out, wearing groundsheets, and carrying their packed lunches, to the starting point at Birdcage Walk.

Gathering in Westminster on an overcast and chilly morning that threatened rain, the newspaper vendors added to the excitement of the day proclaiming that Edmund Hillary and Sherpa Tenzing had given the Queen their very own coronation gift by conquering Everest and the Kiwis in particular were overjoyed. As the rain-dampened Procession of some 20,000 troops made its way from Westminster Abbey along Whitehall, up and down the Mall, through Piccadilly, East Carriage drive and Oxford Street, before heading along Regent Street, Haymarket and Victoria Embankment back to Westminster, Fred's contingent were once more upstaged by the Canadians behind them, as the Mounties on horseback in their bright red uniforms, stole the show.

For the first three miles of the march the noise from the cheering crowds along the whole route made it very hard for Fred and the men to keep in time as they marched as they could barely hear their accompanying band. Nothing in their drill training at Pirbright could have prepared them for the deafening roar of the crowd. It was an incredible day and Fred secretly hoped that his English family were watching, on the streets of London if not at home or in a pub, watching on a new-fangled television set.

The loudest cheer for the Australian contingent could be heard as they passed the so-called 'Kangaroo Corner', stand 40, the Australian stand on the Mall filled with 1500 proud Australians who had made the trip to London just to witness this momentous day.

Completely exhausted after the march the men were still so pumped with adrenaline that they headed back into town from the Earl's Court camp to celebrate some more with the cheering crowds. Fred still had not got the taste for the English beer but was happy to join in the celebrations. He knew not to overdo it though as the following day he was to receive his Coronation Medal from the Queen at Buckingham Palace.

It was such a thrill to return to Buckingham Palace just 24 hours after the Coronation where the whole contingent were once more on parade. The men were called for and then marched through to the lawns in the Palace grounds to stand in lines to be presented to the Queen and the Duke of Edinburgh.

Once Fred had received his Medal, silver, shiny and very heavy, decorated on one face by the beautiful young Queen herself, Sir Edmund Herring called for hats off and three cheers for Her Majesty to which the men responded enthusiastically, before the Royal party returned to the Palace.

The men then marched again, this time to Kensington Gardens which was to be a brief camp respite from Earl's Court. The following day on 4th June, the men were marching again, this time from Earl's Court to Horse Guards Parade to see the Trooping of the Colour, before returning to Pirbright ahead of a week's extended leave.

Fred could never have imagined that he would have the chance to get this close to the Queen. He felt so proud and yet sad that none of his family were with him to witness such a momentous occasion. Canon Watson would have been so proud of him. That this lad from Barnardo's, this Fairbridge farm school boy could have travelled so far, seen so much of the world, survived 47 sorties with Bomber Command, cheated death in Korea and was now on a round the world trip once more to honour the new Queen.

On Saturday 6th June, Fred was to glimpse Her Majesty again, this time from afar, as he set off to sunny Epsom Downs for her favourite horse race of the calendar, The Epsom Derby. The papers were full of the news that Sir Gordon Richards, Britain's champion flat jockey, for longer than Fred had been alive, had just been knighted by the Queen and was to be racing against the Queen's horse, Aureole in the big race.

Fred was bemused to read that Sir Gordon had been trying to win the Derby since 1924, the year Fred was born, and thought that was enough to put a few bob on him riding a horse called Pinza at 5-1 joint favourite. Betting against the beautiful young Queen felt a little wrong to Fred but he had a flutter anyway. It was a 27-strong field so anything could happen, Fred thought, and he was sure the young Queen Elizabeth would forgive him. She loved her horses, didn't she?

Fred jostled in the crowd to get a decent view of the race and was delighted when Pinza thrilled the cheering crowds as it cruised past the weirdly named Shikampur, with three furlongs remaining to take a clear lead and win the race. 'Sorry Ma'am' Fred shouted to himself as he queued to collect his winnings, 'nothing personal'.

Fred toyed with the idea of using his winnings to travel to Nottingham the following week to watch the First Ashes Test at Trent Bridge but decided against it as he wanted to savour more of his 'home' city before the contingent were due to head back to their ship in Portsmouth at the end of the week to prepare for the Spithead review.

On the morning of Sunday June 14th there was no church parade for Fred as he was once more on an early morning train at Brookwood heading back to Portsmouth. The city was filling up with visitors excited about Monday's Spithead Review, so it wasn't until 2.20 in the afternoon that the Australians embarked on HMAS Sydney in Portsmouth Harbour for their rehearsals.

The following morning was an incredible spectacle and a huge show of naval strength as 280 warships, fleet auxiliaries, merchant vessels, tall ships and yachts representing every navy in the world was dressed and lined up to take the Queen's salute as she sailed past in HMS Surprise. Fred thought he had seen lots of ships when he was waiting in New York harbour back in '43, about to head across the Atlantic to

England in a 15-strong convoy to start his time in Bomber Command, but this flotilla was truly on another scale.

The entire crew of the HMAS Sydney lined the quarterdeck and Fred once more joined in the hearty three cheers to Her Majesty above the deafening cheers of sailors lining the decks of all the ships in the Harbour.

It had been a momentous time in England. As the Sydney sailed out of Portsmouth on its Westward journey home it felt to Fred like this was the last time he might see the old country. As much as he would like to bring his future wife and children to England the distance and cost would probably make that hard, so Fred resigned himself to saying a final farewell.

He had a heavy heart that he hadn't found any of his English family, but was hopeful that despite the ravages of war, they were still out there somewhere. Hopefully the ability to come back from anything ran in the family?

After a week back at sea, Fred quietly celebrated his twenty ninth birthday and as he lay in his hammock in the crowded under-deck, he pondered his future in the Army. With Eisenhower looking like he was going to get his son home and bring the Korean war to an end soon, Fred was hopeful that there would be a period of relative quiet for him back at HQ as he worked his way up the career ladder as an instructor. He decided he would definitely sign up for another six years in the RAR when his current term ended in September. He owed the Army that and in any event he could see no other career he wanted more now.

Having crossed the Atlantic in foul weather with a lot of fog to contend with, the first stop in North America was the naval town of Halifax, Nova Scotia, and more marching, this time through the streets of this dull grey Canadian naval city. It was a thankfully sunny day when the men embarked on a six-mile route march around the city, taking only ninety minutes to complete the route, a walk in the park compared to their trek around London on Coronation Day.

The troops were then entertained by the Ents Committee of the Naval Dept HMCS Scotia who held a reception in their honour. Fred was relieved that the beer was properly cold and a lot better than the warm ales he had put up with back 'home' in England. After three nights in Canada, the Sydney sailed down the coast to Baltimore arriving two days before American Independence Day.

Fred wanted to seize the day and being so close to Washington, DC, he decided to hitch a lift with a couple of his mates to the capital. It was thrilling to sit in the back of open top Cadillac and to see the US capital close up. Walking along the clean, majestic Mall and along the Potomac to Arlington cemetery, seemed a world away from the grey of bombed out London. The rotunda of the National Gallery of Art seemed like a huge church building to Fred.

He paid his respects at the Tomb of the Unknown Soldier and leapt on a tram back in DC to Dwight's White House and on to the Capitol building. The city was bedecked with stars and stripes as it was gearing up for the July 4th celebrations and Fred would have loved to stay to see them but he and his colleagues were due to march back in the small town of Catonsville, Maryland, a quiet suburb of Baltimore.

Greeted by Sir Percy Spender, the Australian Ambassador to the United States, the men enjoyed the smalltown feel of Catonsville's July 4th celebrations which felt so much different to the grand formality of the London Coronation Parade.

As the men picnicked in the grounds of the beautiful Episcopal Church of St Timothy's – where they were told Lincoln's alleged assassin, John Wilkes Booth had been baptized – Fred thought he preferred the less formal United States as it reminded him of Oz, even though he loved some of the English traditions of Empire he had been schooled in.

The States felt more modern and better ready to face an uncertain future. Perhaps it was the sunny July weather making him feel more positive in stark contrast to the greyness of Blighty. As he drowsed in the post parade sunshine, after a couple of beers, Fred didn't want to worry too much about the future or over-analyse. Life was for living.

Back on board the Sydney the contingent left the USA the following day for the Caribbean and arrived in Kingston, Jamaica four days later on 9th July. On shore the men were taken aback by the palm trees and beautiful flowers lining the streets of Kingston Town.

When Fred found a bar some of the locals were still talking about Winston Churchill's visit earlier that same year, and Fred was happy to share tales of his part in the war effort. The Jamaican bar owner was a great patriot and already looking forward to the Queen's visit planned for that November, as her and the Duke of Edinburgh's Coronation Tour started. Fred was more than happy to share his Coronation Day stories too, as the Appleton white rum flowed.

With a heavy head and a heavier heart in leaving Kingston Town, Fred returned to the Sydney as the contingent prepared to sail to Colon and the Panama Canal. The vast aircraft carrier had only a foot clearance either side in the narrow canal and onto Gatun Lake across the Isthmus of Panama.

En-route to Hawaii, the men were called on deck in uniform and Fred had to help arrange a formation of the men into the number 10,000 to celebrate the 10,000[th] deck landing on the vast HMAS Sydney.

Later in July the ship docked at Pearl Harbour, and the damage done to the Pacific Fleet was still front of mind to the local naval officers.

The party received the most enthusiastic of American welcomes. United States bands in white tropical uniforms and Hawaiian singers and dancers in their trademark garish patterned shirts and hibiscus-decked hair, greeted the men from the wharf after the carrier had berthed.

A naval rating stepped up to the microphone and made a speech expressing the hope that those on board would spend a happy time ashore during their visit. The singers and dancers were loudly cheered from the deck and as the HMAS Sydney band played on the flight deck. The penny dropped with Fred that this was the first time since they left Melbourne that the men could properly relax, Australian-style, on the beach.

Fred and his mates hitched a lift along the coast to Honolulu and tried their hands at surfing at Waikiki Beach. Walking in shirt sleeves along the front, on lawns shaded by huge palm trees, or feeling the hot white sand scorching their toes, this really did feel like a proper summer holiday experience for the men as they prepared to say goodbye to America and embark on the long stretch back across the Pacific Ocean to New Zealand, and then home.

The guys in the Schofield barracks told them that the Hollywood film producers, Columbia Pictures, had only just finished filming a blockbuster movie on the island, with a working title of 'From here To Eternity', about the bombing of Pearl Harbour which had seen the film stars Burt Lancaster and Deborah Kerr in town, filming a beach scene at Kuhio beach and at the barracks.

Fred found it hard to believe that this was the same country as the bustling New York or pristine Washington, DC he had seen on the East Coast. The Australians felt much more at home here in the warmth, and the slower pace of the Pacific Ocean resort.

It was time for the Anzacs to head home and the longest most boring stretch of the journey. Crossing the Equator one more time Fred recalled his first crossing and the initiation ceremony the Captain had organized on board the Ballarat when he was informed he was just a 'pollywog' who had to show respect to King Neptune and was congratulated by the

Captain and the crew. Now Fred was most definitely a 'Shellback', a son of Neptune, as, incredibly for such a young man, he had crossed the Equator on countless occasions. Sadly, Neptune, or at least the Ballarat version of him conjured up by the Ship's captain, was a more vivid memory for Fred than his own blood father, Captain Willson.

As the vast hulk of the Sydney approached Auckland, the men were once more called on to perform for the aerial cameras, this time they seemed to take an age to make a formation that spelt the word ANZAC and created a Kiwi and a Kangaroo to celebrate the end of the amazing journey for their New Zealand colleagues.

They docked in Auckland in a rain shower, on the 10th August. Fred had fond memories of his brief exploration of Auckland from before his journey to war ten years earlier. It somehow felt a little gentler than the Australia he had left. More like the English countryside he had witnessed in the East of England, as a rear gunner. But with a much warmer climate.

Chapter Sixteen

Settling Down

On the 14th August the HMAS Sydney finally arrived home and Fred caught sight of the Sydney Heads before they docked in the Captain Cook graving dock at Garden Island. 2000 relatives and friends were there to greet the ship's return from its 31,000 mile voyage and some of the families managed to break through the cordons to greet their loved ones. The following morning, thousands of residents lined the streets of the city, at times ten deep, for the formal homecoming march.

Led by mounted police and the RAAF band the Contingent were joined by four platoons from the HMAS Sydney as they swung down Martin Place towards the Cenotaph and Fred and the other sergeants yelled 'Eyes Right'. The only sound that could be heard was their own stomping feet as they marched past the wreaths laid at the Cenotaph earlier to mark the capitulation of Japan eight years ago.

As the march reached the Town Hall, Governor General Sir John Northcott took the troops' salute and as they were showered with confetti raining down from office workers cheering from open windows above them it was great to be home to such a warm welcome.

Fred smiled to see his 'old friend' the Defence Minister Josh Francis, the man he had entertained in Korea and who had chosen him for the Contingent, clambering on board to attend a welcome party on the Sydney, and was sorely tempted to remind him about his Korean Christmas speech fiasco, but thought better of it.

Some of the sweethearts and wives were aggrieved when after a short time at the end of the parade the men were swiftly herded onto coaches back to their barracks. Fred did feel a pang of regret that he did not have family members to greet him on his return.

The army was his family now, and next month he would sign up for another six years with the expectation that life would certainly be less eventful than it had been for the last six years. From the frontline in Korea to an around the world voyage, and the honour of a Coronation Medal, he had packed a lot in and was ready for a slightly quieter, more predictable, army life as he grew older.

Fred got his wish. After two weeks leave, where he headed back to Western Australia to catch up on old friends in Perth and drop in to the Old Fairbridgians Association clubhouse at Pinjarra for a game of billiards, he signed up again for six years commission and commenced his duties as an Instructor for 30 Cadet Battalion.

When the film opened in Perth, just after Christmas 1953, Fred took great pride in explaining to anyone who would listen, that he had been to the barracks and the beach featured in 'From Here To Eternity', adding that he had actually visited the real Pearl Harbour featured in the film.

Promoted three times in the next two years, by October 1956 Fred was transferred to a posting at the Army Command and

Staff College in Fort Queenscliff, Victoria. The Fort had a rich military history. The black stones of its famous lighthouse had been individually shipped from Scotland over a hundred years before.

Despite its history the red brick facilities were a little more contemporary and Fred quickly settled in here. Fred found Queenscliff to be a charming little town and when he wasn't working he would find himself on one of the four full sized tables in the Billiards room on Hobson Street.

Too old to join the 'odgies and widgies' in the popular milk bars in town, during the long summer evenings Fred would fill his time walking the boardwalk of the Fishermen's pier or gazing out at the couta boats crossing the rip in Port Phillip Bay, before retiring to the bar of the Queenscliff Hotel on the front, that Fred felt had probably seen better days but poured a decent cold beer.

He threw himself back into his work and took every opportunity to further his training and education, but it was events outside of work that provided the most excitement. After years of resigning himself to living the bachelor life, Fred was to find love.

The moment he cast eyes on young bank teller Vera Thwaites, in her Queenscliff branch office of the Bank of Victoria he knew she was the girl for him. At 19, she may have been many years younger than his thirty-three-year-old self, but he was sure he could charm her parents to have no fear that he loved their daughter and that this would never change.

The Thwaites were a long standing Queenscliff family of fishermen. Vera's grandfather, Tom, was a local legend, having designed and built his own couta boats, one of which was named after Vera's grandmother, Eunice, and been a mainstay of the town's lifeboat service for years. He had been commended for bravery for saving two men from drowning in the rip and he had successfully fought for Queenscliff's ageing lifeboat to be replaced.

Even the Thwaites' family's springer spaniel, Silver, was famous in this town. The brave dog had swum all the way to their Station Cottage home, in Wharf Street, after falling overboard as their fishing boat came through the Heads.

Coming from that stock, the strong-willed Vera was no pushover, but she was drawn to this charming soldier with his broad smile and cheeky sense of humour. They began dating and very soon Vera knew that Fred was the one for her. She had no idea what being a military wife might be like, but she just knew that she wanted to be with Fred and raise a family together.

Their courtship lasted four years. They both worked incredibly hard and saved up as much as they could. At weekends Vera looked forward to the dances at the RSL Hall and the Saturday night movie showings at the back of the Grand Hotel. As they held hands outside the new American style deli with its donut machine in the window, Fred would regale Vera with stories of his time in New York, and they would dream of walking out together in Central Park.

Vera longed to see London, where the Thwaites family had originated, though Fred was cagey about his English childhood in Barnardo's, as he did not want to queer his pitch with her father. In the winter months, when the hotels and guest houses were quieter, the couple loved to walk the boardwalk to the fishermen's pier or build small fires on the Front Beach to warm them as they stared at the stars.

The couple's love for each other was sorely tested when Fred was transferred to the Pacific Islands Regiment following an Army restructure. Papua New Guinea had spelt trouble for the Australians for some time.

This was the country where, as Hank Nelson has noted, 'Australians fought the battles of World War 2 closest to Australia, the theatre where most Australians went to war and where over 8,000 Australians lie in military cemeteries.' Resisting Japanese advances at the Kokoda Track in late 1942 was a significant Australian victory. Port Moresby and Papua New Guinea mattered to Australians, even if for most of them it remained an exotic tropical mystery.

The locals were hankering for independence, but it was important for Australia to retain control of the Islands, given their strategic positioning as a buffer to Indonesia, which had its own designs on the islands.

While more and more native troops were being recruited into the Army, discipline was a challenge for the 75 Australian officers serving in Papua New Guinea. The PIR needed experienced officers to take charge of the battalion and in particular the native troops who had been very ill-disciplined.

A riot following a wage protest in January of 1961 had resulted in 50 men from Taurama Barracks in Port Moresby being fined by the Commanding Officer, Lt Colonel Norrie, and sent on patrol to 'cool off'. As part of the restructure following a review, the experienced instructor Fred was to be sent to Taurama to help take control of this highly charged workplace. It was a challenging and exciting opportunity for a soldier. But it could not have come at a worse time for Fred, personally, as he had just found the love of his life.

He was torn. The Australian army was his life and to be an RSM was a great honour. He was to oversee the battalion in conjunction with the commanding officer of the day. He was to head the group of NCOs, a mix of Australian and newly promoted indigenous soldiers. As well as instructing newly appointed officers in sword drill and parade duties, he would be conducting the various parades and ceremonials expected as a showcase infantry regiment. His time in London, changing guard at Buckingham Palace, had been well spent.

His love for Vera was beyond question, but unless they married she could not travel with him, and in any case it would be a huge wrench to ask her to give up her promising career in the Bank and leave her family and her Queenscliff life for the uncertainties of Papua New Guinea, and the biggest town in the South Pacific. For now, she would stay where she was. For day after painful day apart the couple had to make do with exchanging letters, and Fred became a copious writer in what spare time the Army gave him.

There was nothing for it but to accept the posting and trust that their love would survive the distance, at least until Vera could join him at Taurama. Arriving just before the March birthday celebrations of the 1st Battalion, with a trooping of the colour and regimental parade in searing heat on the cinder parade ground, overlooked by the green mountainous jungle that surrounded the barracks, Fred hadn't quite prepared himself for the tropical savannah climate of Port Moresby.

Thankfully, for once in the rainy season, the rains held for the parade and Fred was impressed by the pipe and drum band's performance, though he wondered if the old Barnardo's musical troupe master at Dickies would be equally impressed.

From the moment he first walked off the plane and into that wall of hot and humid air at Jacksons Airport, Fred could see this posting in New Guinea was going to be a tough one. It would need his complete attention. He was also acutely aware that he could not afford to lose Vera and he wrote to her as often as he could.

After a month in Port Moresby Fred could wait no longer and wrote a love letter to Vera like no other he had written before.

In it he said:

'I was going to wait till I I saw you before I said anything, my darling, as saying it personally is so much nicer. But I can wait no longer for it is the most important thing there ever was. We love each other deeply, and being apart has made me realize that the only thing that I have ever really needed, my wonderful beautiful darling, is to be with you forever and love and be loved by you forever. It would make me the happiest man alive, if we could become as one wonderful family, with you as my wife.

My darling, would you consider to marry such as me? I have not got much money, and don't ever think I will be rich, but I love you with all my heart and soul, and will try with all my being, to make you a loving and happy partner through the rest of all my life.

Yours everlastingly, Fred

Fred included with the letter one of his home-made crosswords which he and Vera loved to exchange. This one was at the same time the easiest and the hardest to complete. Question One. Three letters. Please reply with YES.

Vera Thwaites was in no doubt. She wanted to become Mrs Wilson. The answer was yes and soon plans were being made for her resignation from the Accounts Department of the Bank of Victoria, Queenscliff branch, and a move to a newly built married quarters at Taurama Barracks. After seven years' service with the Bank, Vera received a strong letter of recommendation from the Bank Manager Mr. Johnston, who was reluctant to lose her and afraid for her fortunes as a lone white woman in Papua New Guinea.

The plans were exciting. A three-bedroom marriage quarters, seven feet six inches off the ground, with a large lounge and diner, kitchen and bathroom, with a laundry under the house, and overlooking the expanse of the Taurama parade ground, was completed for them ahead of their Summer wedding at the Barracks chapel in December 1961.

The couple were even to have a house boy, Gesse, a kindhearted young Papuan whom Fred took a fatherly concern for, always concerned to ask after the welfare of his young wife and 'pikininis' as Gesse dubbed his children.

Fred could not have been happier. His search for love and the family he had never really had, was finally over. He was hoping for 'pikininis' of his own. However much he had always cared about the men in his charge, from his brothers in arms in the Lancaster or Flying Fortress surviving bombing raids, to his comrades under attack in Korea, or the homesick young army cadets he had

responsibility for on the Coronation Contingent 'cruise' to London and back in 1953, this camaraderie, even under the most extreme conditions, had never filled the void left when Fred lost his family as a young boy. Now, with the love of his life, he had felt a warmth and intimacy that he had never experienced before. More than that, he now had the chance to raise a family of his own.

That wish was granted a few months after their marriage when Vera told Fred she was pregnant and their baby son, Anthony, was born in January 1963. The couple took great pride in showing off their baby son to the Governor General Lord De L'Isle, and his daughter, the Hon Catherine Sidney, on their visit to the Taurama Barracks to receive the trooping of the colour.

Fred knew he would need Vera's support, as this was a tough professional assignment, after years at the Staff College, and the quiet contented life he'd had as an instructor in Queenscliff. For four years from 1962 to 1966 the regiment patrolled the border with Indonesia during the Indonesian-Malaysia confrontation.

As Australia's northern neighbours, Indonesia's President Sukarno's policy of 'konfrontasi' with Malaysia troubled them. A number of incursions took place, and these patrols were often conducted in rugged terrain, draining PIR resources. Amid growing concerns about Indonesian intervention along the border, the PIR began training for guerilla operations.

As the Federation of Malaysia came into being and the Indonesian confrontation ramped up a notch, the Menzies Government authorized a second battalion for the PIR, the building of new barracks at Taurama and the consolidation of the Training Depot at Goldie River, in 1963. PNG Command was formed in 1965. In March of that year, a month after Vera had given birth to their darling daughter Susanne, Fred was focused on the visit from Major-general J W Harrison who inspected Taurama on their Battalion birthday celebrations. In April 1966 the Army appointed Brigadier Ian Murray Hunter as head of PNG Command.

A third of the rifle companies time was spent on patrol. Fred's Korean patrol experience was invaluable, though this jungle heat was not something he had ever experienced before. He had felt the extremes of cold near the Imjin River and frozen to a bicycle saddle in the rear cockpit of a Lancaster bomber, but had never sweated like he was now.

The patrols were tough going, not least because for Fred they took him away from Vera and the children. The no-stop patrolling programme was vital for the Australian Army to gain and maintain the goodwill of the territory's people, to report on the habitation and gather topographical information. Moving through the mountains of jungle covered terrain in the Southern Highlands and Western Districts, Fred oversaw platoons from A Company as they set up administrative patrol posts at Nomad River.

The jungle dangers were real here. The crocodiles in freshwater swamps, the wild pigs and notably, the cassowaries with their murderous toenails that could sever an arm with ease, all posed risks to Fred and the men. The Papuan climate itself was a real challenge and dengue fever and malaria were constant threats, as were the conditions caused by the torrential rains in the wet season.

Keeping to well-trodden trails sometimes helped, and the historic Bulldog and Kokoda Trails were often used in training, as their steep climbs and river crossings posed strong challenges for the men. With the possibility that the rifle companies might be deployed as part of Australia's contribution to the US war in Vietnam, this kind of training on patrol was invaluable.

The Kokoda trail held particular importance to the Australian soldiers as this route to the northern goldfields in the Owen Stanley mountain ranges, was the place where Australia had fought back successfully against the Japanese during the Second World War, albeit at great cost in terms of Digger lives. With the help of the legendary 'fuzzy wuzzy angels', indigenous bearers who carried the fallen to safety, this was the closest conflict to home that had seen Australian soldiers and airmen give their lives for their country.

Treading in their footsteps was humbling for Fred. Looking at the young men in his charge now, he knew that the lads who had given everything then would have been as young and full of life as these diggers. He felt a great responsibility to train them well but also hoped that they might be spared the kind of privations he witnessed in Korea if they were to be called to Vietnam.

He didn't speak to Vera about the possibility of their call up to fight the VietCong. She was troubled enough by his absences on patrol in PNG and fearful of the reputations of some of the indigenous tribes' people Fred was to encounter on the trails. The Kukukuku people had the reputation as the fiercest head hunters in PNG.

The Chambri tribe, who the locals called the Crocodile Men, lived in the East Sepik province where Fred often patrolled, and their ritual cuts to their backs gave them a frightening appearance as threatening as the crocodiles themselves. That was bad enough without the threats from snakes as the men slept in their hastily assembled hammocks under mosquito nets.

Vera tried not to think too much about the risks to Fred's life as she played with the children on the camp or explored the cove at the far end of Ela beach at Port Moresby. As she gazed out to the hills of Touaguba across Fairfax Harbour, she had to hope that he would keep himself and his men safe. She knew what she had signed up to as an army wife and was sure that the Fred she knew would not knowingly put himself in danger.

Fred knew everything had changed now he had his longed-for family. He didn't just have to think about his own safety. He had to be there for Vera and the children. It made him a little more cautious, while at the same time oddly giving him a greater sense of security to be himself. It was as if he knew who he was now. He was rooted in a family of his own. The pit in his stomach left when the Captain died, and when his Mother gave him and Phil away to Barnardo's as small boys, was now filled with the love of and for his own family.

He still missed his brothers, but as his memory of them faded he no longer felt their absence hanging over him as it had for so long when he was a single man, alone in his own thoughts. Vera, Anthony and Susanne were his focus now. His world. He lived for them.

When national service was introduced in 1966 the Australian Army was overseeing the training of teachers to prepare the Papuan Army for independence. The 'Nashos' – national service conscript teachers or Chalkies, were to be based at barracks around the islands and Fred was to be in charge of the group of education sergeants based at Taurama.

The Sergeants' mess at Taurama was a harmonious place under Fred's command. He was well respected by the national service conscripts and his quiet, modest manner was well received. He liked to greet the newly arrived men in person with a handshake and walk them to their mess accommodation that was to be their home for the 15 months they were to serve in PNG.

Fred was respected by the men as an enthusiast, a hard worker and, above all a family man, who understood how the Nashos might be missing home and family and tried to create a happy environment in the mess at weekends and on special occasions. One of the Chalkies, Terry Edwinsmith, recalls how he would walk with the RSM from his office back to the Sergeants' Mess at morning tea or lunchtime.

He took the welfare of the men under his charge very seriously. Whilst the new investment in the Taurama Barracks as part of the Australian Government's renewed commitment to a stronger military presence in the territory had created a better environment for the men, Fred wanted to go further.

A family man himself now he planned to create a recreational facility added as an annex to the newly completed Sergeants' Mess. Outside the terms of the Government contract, Fred would devote his weekends and time off with a few of his engineering mates in the construction of the annex.

It was a typical hot and dry Port Moresby day when, taking a break from working on the new roof of the annex building that was his pride and joy, the shock of a freezing cold drink triggered something in Fred's heart. The heart that had carried him through the stress of nightly Bomber Command missions in the freezing cold and a year of bombardment in the trenches of the Korean War had given up on him prematurely. Nothing in his Barnardo's or Fairbridge schooling or years of RAAF and Army drill had prepared Fred for this moment.

As Vera watched proudly from their married quarters overlooking the mess, she was powerless to help as her beloved husband suddenly fell to the ground clutching his chest. His mates had clambered down from the metal roof they were assembling but were struggling to revive him.

She screamed and, leaving the children with their faithful houseboy Gesse, dashed to be with him. By the time she got to him, the efforts of his mates to revive Fred had been in vain and all life had drained from his red face. He had no last words of comfort for his true sweetheart Vera.

Vera held him in her arms, shaking with shock. She could not believe that after less than seven years of married bliss and with Susanne and Anthony so small and vulnerable, she had been robbed of her beloved Fred, the only man she had truly loved. The children had lost a wonderful father and the Australian Army had lost a faithful servant.

The next few days were a blur for Vera who was, understandably, in a state of complete shock. Her Fred gone. The Regiment took control of the funeral arrangements and practically everyone turned out on the parade ground to show their respects at Taurama, marching behind RSM Wilson's coffin draped, in the Australian flag before he was finally laid to rest in the cemetery on the Barracks.

At the age of just 43 he had achieved so much in his too short life. The Barnardo's boy from the streets of London had risen to the rank of Regimental Sergeant Major in the Australian Army. He had served his country and the Commonwealth with distinction. Chosen to represent his country at Queen Elizabeth's Coronation. Changed guard at Buckingham Palace.

From freezing in the rear cockpit of a Lancaster Bomber with Bomber Command, helping to wipe out German armament factories and railway lines ahead of D-Day, to the wet trenches and dangerous night patrols of Korea, Fred had thrown his whole life into serving his country and the cause of freedom and died doing what he loved most.

Vera could not have been prouder as she heard the Commanding Officer sum up her late husband's career. She was just distraught that he had been taken from them at such a young age and with no warning. The army doctors told her they believed Fred may have had an undetected heart condition which had been exacerbated by the extreme cold of his drink on such a hot day. No medical explanation would bring her Fred back to her and the children. Vera now faced a painful return to Queenscliff, leaving the Papua New Guinea she had grown to love and raising the children alone, without their loyal houseboy Gesse, but at least with the support of her concerned family. Poor Gesse was inconsolable. He loved RSM Wilson who had only ever shown him respect and concern for his family and the little Wilson pikininis were delightful to look after.

Chapter Seventeen

Going Home

The Wiltshire lads huddled around a wireless to listen to the King. 'Today we give thanks to God for a great deliverance.' At this hour when the dreadful shadow of war has passed far from our hearts and homes in these islands, we may at last make one pause for thanksgiving and then we must turn our thoughts to the tasks all over the world which peace in Europe brings with it.'

Prime Minister Winston Churchill may have also said 'we may allow ourselves a brief period of rejoicing' but Victory In Europe Day in Tarmstedt in Lower Saxony in the North East of Germany passed with little fanfare for Phil and his colleagues. It was made clear to them that their work was not done here.

Any immediate thoughts of returning home should be put on the back burner. There were many Prisoners of War to be taken, Nazi literature to be publically burnt in villages and, critically, thousands of Russian and Polish refugees to be evacuated to Displaced Persons Camps. There was some respite on 24th May in the Brelingen Area as 40 Polish girls were transferred from Hanover to take part in an HQ Company Dance in Brelingen Village Hall.

There was a reminder of the ferocity of war a few days later on the 27th May when the SS murderer, Friedel Heinz, was caught by Americans in the Wittingen area where the Battalion were posted and was brought in to camp. He tried to escape and was finally shot after running 300 yards. 11 bullet holes were counted in his body.

The following day Heinz's father shot himself in a churchyard at Waddekath as a small task force from the Battalion was about to arrive to arrest him after he had shot the local burgomeister. The new burgomeister brought back a weapon and dum dum bullets used in the assault. The Division continued to search for members of the SS and SA and a number of arrests were made.

In June, Phil picked up some more Polish words as his division were guarding the Polish camp at Lessien. More than 1000 Poles were counted locally not in camps. The Division were also tasked with establishing roadblocks to prevent German civilians from infiltrating from the Russian zone to the British zone.

That same month, exactly a year after the Wiltshires had first set foot on French soil, on Sunday 24th June the men were transported to Celle in a convoy of trucks and to the beautiful and ancient church to form part of the 2000-odd congregation of men to witness the investiture of Field Marshal Montgomery, below the chancel steps.

Major General Thomas read the lesson and as the men were about to sing the Hymn 'For All the Saints' the silver bugles of the Somerset Light Infantry struck up the last post outside the church. As they got to the fourth verse, Phil's favourite, he could barely sing the words as he took in their powerful resonance for the men gathered in that church.

'O may thy soldiers, faithful true and bold.

Fight as the saints who ably fought of old.

And win with them, the victor's crown of gold.

Alleluia, Alleluia.'

Not for them, the victor's crown of gold. He didn't see himself as a victor. A survivor, yes. But the thought of victory felt hollow when it was won at such a cost in terms of blood spilt and nerves shattered, and after so many bloody battles.

As Monty addressed the congregation and reminded them of their remarkable achievements in battle, Phil's eyes were drawn to the Remembrance Shield that was hung over the west door of the church, and round the richly-painted walls of the lower gallery, smaller shields which Phil would realise later were each commemorating battles the Wessex Wyverns had fought in their advance from Normandy, through France, Belgium, Holland and into Germany. Each shield was encircled by a freshly made wreath of green foliage and on each side of the chancel in the church hung the sign of the Division, the Golden Dragon of Wessex, the Wyvern, the emblem of Harold at the Battle of Hastings and the Kings of Wessex.

All Phil could think of as Monty spoke was of the many men they had lost since they disembarked into the choppy waters of Seine Bay in a stiff gale this very day last year.

After the service, as they marched proudly past the Field Marshal, where he took their salute from the dais erected in front of the stunning white and red Celles Castle, with its beautiful French park and grounds, Phil's overwhelming sense was of relief. He had survived to return home to live a normal quiet life.

As he attended the gymkhana that followed the service at the local German Sports Platz alongside the river, and played a game of skittles at the makeshift skittle alley one of the lads from the Somersets had erected, all he could think about was getting home to a proper game in the Swan.

With the war over Phil was keen to get home. He thought about how the changing seasons would be affecting the Watsons' garden. He knew how much they loved to sit out in the long summer evenings as the shadows lengthened under the Cedar of Lebanon. Mrs Watson's homemade elderflower cordial was a real treat after a long day mowing the lawns and keeping weeds at bay on the grass tennis courts. Phil was under no illusions.

Although Colonel Watson had agreed to be his legal guardian when he left Barnardo's and his kindly daughter Ina was named as next of kin in the event of the enemy getting the better of him, Phil knew he would never be their proper family. But that didn't stop him loving the Watsons and wanting to be back looking after their beautiful, peaceful garden in sleepy Southrop.

As the summer approached, and to relieve the boredom, the regiment were offered the chance to travel to Hannover to watch an Army football eleven play some of the stars of Liverpool Football club. However much fun this was for the lads, Phil, oddly, looked forward more to the route marches they were to undertake in the verdant Hartz Mountains in August. This was the Kingston school textbook Germany of castles and Hansel and Gretel houses that Phil was glad had not been destroyed by the Allied bombing or Hitler's neglect.

Since his time in the Woodford Garden City Cubs and the Barnardo's Kingston Hill Scouts troupes, Phil had always loved the outdoors, and camping in these dense forests without the threat of enemy fire was something he relished. He still took care to find pinecones to sweep the grass after they had pitched camp and to place under the tent to provide a natural spring mattress at night. He had forgotten little from his youthful reading of Baden-Powell's 'Scouting For Boys' whilst in Barnardo's.

Christmas 1945 in Unterluss was largely uneventful, though Phil did enjoy having his morning tea served by the officers, and seeing the smiles on the faces of the German children who came to the Christmas Party laid on by the Battalion.

The Christmas Eve Carol service in the Canteen was a very poor substitute for the beautifully simple Midnight Mass at St Peter's in Southrop, but Phil relished his company winning the best decorated dining hall competition on Christmas Day, before tucking into his first ever taste of goose, and the couple of days holiday the men were granted to play darts and skittles and enjoy the free beer in the Mess.

The Fancy Dress football match, officers v Sergeants on Boxing Day raised a few chuckles but generally the men were very much in the mood for going home to England. They knew they had important work to do to oversee the resettlement of refugees, but they felt like they had been largely forgotten now that the conflict was over and the war won.

After a few months of seeing his battalion colleagues gradually dwindling in number as they joined the ranks of other regiments, by April the 5th Battalion was completely disbanded.

On April Fool's Day, 1946 Phil and 60 other men learnt that they were to be posted to the Green Howards before eventually returning to England. This was no joke. It was a further eight months before he got his wish and made it back to Southrop, after dispersal at York.

His last train journey was disrupted by a French train strike and Phil smiled at the thought that life was getting back to normal in France. He wondered if Mr. Attlee's Government would fare any better than dear old Winnie.

His release papers included the testimonial, 'a very conscientious man who is always willing. A rather quiet type of temperament, and habits, who is most loyal and respectful. A good reliable and trustworthy man. '

Phil thought that his mentor and guardian Lt Col Watson would be so pleased to read that he had made this impression on his superior officers. Not that Phil wanted to speak much about the war. It was all too painful to recall and in truth his nightmares were still haunting him.

He was so glad to be home in Southrop, where he was pleased to find he still had his job tending the gardens for Col Watson and his family. The peace and quiet of the village was just what he needed, although sometimes perhaps he had too much time to dwell in his own battle-scarred memories.

Physically, little seemed to have changed in the village apart from the conversion of RAF Southrop into a camp for displaced Polish families. Phil joked with his mate, Coxy, that he was never going to be able to escape the Poles and he hoped these ones would be a little less trouble than the refugees they had to deal with in Germany.

He understood their desire to get home. He had felt it himself as soon as hostilities had ceased. No one would choose to continue to live in the conditions the camps were in when the Allied forces liberated them.

At times on those crisp Autumn evenings when he was tending a bonfire burning off garden rubbish at the Lodge he would recall the fierce heat of the flames the Wiltshires had deployed to destroy the camp huts at Bergen Belsen and buried the bodies of the dying refugees they had been unable to save. Those flashbacks would overwhelm him and compound the tears from the eye-watering smoke as it blew back into his unshaven face. The horror of war had not ended on VE Day.

As the autumn of 1946 approached, the garden needed a lot of tidying up, but Phil was happy as that would mean he might have some more work here for a good few months at least. He had collected his war payments from Lechlade Post Office, and he knew they wouldn't last forever. He wasn't really cut out for farm work and in any event all the local farms had all the help they needed as the sons of the families returned from the front.

He knew he would have to look further afield to Oxford or Swindon, and some of the lads in the 5th said that Swindon was particularly good for work with the Woodbine factory at Wills, Turntable makers Garrards and the GWR Rail works always looking for men. He didn't really think of himself as a factory man. If he could, he would like to carry on working outdoors, but beggars could not be choosers.

For now, Colonel and Mrs Watson were happy to keep Phil on. They had employed a housemaid from Barnardo's while Phil was away at the front and the young Amy was pleased to have a kindred spirit to talk to of an evening. He was a little shy with her at first, but she was fun to be around and didn't press him to talk about the war when she could see it made him uncomfortable.

On their days off the pair would pack a small picnic and cycle to the River Thames at Lechlade or Kelmscott. He was starting to feel himself again. Amy was engaged to be married and her fiancé was uneasy about her friendship with the young former signaller, so the picnics stopped some time before Phil left Southrop to find another job.

The Watsons had been good to him, but it was time, now he was in his late twenties, to strike out on his own. The NAAFI Bakery in Upper Stratton on the outskirts of Swindon was looking for workers and though he would have preferred a gardening job, they were hard to find and at least he would be making something worthwhile and using some of the skills he had acquired at Barnardo's.

He had saved up some money during the war, enough to find lodgings in a terraced house in the town, in Kitchener Street, and cycled the couple of miles each way every day to the bakery in Headlands Grove. He enjoyed learning the art of cake making and decoration and he really felt he had a flair for it. His shyness was tested, working with so many women in the kitchens, but they took him under their wing and made 'the Cockney' the butt of their gentle ribbing.

It was at one of the NAAFI dances that he met the young Joyce Carter, a quiet and pretty twenty-year-old girl from a large local Stratton family. She was charmed by his shy smile and the two soon fell in love. Her father, Albert, was a little wary of the Londoner from an orphanage, he had already lost one of his girls to a Cockney, but at least this one had served at the front alongside the Wiltshires and seemed to care for his Joyce. Phil got on with Joyce's older brother, Eric, who was a similar age and drove an ambulance in the GWR works.

Their courtship lasted two years and they enjoyed a number of cycling and camping holidays together. On one occasion returning home on their cycles having been to see the stones at Avebury, they were belting down a hill to the village of Wroughton, when having reached the bottom Joyce told Phil that her favourite beret, that he had bought her had fallen off at the top of the hill. Phil walked all the way back to the top of the hill to retrieve it for her, all the while with a smile on his face.

These were heady days. Swindon was booming after the war with new council housing being built for the workers who were needed in the busy factories and works. Though the Railway Works was starting to decline in scale, other businesses like Wills and Co and Garrards were expanding and taking on more men and women. It was a good time for Phil and Joyce to start a family and after their St David's Day wedding at the redbrick St Philip's Church in Stratton, and a short honeymoon in London, staying with Joyce's sister Hilda and her family in Putney, and visiting all the tourist haunts, Joyce was soon pregnant and their firstborn son, Barry John Wilson, was born on Christmas Eve, 1952.

The couple were living in Stratton with Eric and his wife Bet in their small council house and as Joyce's brother and his wife had three little ones of their own it was clear that Phil and Joyce would soon need to find a place of their own.

Thankfully, before Barry's second birthday they were allocated a prefabricated bungalow at No. 6 East Close, Stratton St Margaret. The bungalows had been built during the war to house workers from the Short Brothers' aircraft factories at the nearby villages of South Marston and Blunsdon, which had been set up after the main MAP factory in Rochester, where Phil's brother Henry had worked during the war, was bombed.

Not too far from Joyce's family, and close to the area she had grown up in the East Close prefab had a large garden complete with an Andersen shelter, which Philip turned over to growing vegetables. At last he had a garden of his own to tend and apply all those tips he had picked up during the war, though without the swanky glasshouses to pot out in.

Life was looking up. Phil's only regret was that he hadn't found a job working outdoors, but his garden and the nippers took up all his time. He was soon to get his wish when Garrards, the booming record player factory in the Town run by the sports mad Mr. Herbert Slade advertised for an assistant grounds man at their prestigious Sports ground in Stratton Road. All the significant employers in the Town were competing to provide the best sports facilities for their workers and Garrards were no exception.

Mr. Slade had been the Chairman of the Swindon and District Football League and the Swindon Cricket Club so ensured that the Garrards ground was his pride and joy, complete with a pavilion, grass tennis courts and a bowling green. There was even a grandstand and, thankfully for Phil, numerous flowerbeds to maintain. Though his soccer playing days were behind him, Herbert Slade himself played bowls for the Garrards team so the pressure was always on to keep the grounds pristine.

It might not be a country garden to rival Southrop Lodge or Tongwood House's walled gardens, and it didn't exactly pay a King's ransom, but it was a job he could take pride in and, crucially for Joyce, it came with a tied cottage. The Late Victorian semi-detached house at 67 Stratton Road had been empty for some time so Phil spent months clearing and setting out a new garden in any spare time he had from the job. All those years of listening to the Head Gardeners at the posh estates he had been billeted at during the war, on top of his early Barnardo's grounding, was finally going to be put to good use.

He even had a tractor which the farmer boys he had fought alongside in the Wiltshire Regiment would have been proud of, though 'Daisy' as he dubbed her, would not be pulling the plough but rolling immaculate pitches for the summer cricket season.

Life at 67 Stratton Road was largely a happy one in the early days of their growing family but as the 1950s gave way to the 1960s Joyce started to feel the pressure of raising three young children on Phil's meagre wages and with him working all the hours under the sun. They had just about managed when they just had Barry and Julie to feed but when their third child Michael came along in 1958 the house just didn't seem big enough for their growing family.

Joyce screamed at him that it didn't help that Phil insisted on taking pity on every gentleman of the road that knocked on their door on the way to Oxford from Swindon and feeding them like he was Doctor Barnardo! Word had got round that the man at 67 was a kindly soul and couldn't turn anyone away, and it was costing them dear.

Phil was torn. The house came with the job he loved and made sure he was only a stone's throw from his work. He was not going to give up the job just to get one of the new Council Houses that were popping up all over Swindon.

Joyce wanted more room to breathe and, ideally, to be nearer to Eric and Bet in Meadowcroft, where they had been happy newlyweds. Phil knew the Council Houses came with only the pokiest of gardens and if he wanted to grow more vegetables he would have to apply for an allotment. In any event Barry and Julie were happily settled at Grange Infants School and a move would be disruptive for them. He thought Joyce was being unreasonable. They could not agree on what to do for the best.

One fateful night, something popped in Phil's head. The pressures of working all the hours he could after little sleep, coupled with his inability to deal with the arguments with an ever-frustrated Joyce at home over how she could possibly make her meagre housekeeping money stretch to feed the little 'uns, got to him. He had what can only be described as a nervous breakdown.

At once, his head was filled with everything that had gone before. The feelings of loss from his childhood he had kept at bay. The horrendous nightmares filled with mortar fire and blood-splattered infantrymen screaming in pain. The daily fear of poker-hot shrapnel piercing your skin. It was just too much to bear. He didn't know how to deal with it.

Nothing had prepared him for how he was feeling right now. There was no one he could talk to. Joyce wasn't in any mood to be understanding. Even his best mate Coxy would not understand and in any event they had drifted apart in recent years. He lashed out. He couldn't control his new foul temper.

He felt like he had lost control of his mind and didn't know how to get it back. He withdrew further into himself.

Over time he became more and more detached from his family. He gave up his scouting work that had given him so much pleasure. When Garrards were acquired by Plessey Semiconductors he took on the role of grounds man at the less prestigious sports ground nearer to their new family home in Upper Stratton. Joyce had persuaded him to take up the council tenancy when their fourth child, David, who Phil had actually wanted to name Winston Spencer, after the 'great man' himself, was born in 1965, the year of Churchill's death. He had lost his treasured large vegetable garden and the job he loved. The Plesseys job meant the grass tennis courts that had been his pride and joy were replaced by hard courts that required little skill in maintaining. There was not even any room for flower beds.

Altogether, despite being solely in charge, the new ground gave him much less satisfaction and life on the council estate felt joyless compared to their early Stratton Road life where he had been happiest. It may have been a newly built house in a well-maintained cul-de-sac with a small green outside for the kids to play, but there was no piano, barely enough room for a record player in the front room. There was little joy for Phil. The rented television set became an unwanted intrusion. It was his turn to resent the house being filled with neighbours, friends and family of Joyce or the children.

Working alone now, away from the family home, gave him little pleasure. He withdrew further into himself and watched as his children left home. At times, the train set that he had carefully constructed in the boys' bedroom gave him some distraction as he had created a dream model village on plasterboard that he would have loved to live in, complete with a pub with cycles perched outside, a church on a hill and thatched cottages with tiny tinned baths hanging on the outside walls.

Summer after summer he holidayed without Joyce and often alone, though did on occasion take Barry, or later the young David, with him on cycling and camping sojourns to the south coast or the coastline and hills of North Devon, where he loved to walk. He was searching for the peace of mind that had alluded him since his breakdown and hoped that the countryside would help him find it. The early mornings, dragging on his first woodbine as the damp of the dew still lay like tears on the flattened campsite grass, were the closest he came to grabbing back the hope and the joy he once had.

There was always hope in a new dawn, and joy in the birdsong, before 'normal' life could blow it away like sea spray on a wave crashing on the shore. As the nicotine coursing into his lungs woke up his reactions and returned him to the realities of his life now, Phil knew he had to find the strength to get through for the sake of his children.

He had to try to find a way to get out of this 'city of destruction' that was his state of mind just like the Pilgrim in his battered copy of Pilgrim's Progress. Bunyan may have charted a route out, but Phil was struggling to find it despite all his map-reading skills and scouts training.

When death came it was quick for Phil but painfully slow for his family. The second of his strokes that rendered him unconscious happened overnight in the run-up to Christmas 1987. As he slept alone it was only his failure to wake the rest of the family up with a cup of tea that alerted them to this. As the ambulance crew pelted across the snow-splattered green outside 27 Pinnock's Place, he could not be revived. At 65, after a lifetime of smoking unfiltered cigarettes and living on his nerves his body had finally given up.

His children gathered at his hospital bedside and tried to break the tension with stories and funny anecdotes from his life. His only daughter Julie was inconsolable. David, home from University for the Christmas break, stroked his Dad's thinning hair and spoke to him in the hope that he might be heard. There was no response. The only comfort for Joyce and the children was the reassurance from the nurses that Phil was in no physical pain. The twitches had stopped too so David hoped that his dying Dad's wartime nightmares had ended for good.

On Christmas Eve, at his bedside in a side room at Swindon's Princess Margaret Hospital, the tension was broken for David and Julie when the priest from the local Christ Church wafted in to their Dad's room looking like Count Dracula in his long black cape and, ironically, reeking of garlic, to render a blessing to Phil. It was all his grieving children could do to contain their laughter.

After three months in hospital, the last two closer to the Stratton Road home he had loved so much at the older

Stratton Hospital, where, the family all knew, you were sent to end your days, Philip Charles Wilson passed away on 13th February 1988. As the funeral cortege inched its way from their Pinnock's Place home to the Upper Stratton Baptist Church in nearby Green Road it passed the home of his sister in law Bet at 34 Meadowcroft where Phil and Joyce had first lived in those happier times as a newlywed couple with baby Barry.

The Barnardo's boy had come full circle. He had 'survived' the war but paid a huge price with hauntings that he had only been able to suppress for so long. The hole that was left in his life by his abandonment as a ten-year-old child remain unfilled. Just as there had been no one on his side of the church on their wedding day, there was no one from his own blood family to mourn him. He had gone to his grave not knowing the fate of his mother Kate or his two brothers. It would be another twenty years before the truth of Phil's life and the whereabouts of his family would become known. Twenty years too late.

Chapter Eighteen

A Life Apart

Kate and her son Henry, Rhyl c. 1970

Henry was anxious to place Lily and their young son Anthony, who had unknowingly been given the same name as his Australian cousin, out of harm's way. Lily's Aunt and Uncle had moved to a small village called Kimnel Bay near Rhyl on the North Wales coast to manage a small chicken farm and as they reached retirement age Lily's Mum and Dad, Joe and Annie, planned to join them. Miles away from the Medway 'Bomb Alley', Lily could see the sense of moving there too. Kate would go with her to help with young Anthony and Henry would join them as soon as he could.

It was a wrench to be apart, but as Henry's work at Short's was all consuming at least Lily knew he was relatively safe thanks to the Short's tunnels and the vast air raid shelters alongside the factory. Kate relished the fresh sea air at Rhyl and took to her grandmother duties like a duck to water, braving the wind and the rain in winter for bracing walks on the front.

She thought Henry would love the sweeping white sands of the beaches here even if Prestatyn could not compete with the Merrie England of his Ramsgate youth. A popular resort, with its children's paddle boat pool and lido on the front, it was a safe place to raise a family.

The local holiday camps had been given over to the military, so the town was full of young squaddies undertaking their initial training before being sent to the front. Kate was relieved that Henry was still working at Short's. She would dread to think where Fred and Phil were. She saw them in the fresh-faced laughter of the innocent young, uniformed men walking along the windy promenade. All she could do was pray that they would be kept safe from the bomb and the bullet and see this war through.

She held young Anthony close to her and vowed she would do all she could to protect him and Lily from harm.

When the Allied victory finally came in the summer of 1945, Kate and Lily gathered with her parents on the front, joining the large crowd of revellers on the Promenade as the rain fell and the service of celebration had to be transferred indoors at the Rhyl Pavilion. Lily hoped that would mean that Henry would soon be home, but he had other plans. He had decided to follow his late father, the Captain, and join the Royal Army Ordnance Corps at Colchester barracks, signing up for three years. Though she and Kate had managed without him, they were uneasy about Anthony growing up without his Dad around, but Henry was determined to do his patriotic duty.

When he was finally discharged from the depot at Winchester barracks in 1948 Henry found work as a bus conductor in Rhyl and he and Lily settled down to raise their growing family. As David, a name also later chosen by his uncle Phil for one of his sons, and Diane were born in the 1950s, they felt their family was complete at their council house at number 30, Edgbaston Road, just up from the Rhyl seafront.

Kate was later blessed with great-grandchildren when Diane had Joanna and Jamie in the 1970s and Kate was in her eighties. It was around this time that David recalls Kate admitting that she had two other sons and that she did not know where they were. Too upset to talk about it she took to her bed and stayed there for the rest of the day, never to talk of them again. It was just too upsetting for her to deal with.

Kate died in 1980, in her early nineties. She had tragically not seen two of her boys for nearly fifty years. She did not know that Fred had sadly passed away and Phil did not know that his 'Ma was still alive, but she was surrounded by her eldest son and two more generations, in her final days.

Henry had blocked his brothers out of his head, as the years went by. He got on with his life with Lily, raising their family and working hard to keep food on the table. He worked for Crosville Motor Services as a bus conductor on a Bristol double decker bus for thirty seven years before retiring early after sustaining minor injuries in a bus crash. He passed away

in June 1987, just six months before his younger brother Phil
and fifty five years after they had all been parted.

Postscript

When I started researching my Dad's life I had the sketchiest of information to go on. As a child I had completed my own rudimentary autobiography for a school project and whilst my Mum's Carter family history bound up with the Swindon Railway works and the South Wales coalmines before that, was clear and emphatic, quizzing Dad elicited only that his mother was called Catherine or Katherine (neither was in fact accurate) and that the family name was changed to Wilson following some kind of scandal.

Dad was proud of his Barnardo's history and sad that a brother he had been close to had been sent to live in a different children's home in Australia when they were very young. Dad said he had made many attempts to find his brother Fred, but all to no avail.

That was all we had to go on. When I interviewed Dad in 1977, tragically he was unaware that his own mother Kate was in fact still alive and living with his older brother Henry, less than two hundred miles away in North Wales. There was also no reason that he should have been bereft of family when he married Joyce Carter in Swindon on St David's Day in 1952, given that only twenty miles away in the same County, his mother's Flippence clan was still a strong presence in the Pewsey Vale.

A further sadness to me is that on one of the rare occasions that Dad and I holidayed together, when I was thirteen and had been given my first grown up bike as a present, just the two of us cycling to the south coast from Swindon and back over the course of his week off work, on the first night we camped in Savernake Forest just up the road from Milton Lilbourne, where Kate had been born, and where Dad's own grandfather was buried.

To think that he spent his whole adult life not knowing his mother or seeing his siblings, again is hard for me to comprehend.

I didn't really know my grandparents on my Mum's side as the feared patriarch Albert, who had worked as a colliery boy in the Welsh valleys before moving back to Swindon with his family, and a job on the Railways, who had served with the Wiltshire regiment in India and the Dardanelles in the Great War, had died when I was nine. I do remember he had a booming voice resulting from his deafness caused by a lifetime as a GWR boilermaker and an Alsatian dog that scared me.

Relations between him and my dad were strained as Albert had no sympathy for Dad when he had a breakdown and Joyce struggled to cope with his moods. One of their ferocious rows prompted Grandad and my uncle Eric to pay Dad a visit and issue him a warning. From that night, Dad never joined any of the extended family holidays and spent the rest of his holidays alone or with his children.

I knew the Carter legacy and I knew I was grounded in Swindon. What I did not know, until I left Swindon after University and was living in South east London with a young family of my own, was my father's London heritage. It took

Dad's death to prompt me to search for answers. To understand how Dad could be left alone in the world at such a young age. To properly appreciate Dad's wartime experiences in a bid to explain what I saw as his strange behaviour, when I became aware of it as a young adult.

Sleeping in his own bedroom apart from my Mum even though we only had three bedrooms for the six of us. The insomnia, the nightmares that made his legs twitch violently when he was napping on the settee in front of the telly in our small front room. The times I would catch him over breakfast before I walked to school staring into the distance lost in his own thoughts as he smoked another Woodbine. Tears in his eyes as he tended his beloved bonfire in the small patch of back garden we had in Pinnock's Place.

We never discussed any of this behaviour as a family. It was a given that it was just how he was. As the youngest I felt that I wasn't being let in on a grim family secret. Every Remembrance Sunday, Julie and I would be moved to tears watching the telly with him as Dad was unable to watch as his comrades marched past the Cenotaph. It was too painful for him to bear.

When Barry and his wife Susan offered to take Dad to Normandy to revisit his wartime haunts, he politely declined. The haunting would be too real, and he just could not face it. My brother Mike and I went with them instead to witness the D Day beaches, and my seventeen-year-old pacifist self was moved to tears by the rows and rows of immaculate white gravestones in the Commonwealth war graves of Normandy.

I was beginning to understand what had shaped my Dad and felt proud of what he had endured.

After returning from the War, Dad never again left England, apart from one skirmish across the border at Hadrian's Wall with my brother Mike and I when we drove Mike's 'red Ken' Mini to the Lake District and up to the Scottish border. By then Dad had retired due to ill health following a stroke and Mike and I were desperate to build a closer rapport with our father before it was too late.

It is wonderful to see the serenity of his smile in one of the few blurry photographs I have to treasure of Dad in his cap, resting on his walking stick half way up a Cumbrian fell and taking in the view of his beloved outdoors.

It is one of the few moments I remember where Dad was truly happy. I do recall his proud look when he gave my sister Julie away at her wedding, when I was ten. His beaming smile during the Queen's Silver Jubilee in 1977 when the fantastic elaborate cake he had made for our street party, complete with Grenadier guardsmen guarding Buckingham Palace, was lauded by our neighbours.

How much happier he might have been and beaming with pride had he known that his very own younger brother, his beloved Fred, had changed guard at the Palace and marched through London in the Coronation Parade.

I did not witness any intimacy between my Mum and Dad. As I said, by the time we were living in the council house in Pinnock's from when I was three years old, Dad slept in his own bedroom, in a sparsely furnished bedroom where, not much of a reader, he kept the four books he possessed. A biography of Doctor Barnardo, David Niven's autobiography 'The Moon's A Balloon', Spike Milligan's 'Adolf Hitler; My Part In his Downfall' and The Pilgrim's Progress (Dad's gift from Barnardo's).

I believe he kept Niven and Milligan's writing as they mirrored in part Dad's wartime experiences. He said Spike captured the madness and humour of squaddie life all too well, particularly to relieve the long months of boredom before they finally went to the front.

As the youngest of four, the family joke was that I was an after-thought or that I was found in a Coop carrier bag near the Stratton Road tied cottage I was born in, Dad wanted to name me Winston Spencer in a tribute to the great war leader who had died a few months before I was born in 1965. He spoke warmly of Monty and did not truck criticism of him.

The only time I remember going to the pictures with Dad, we took the bus into town to the ABC in Regent Street to see the blockbuster film 'A Bridge Too Far' about the failed Operation Market Garden, as I think Dad wanted me to understand something of his wartime past without having to talk about it.

Our relationship was never particularly close, as his age and his physical tiredness precluded us having the kind of father/son bond that some of my schoolfriends seemed to have with their Dads. We didn't go to the match together and by the time I joined the Cubs he had already stopped being a scoutmaster so I couldn't make him proud of my knots or when I did my best during Bob a Job week in Stratton Cubs. I was always jealous when Barry and Julie spoke so warmly about their Stratton Road childhood as it seemed Mum and Dad were happier then, in themselves and with each other.

The house in Stratton Road came with a piano which Dad played, and Barry remembers he also played the mandolin. He had a musical ear and could transpose musical notes. He had clearly availed himself of the Barnardo's musical boys training.

He was a hands-on Dad. He had to be particularly hands on when Barry and his friends found a live artillery shell and brought it home to Stratton Road, scratching it with their penknives and throwing it up into the air to see how it landed.

When he discovered this on returning from work, Phil immediately recognised the danger and called in the bomb disposal team to detonate it safely. The crater it left was talked about for weeks and the story of the near miss made the local paper.

On another occasion as they were camping out in the back garden that led to the Garrards sports ground, a sound of breaking glass was heard from the Garrards sports pavilion and Phil knew at once that this spelt trouble. He gave chase struggling to keep his trousers up.

My brother Michael is so proud of the fact that Dad travelled all the way to Bristol by train, walking miles from Bristol Temple Meads Station to see him perform in a school play at

Clifton College, despite feeling so uncomfortable among so many posh parents at his public school.

Dad walked everywhere. His route marching days had prepared him well for long walking holidays, first with Joyce in their beloved North Devon, and then with the Scouts as an Assistant Scoutmaster with the 1st Stratton St Margaret Scouts based in Ermin Street.

At one camp in the Malvern Hills near to Eastnor Castle, Barry recalls how on arrival he was informed that his Dad had already managed to walk the length of the range of hills. On another occasion he walked thirteen miles from his home in Stratton to join another Scout camp at Filkins, close to his former home in Southrop.

After his breakdown, he returned to the North Devon coast on his own on a number of occasions. Combe Martin was his favourite spot.

As the spoilt youngest and a Mummy's boy, I was much closer to my Mum though I never felt torn by this until I had my two consecutive summer holiday weeks with Dad, first on a youth hostelling and hiking holiday to his favourite North Devon and then the memorable bike ride the following summer camping, as we travelled through Wiltshire to the New Forest. Dad always preferred his own company to the family holidays and so the three Butlins trips and caravan holidays I remember with my Mum's brother David and his family did not include Dad. I thought nothing of it, other than knowing that the cricket season and tennis tournaments kept Dad really busy at his work as a grounds man at the Plessey Sports Ground during the school summer holidays.

I knew Dad was older than my mates' Dads. I got some stick at school because of his age and unkempt appearance with his wellies and wooly hat he wore to work the bullies said he looked like the comedic television character Compo from Last of the Summer Wine, but I was proud that he had fought in the Second World War . Even as late as the 1970s the legacy of the war still loomed large in our life. When we camped in Savernake Forest we used his Army issue billy can set to cook with.

He astonished me when, as a fit fifty-five-year-old, he carried my rucksack and his own with ease, when we climbed Dunkery Beacon in Exmoor and I struggled with the weight of my pack. He had clearly coped with far greater weights for weeks on end as a signaller during the fateful years of 1944 and 1945.

As we traversed Salisbury Plain on our bikes and Dad stopped for a fag break and one of his Woodbines, he decoded signals that were being used by the Army in a training exercise. He deployed those signalling skills with his Scout group teaching them semaphore and Morse code and his firstborn Barry proudly became the first scout in Swindon to have the Signallers badge sewn onto his camp blanket.

I must have been disappointment to him given my lack of physical strength and resilience, the way I failed to maintain clean shoes or keep my hair at a tidy short length but he kept those feelings to himself. I wanted to make him proud of me but didn't know how to start.

He taught me how to fish but I was a very poor angler without sufficient patience. I did briefly take to youth hostelling after our Devon holiday and briefly showed interest in the amazing trainset he had created complete with a beautiful hand-crafted model village of pub, church and thatched cottages.

Cycling, as it was with Barry before me, was a shared love of ours. One summer we cycled around villages that he and Mum had toured during their courtship, including Lechlade and Southrop, though I have no memory of him mentioning that he had once lived and worked there.

He never made the connections. He was not the sort of bloke to have mates or to go to the pub and pretend that the blokes you were drinking with were your mates. He was a solitary man, happiest in his own company. I got the impression that the television was an annoyance to him, dominating as it did our front room and our social lives.

He showed no passion for sport as he got older, despite his job as a grounds man, and he rarely listened to music, though we did have a record player. I remember him playing along with the spoons as Mike and I were jamming in the front room on guitar and my newly acquired secondhand bass. He spoke fondly of the Barnardo's bagpipes but it was unclear whether he could actually play them as we didn't possess a set.

On reflection, to me Dad seemed like a broken man. Constantly tired after work, he did little but snore and twitch on the settee in the evening while Mum and I watched telly and got on with life. The only joy I could see he took was from our small garden and his baking, he was particularly proud of his roses and the beautiful lavender bush he had planted in our front garden. I wonder now if they reminded him of Normandy. He loved to bake and decorate cakes for family and friends and did so with real skill and creativity, never accepting a penny in return. Some of my fondest childhood memories are of watching flour-drenched Dad bake and being allowed to pinch some of the marzipan or icing sugar as he did so.

My Dad proudly posing in front of his Silver Jubilee cake as Mum organises the Pinnock's Place street party, 1977

A childhood in Barnardo's may not have given Dad any love in his early life but they did teach him some very useful life skills which helped him survive the hell of War and gave him some joy as he grappled with his demons in the aftermath.

When he finally cracked, Mum bore the brunt of Dad's breakdown, which seems to have occurred before I was born and resulted in a fracture of relations between Mum's family and Dad. My Grandfather had intervened to protect Mum and warned Dad to behave himself. There was little solidarity from one Wiltshire Regiment veteran to another.

Things were never quite the same again between Mum and Dad and though they would have never countenanced divorce they lived very much separate lives. Mum went out to work at her cleaning job in the evening as Dad returned from the Sports Ground and at weekends Dad worked Saturday and Sundays with weekend football or cricket fixtures to deal with, and otherwise spent time in his own world in the garden while Mum went to the Gospel Hall or later the Baptist Church.

I saw no animosity between them, but neither was there particularly any love and affection. We kids joked that the only time they addressed each other remotely affectionately by their first names was Christmas Day and even then Dad would be in the kitchen all morning preparing the Christmas Dinner and collapse into his armchair wearing his new slippers after the Queen's Speech and too many sherries.

A shy and withdrawn man, his children have very much inherited this trait, balanced in part by Mum's love of people and concern for the underdog. Mum thrived with people around her and loved having young people in the house. The teapot was always warm. The Dad I knew would be happiest alone and seemed to resent the intrusion that others wrought though would never say as much.

The loss of his mother's love and the separation from his brothers as an impressionable and sensitive child had clearly left its mark. The kindness he received from the Thomas's and the Watsons, helped to heal some of those wounds and guided him through his teenage years and into adulthood but what he saw at war drove him deeper into himself and left him damaged in a way that not even love for and from his wife and children could properly repair.

Finding Fred

In an unhappy period of my life following my divorce and separation from my two boys I developed an obsession with finding out the facts about my Dad's life and his family. Going through the motions in a job I was bored with and struggling living alone in my rented terraced house in the small Cambridgeshire city of Ely, I filled my time searching the internet for answers.

A decade before, just after my son Calum was born, I had discovered through writing to local newspapers in western Australia, that my Dad's brother was alive in the 1950s as I was sent a photograph from a former friend of his in Perth of him in an Army uniform holding a child. From the posture the child did not appear to be his own and the correspondent confirmed this. The date on the back of the photograph was 1953 and the physical appearance was uncannily similar to a younger Phil. They were clearly brothers.

The Australian Army records were helpful, and I eventually received a copy of Fred's full military record dramatically stamped through with 'Deceased', which confirmed that he had indeed died in 1968 at the age of 43. I knew his widow's name was Vera and that he had two children, though I did not yet know their names, merely their dates of birth.

Unusually it seemed, after service in Korea and a return to England with the Anzac Coronation Contingent, Fred had died serving in Papua New Guinea and I reasoned that the numbers of Australian servicemen posted to what I assumed to be small islands would be small he might be easy to track down. I stumbled across a site that had been set up by 'Nashos' - Australian national servicemen who had served as teachers in PNG. I emailed them to see if any of them recalled my Uncle and, thankfully, got a lucky break.

Terry Edwinsmith, a former Chalkie, who had gone on to be a primary school teacher after undertaking his national service in Port Moresby, had warm memories of my Uncle Fred, his RSM who had made such a mark on him as he welcomed him to Taurama Barracks in 1967. Terry was able to send me photographs of the Barracks and an account of my Uncle Fred's death and his funeral.

Terry and I later met in London when he and his wife Jenna were in England visiting relatives, and as we had tea in the smart Richoux coffee house on Piccadilly, it was emotional for me to meet someone who had actually known my uncle Fred. It somehow made him real to me after all these years of desk research.

I was to get an even better lead later that year. Searching the site for background information I saw that Fred's daughter., my cousin Susie, had been in touch with the veterans group to seek their support for her campaign to reinstate her late father's and other military graves at Taurama barracks where he was interred following vandalism. Susie saw my appeal online for anyone who might know anything about RSM Frederick Alexander Wilson and tentatively replied that she might be the daughter of the person I was looking for.

I had found my Australian cousins and Susie had found some answers to her own questions about her Dad who had died before she was three. It was the middle of the night in Ely but this was too important to wait. I asked Susie for her number and immediately called her at what I knew was a reasonable hour for her at home in Victoria. We were both in tears as we talked, and we realized that our families were at last to be 'virtually' reunited after nearly eighty years.

Susie and her older brother Anthony knew nothing about their Dad's early life other than a vague knowledge that he had been born in England. He had been vague to friends of his wife about his Western Australian upbringing, and they had suspected he might be hiding something from them. I was able to tell her a little about the complicated Wilson family history, of Fred's Barnardo's life and his voyage to Australia. Of his Fairbridge Farm School life and his dream to fly with the RAAF that brought him back to the country of his birth.

Susie shared information about her wonderful mother Vera and the heartbreak she suffered, compounded when Fred's medals and treasures mementos of their life together were lost in transit from Papua New Guinea when she returned as a young widow with the children back home to Queenscliff.

Vera had eventually remarried but Fred had remained her first love, and it was with him she wanted to be interred in Taurama. This was how Susie had discovered the fate of her late Dad's grave and she and Anthony had been fighting for it to be restored. Susie, like me, has two sons, and Patrick and Bryan call Fred 'soldier Grandad'. Her daughter Carly, a talented actress, has written and produced a play based on Fred and Vera's tragically short love story.

The more I have learned about the Wilson brothers' lives, the prouder and sadder I have become. Proud because all three men gave their all for the war effort in different ways and despite their childhood traumas went on to live good lives and raise decent families.

This pride is tinged with sadness because of what might have been had Kate not lost touch completely with her younger boys and instead sought to reunite her family. I believe that my Dad would have found life more tolerable if he knew he had his Mum and brothers in his corner and on his side of the church when he married the love of his life. There to share the joys of parenthood and the pride in their grandchildren and nephews and nieces.

Fred channelled his newfound love for family beyond his beloved Vera and the toddlers Anthony and Susanne to encompass support for all the families living under his watch on Taurama barracks. It was this generosity, made possible because he himself had found love in later life, that ultimately contributed to his tragic early death.

The older brother Henry devoted his whole life to looking out for his mother Kate. He had been left 'in charge' by Barnardo's at the age of twelve and that sense of responsibility never left him. He and Lily shielded her from German bombing and cared for her right to the end. After a fall at the home she shared with Henry and Lily, contracting pneumonia in hospital at the age of 92, Kate went to her grave not knowing what had become of her three other sons.

At least she was reassured that her Bertie had been looked after, though it would have pained her to find out that he had died young in 1957 at the age of 44 after losing a painful fight with cancer, leaving a widow and four children to mourn his loss. She had no idea what Fred and Phil had achieved in their lives. How they had overcome their orphanage childhood and proudly served their King and country, just as the Captain had hoped they would.

Sadly, there is no happy ending to this story. Like too many mothers of her generation Kate had to live with the agony and guilt of the separation from her children driven solely by her incapacity to afford to raise them as her own or to feed them.

We who came after and proudly carry the Wilson name, cannot rewrite our history. The only comfort we can take, through the years of patient and, at times painfully slow research, is the healing of the branches of a family tree which it might have seemed had been severed forever, nearly a century earlier.

Acknowledgements

I am indebted to the Wiltshire Regiment Museum, the Australian War Memorial, the Old Fairbridgians Association, Barnardo's Family History Department and the Ministry of Defence for access to Fred and Phil's records. I have drawn heavily from the brilliant resources of the British Newspaper Archive and Trove in Australia and from the National Archives.

Much has been written about the experiences of Barnardo's and Fairbridge children, and of the wartime ordeals of Australian aircrew in Bomber Command, and I have benefited from these accounts. For the account of Fred's time in the Korean War I am grateful to Peter and Thompson and Robert Macklin's book, 'Keep Off the Skyline: The Story of Ron Cashman and the Diggers in Korea', and to the Australian Army Unit War Diaries of 3 Battalion, The Royal Australian Regiment.

This book could not have been written without the support and encouragement of my family and friends. My cousin Susie has kindly shared her late father's Fairbridge Farm School file. My brother Barry has helped me undertake much of the family history research. My wife Katie has lived and breathed the book since we first met and encouraged me to persevere when it felt like I would never finish it.

David Wilson

Further Reading

Barnardo's and Fairbridge

Frank Norman – Banana Boy

John Lane – Fairbridge Kid

Roger Kershaw and Janet Sacks – New Lives For Old

Leslie Thomas – This Time Next Week

Frank Dixon – Looking Back (The Garden City, Woodford)

David Hill – The Forgotten Children

Alan Gill – Orphans of the Empire

Gillian Wagner – Children of the Empire

RAAF and Bomber Command

622 and 214 Squadrons Operations Record Books (National Archives)

David Scholes DFC – Air War Diary: An Australian in Bomber Command

Murray Peden – A Thousand Shall Fall

Hank Nelson – Chased By The Sun

R James – Avenging The Shadows

Laurie Brettingham – Even When The Sparrows Are Walking' – the origin and effect of No 100 Bomber Support Group (1943-45)

Don Charlwood – No Moon Tonight

Leo McKinstry – Lancaster: The Second World War's Greatest Bomber

Kevin Wilson – Men of Air: Doomed Youth of Bomber Command

Peter and Maureen Wilson – 'We Will Remember Them' – A Private Tribute to 622 and 149 Squadrons

Normandy Campaign

Alexander Baron – From the City, From the Plough

Anthony Beevor – Ardennes 1944: Hitler's Last Gamble

Patrick Delaforce: The Fighting Wessex Wyverns: From Normandy to Bremerhaven with the 43rd Wessex Division

Ken Ford – Assault On Germany – The Battle for Geilenkirchen

William Gould: An Infantry Signaller

Charles Messenger – The D Day Atlas

James Holland – Normandy '44

Chris Tarrant: Dad's War

Wiltshire Regiment – The History and War Diary of the 5th Battalion: Wiltshire Regiment, 1944-1946

Korean War

Peter Thompson and Robert Macklin – Keep Off the Skyline; The Story of Ron Cashman and the Diggers in Korea

Australian Army Unit War Diaries, Korea – 3 Battalion, The Royal Australian Regiment

Coronation Contingent

Annette Gaykema – Blog Article – Coronation Contingent of 1953, Australia War Memorial (2009)

Papua New Guinea

Darryl R Dymock – The Chalkies

Terry Edwinsmith – Nashos Blog – Frederick Wilson: A Boys' Own Adventurer.

About Take A Leaf

Take A Leaf was established in 2021 by Katie and David Wilson to provide family history research support for the growing number of people who wish to know where they come from.

Borne out of their shared love of family history and their experiences in discovering numerous fascinating tales involving their own ancestors, Take A Leaf combines the couple's love of books and social history.

In time, Katie and David dream of running a teashop and bookshop in the West of England under the Take A Leaf umbrella. In the meantime, Boomerang Boy is the first of what we hope will be a series of publications exploring the past.

http//www.takealeaf-tandb.co.uk